Cambridge Studies in Oral and Literate Culture 13

NATIVE AMERICAN DISCOURSE

Cambridge Studies in Oral and Literate Culture

Edited by PETER BURKE and RUTH FINNEGAN

This series is designed to address the question of the significance of literacy in human societies: it will assess its importance for political, economic, social, and cultural development and will examine how what we take to be the common functions of writing are carried out in oral cultures.

The series will be interdisciplinary, but with particular emphasis on social anthropology and social history, and will encourage cross-fertilization between these disciplines; it will also be of interest to readers in allied fields, such as sociology, folklore, and literature. Although it will include some monographs, the focus of the series will be on theoretical and comparative aspects rather than detailed description, and the books will be presented in a form accessible to nonspecialist readers interested in the general subject of literacy and orality.

Books in the series

NATIVE AMERICAN DISCOURSE
Poetics and rhetoric

Edited by

JOEL SHERZER
Departments of Anthropology and Linguistics
University of Texas at Austin

and

ANTHONY C. WOODBURY
Department of Linguistics
University of Texas at Austin

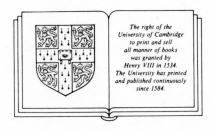

The right of the
University of Cambridge
to print and sell
all manner of books
was granted by
Henry VIII in 1534.
The University has printed
and published continuously
since 1584.

CAMBRIDGE UNIVERSITY PRESS

CAMBRIDGE

NEW YORK   NEW ROCHELLE

MELBOURNE   SYDNEY

Published by the Press Syndicate of the University of Cambridge
The Pitt Building, Trumpington Street, Cambridge CB2 1RP
32 East 57th Street, New York, NY 10022, USA
10 Stamford Road, Oakleigh, Melbourne 3166, Australia

First published 1987

Printed in the United States of America

Library of Congress Cataloging-in-Publication Data
Native American discourse.
(Cambridge studies in oral and literate culture; 13)
Includes index.
1. Indian literature – History and criticism. 2. Indians – Languages – Discourse analysis.
I. Sherzer, Joel.   II. Woodbury, Anthony C.   III. Series.
PM155.N38   1987   897   86–28382

British Library Cataloging-in-Publication Data
Native American discourse: poetics and rhetoric. – (Cambridge studies in oral & literate culture)
1. Indian literature – History and criticism
I. Sherzer, Joel   II. Woodbury, Anthony C.
897   PM155
ISBN 0 521 32936 1

CONTENTS

v

PREFACE

This book presents a collection of texts, with commentary and analysis, from Native American communities past and present. Our purpose is to advance a new perspective on the presentation, philology, analysis, and interpretation of oral literature and verbal art. Inspired by the work of two of our contributors, Dell Hymes and Dennis Tedlock, this perspective has broad implications for linguistics, anthropology, folklore, and literature as well as for bilingual education and language maintenance in minority communities. The approach is centered on discourse, which it takes to be the richest point of intersection among language, culture, society, and individual expression. In discourse, individuals draw on their own artistry at the same time as they draw on the special and unique resources of the language and culture of their communities, including lexicon and grammar, norms of pragmatic interpretation, cultural knowledge and symbolism, systems of genres and style and the rules for their effective performance. At the same time, we hope that the texts themselves can be studied, appreciated, and admired on their own terms. Although they cannot be taken as representative of the whole of Native American discourse – it comprises traditions far too numerous and corpora far too vast for that to be remotely possible – they nevertheless can stand as valuable instances of it, fascinating in their own right and suggestive of the richness of the verbal art of the indigenous peoples of the Americas.

The original impetus for this book was a workshop at the University of Texas at Austin on Native American discourse organized by the editors. Our co-participants were Ellen Basso, Judith Berman, Mary Haas, Dell Hymes, Virginia Hymes, M. Dale Kinkade, Bruce Mannheim, Sally McLendon, Barbara Tedlock, and Dennis Tedlock. We are very grateful to all of them for their insights and perspectives on Native American discourse. We are also grateful to Robert D. King, Dean of Liberal Arts at the University of Texas at Austin, for funding the workshop through grants to the departments of Anthropology and Linguistics. Finally, we hope that in however small a way this book stands as a tribute to Native American storytellers, orators, poets, and musicians past, present, and future.

Austin, Texas

CONTRIBUTORS

JOEL SHERZER is professor of anthropology and linguistics at the University of Texas at Austin. His research interests are linguistic anthropology and sociolinguistics, with a focus on speech play and verbal art. Most of his research has dealt with North and South American Indians, especially the Kuna Indians of Panama, among whom he has carried out considerable field-work. His publications include *An Areal-Typological Study of American Indian Languages North of Mexico*, *Kuna Ways of Speaking*, and numerous articles.

ANTHONY C. WOODBURY is associate professor of linguistics at the University of Texas at Austin. His general interests are in grammatical theory including phonology, morphology, and syntax; ethnography of speaking; and oral discourse. He specializes in Eskimo-Aleut languages and culture and has been doing fieldwork in Central Alaskan Yupik Eskimo-speaking communities since 1978. Among his publications are *Grammar Inside and Outside the Clause: Some Approaches to Theory from the Field* (edited with Johanna Nichols) (Cambridge, 1985) and *Cev'armiut Qanemciit Qulirait=llu: Eskimo Narratives and Tales from Chevak, Alaska* (1984), and articles in *Language in Society*, *Natural Language and Linguistic Theory*, *Handbook of North American Indians*, and elsewhere.

DELL HYMES is at the Center for Advanced Studies at the University of Virginia, where he is also professor of anthropology and English. While his chapter for this volume was reaching final form, he was professor of folklore, linguistics, sociology, and education at the University of Pennsylvania, and dean of the Graduate School of Education. His research interests include the languages and traditions of the Pacific Northwest; the history of linguistics and anthropology; sociolinguistics, especially the ethnography of speaking; narrative; poetry. His publications include *Language in Culture and Society* (1964), *Pidginization and Creolization of Languages* (1971), *Reinventing Anthropology* (1972), *Foundations in Sociolinguistics* (1974), *American Structuralism* (with John Fought) (1975, 1981), *Language in Education* (1980), *"In Vain I Tried to Tell You": Essays in Native American Ethnopoetics* (1981),

ix

Essays in the History of Linguistic Anthropology (1983), and "The General Epistle of James" (1986). He edits the journal *Language in Society*.

VIRGINIA HYMES is academic lecturer in anthropology at the University of Virginia. While her chapter for this volume was reaching final form, she was lecturer in folklore, and undergraduate chair in folklore, at the University of Pennsylvania. Her interests include American Indian languages and cultures; the ethnography of speaking; and training in linguistics for social scientists. Her research has focused on the language and traditions of the Sahaptin-speaking people of Warm Springs reservation, Oregon, and on oral narrative in English. Her publications include "Athapaskan Numeral Systems" (1955), "The Ethnography of Linguistic Intuitions at Warm Springs" (1975), "A Sahaptin Narrative Device: From Sahaptin to English and Back Again" (1982); and "Some Features of Warm Springs Sahaptin" (1984).

DENNIS TEDLOCK is University Professor of Anthropology and Religion at Boston University. American Indian languages, verbal arts, philosophy, and religion are at the center of his research interests; he has done fieldwork among the Zuni of New Mexico and the Quiché Maya of Guatemala. His works include *Finding the Center: Narrative Poetry of the Zuni Indians*, *Teachings from the American Earth: Indian Religion and Philosophy* (with Barbara Tedlock), and *The Spoken Word and the Work of Interpretation*. His latest book, *Popol Vuh: The Mayan Book of the Dawn of Life*, was awarded the PEN Translation Prize.

1

INTRODUCTION

Joel Sherzer and Anthony C. Woodbury

Background

The purpose of this book is to present a variety of forms of Native American discourse together with a variety of ways of representing, translating, and analyzing it. The goal is to provide readers with an exploration of an exciting current of research that has been developing over the last decade, linguistically oriented and yet cutting across and relating several distinct disciplines.

The research leading to these papers is a continuation of a long tradition in American anthropology, linguistics, and folklore and at the same time a new and significant development within this tradition. Franz Boas and his students, as well as others involved in the study of Native American languages and cultures, collected and published texts as part of their documentation of them. In particular, the Boasian tradition called for the publication of a grammar, a dictionary, and a collection of texts for each language studied. The texts had a twofold purpose, serving both as data for linguistic analysis and as primary ethnological documentation. Attention to the structure of discourse in and for itself, while perhaps implicit, was not explicit. Texts were presented in block form, with little or no attempt made to analyze and represent the verbal artistry of native performances. This is precisely what is significant about the papers in this book. They take Native American discourse seriously as their starting point, as encompassing an important literature, as having precise and complex linguistic patterning, and as the locus of the relationship among language, society, culture, and individuals.

The history of the set of approaches represented here can be traced to the pioneering efforts of Dell Hymes and Dennis Tedlock. These two scholars have been concerned with the presentation and translation of Native American verbal art and with making texts, in all of their original complexity and richness, available to English-reading audiences. Both Hymes and Tedlock recognized that an important aspect of Native American discourse and a central feature of its verbal artistry is organization into lines and groups of lines. Tedlock determined lines by focusing on such basic features of the voice in oral performance as the alternation between speech and silence, and, within

1

speech, variations in pitch, loudness, voice quality, tempo, and cadence. Hymes, investigating literary structure in already transcribed myth narratives, focused on hierarchic and often numerically constrained rhetorical patterns manifesting themselves as repetitions and recurrences in content and syntactic form, including the recurrent adverbial particles of his "measured verse" (Hymes 1977). This fundamental work has made original contributions in a remarkable range of disciplines. In linguistics, it has contributed to the study of form and meaning in discourse, at the same time locating interesting features that may have diffused over large areas in North America. For literary studies, it has made challenging suggestions for how the verbal artistry of Native American oral literature could be studied, visually represented on printed, published pages, translated, and ultimately appreciated by nonnatives. In folklore, it has led to new techniques for investigating the relationship between discourse and performance, text and context. And in anthropology, it pointed the way to more philological approaches to meaning in myth, and to a text- and discourse-centered approach to the language–culture–society relationship. At the heart of its concern in all of this is the form of discourse, and its relationship to verbal art.

A primary feature of all of this work is the recognition that literary interpretation and imagination intimately intersect with linguistic analysis. That is, Native American verbal art can only be truly appreciated by means of attention to linguistic detail, and at the same time linguistic structures can only be adequately and completely described by paying attention to their function and pattern within verbal art and other natural discourse, a point long emphasized by Jakobson (1968). A term Hymes and Tedlock (and others) have used to capture this intersection of linguistics, anthropology, literature, and folklore is "ethnopoetics." The notion embraces both the native conceptions and performances of verbal art and the analysts' attempts to represent, analyze, and translate it.

Recent research

The enterprise begun a decade ago by Tedlock and Hymes has attracted others and continues to develop.[1] Represented in this book is some of this recent work. The research is characterized by increasingly deep and detailed consideration of the basic issues of discourse form and verbal art, as well as by study of a broader range of texts, languages, and issues. Let us now outline some of the more important emerging issues, at the same time giving some background and context for the five papers presented.

Discourse structure in different genres

It has become clear that formal discourse structure covaries with genre. Analysis of this covariation is a powerful tool for investigating and ultimately characterizing the range of ways of speaking found in a community (see the papers by Sherzer and Woodbury). This includes genres regarded by native participants as verbal art, such as myth narrative and songs, and also informal conversation and such formal discourse types as prayer and ritual language.

The texts presented in the papers in this volume for the most part are or were valued highly as verbal art in the societies in which they were performed. The paper by Sherzer presents a Kuna story recorded in Panama from the same man first in 1970 in spoken form and then in 1976 chanted, as well as a Kuna myth performed in 1971 as a ritual chant by a chief and then interpreted as a formal speech by his spokesman. Central to the analysis is a comparison of these different genres and performances. Woodbury's paper presents a Central Alaskan Yupik Eskimo traditional tale performed in the early 1970s for a small native audience who taped it, and touches on genre in the analysis of a short song that recurs within it. A Warm Springs Sahaptin performance of a Raven myth, performed for a nonnative audience with a tape recorder in 1979, is presented in the paper by V. Hymes. And both D. Hymes and Tedlock deal in their papers with older materials as philologists: Hymes analyzes a Coyote myth taken down in dictation circa 1928–9 in Tonkawa, a now-extinct language of central Texas; Tedlock considers a far more ancient text, the written record from the mid sixteenth century of the Quiché Mayan "council book," the Popol Vuh. In doing so he considers as well a wide range of modern Quiché narrative types recorded in 1975–6, including narrative, sung prayers, and announcements made by town criers.

In addition to its descriptive value in approaching questions of genre, register, and speech situation, such a wide range of text types greatly enhances our ability to consider discourse in its many formal facets. It furthermore helps us contextualize verbal art among the everyday linguistic resources on which it must continually draw.

Resolution of different types of formal units and their roles in discourse structure

Pattern and recurrence can be found in discourse in sound, in syntactic form, and in content. Part of the fundamental insights of D. Hymes and of Tedlock has been to use such devices as lines, verses, and striking typography on the printed page to represent these features and in so doing reveal hitherto hidden aspects of poetically and rhetorically relevant structure. But the pattern and recurrence that exist are present in several logically independent domains of linguistic form (Hymes 1980; Tedlock this volume; Woodbury 1985 and this volume). Thus, it is possible to divide discourse into pause phrases, one spoken after another, bounded by the pauses that naturally occur in any sustained stretch of speech, as Tedlock has done in much of his work (e.g., Tedlock 1983). It is also possible to divide discourse into syntactic constituents such as clauses or other predicational units and take them as lines in hierarchies of "verses," "stanzas," and "acts" manifesting underlying or covert rhetorical patterns, as Hymes has done. These schemes for dividing discourse turn out not to coincide all of the time, although they sometimes do to a significant degree. Because of this irresolution, earlier debates (Hymes 1977; Tedlock 1977) focused on which scheme was best for representing a given narrative in a way that would most reflect its literary artistry. To complicate things still more, discourse can also be divided into recurrent units by phonological phrasing – the division of the stream of speech into tone groups marked, typically, as nonfinal by high or rising intonation and as final by low or falling intonation – yielding a hierarchy of units that need not correspond to pause phrases on the one hand or to clauses or other syntactic constituents on the other. And lastly, recurrent adverbial particles may mark off rhetorical units given in other subsystems, or set up their own rhythm in discourse. In short, someone wishing to use all of these kinds of discourse organization as the basis for presenting a text on the printed page in lines and verse may end up committing himself or herself to a series of different versions and restatements.

Different views continue to be held on the role and importance of these various aspects of structure, but a consensus is developing that they all should be taken into account in some way. In this volume, Woodbury is concerned with this issue explicitly, proposing a general linguistic framework that would take each aspect as a separate but interacting component in a larger "rhetorical structure." And Tedlock carefully distinguishes pause phrases ("lines"); syntactic elements ("clauses," "sentences," etc.); syntactic elements functioning in parallelistic patterns ("stichs"); and phonological phrases ("cola" and "periods") according to their degree of finality. Part of the reason that all have come to be recognized is a growing realization that the interaction of these logically separate formal entities is significant (Hymes 1980). In some cases it is observed that the pause phrase, the clause, the simple phonological phrase, and units demarcated by initial particles all coincide (see Bright 1979; McLendon 1982; V. Hymes this volume). Elsewhere such coincidence does not occur. Sherzer, Tedlock, and Woodbury find in their respective corpora that differences in the types of mapping between units are strongly associated with genre, in particular that the tightest coincidences tend to come in singing and chanting. And Woodbury finds that strict formal mappings between units of different structural types can often be posited as the normal state of affairs for a genre or narrative, and that deviations from it carry specific expressive or other pragmatic meaning. In summary, then, an increasingly synthetic understanding emerges from these papers of the roles of the formally disparate phenomena that organize discourse in recurrent, hierarchic patterns, recasting the whole as a complexly interacting system of systems.

Linguistic description and theory

The different formal aspects of discourse structure taken up in work represented here have all been studied linguistically, but usually in the context of sentence grammar, of word-level phonology, and of sentence-level intonation: they have only rarely been taken up in discourse-level terms. Meanwhile, linguistic work on discourse has been largely organized not around such matters of form, but instead in terms of issues of discourse function, such as textual coherence and cohesion (Beaugrande and Dressler 1981; Halliday 1984; Tannen 1984), speech acts and the social contextualization of talk (Gumperz 1982; Labov and Fanshel 1977), and rules of interaction and negotiation of meaning in conversation (Levinson 1983; Sacks, Schegloff, and Jefferson 1974). The work represented here is important in that it is oriented toward form in discourse both as a way of studying function and as an end in itself. On the one hand, its insights may turn out to be critical in approaching the better-studied aspects of discourse function. Each of these papers points to the danger of investigating grammar in terms of referential function alone. The expressive, poetic, and pragmatic functions of language in its sociocultural context must be accorded equal attention, for, as is shown again and again in the papers in this volume, a particular affix, word, or phrase may by its very presence mark the beginning of a line or verse, create an effective parallel structure, or evoke the stereotypic speech habits of a well-known myth character or neighboring society. On the other hand, this work may succeed in extending to discourse the essentially form-based approach taken in mainstream linguistics in this century, in turn facilitating a better integration of sentence grammar in the broader structural framework discourse provides. This of course implies that development of general, cross-linguistically valid notions of discourse structure must take place alongside intensive investigation of such structures in many languages, and in many genres within them.

Text as knowledge and text as performance

The concept of performance is crucial in the study of verbal artistry. In different ways each of the authors in this volume has endeavored to capture the specifics of the text performances rendered, including features of the voice, aspects of their social and cultural contexts, and conventions of interaction and interpretation shared between performers and audiences.

Also crucial is the relationship between an underlying model or "score" (D. Hymes personal communication) for a text and its actual performance. Of those presented here, some are memorized and performed identically each time; others involve improvisation or adaptation from a relatively fixed starting point, whether it be a story or plot to be realized in linguistic form, or the pure form of a song stanza to be realized in performance with new words and meaning; still others are created anew on the spot. Comparing different performances of what natives regard as the same text has proven a powerful technique for investigating this question (Hymes 1985; Sherzer this volume). In addition to shedding light on questions of cognitive representation, it provides for relatively controlled study of the relationship of language and action to context and situation. It offers an empirical antidote to simple conceptions of the relationship between knowledge and verbal performance in nonliterate societies, a relationship that by its very nature must always be complex and varied.

Philological approaches to discourse structure and artistry

In their papers for this volume, both Tedlock and D. Hymes consider poetic and rhetorical structure in already transcribed materials, bringing to bear on them a comparative perspective gained though their earlier pioneering work with similar transcriptional–analytic issues in other Native American literatures and languages. Tedlock discusses a text remote in time with many technical difficulties, a relatively rich corpus of historical attestation, and a very vibrant contemporary language and culture as resources for reconstructive hypotheses. There is an initial similarity to some of the reconstruction of Homeric performance based on modern Serbo-Croatian bards (Lord 1960), but it differs in that it involves manageable time depth, a contemporary speech community directly descended linguistically from the ancient one – rather than an entirely different one as in the Homeric case – and a sophisticated understanding of the nature of oral discourse in the contemporary community, taken holistically. The paper makes a compelling case that written texts in languages and discourse styles not too different from ones now existing deserve this kind of full philological treatment.

Hymes has a much more recent, better-documented primary text, but supplementary attestation that is scant and ranges over only a short period of time, and no recourse to a contemporary Tonkawa language or culture. His analysis is directed not toward reconstructing the auditory form of performance, but rather to reconstructing pattern and recurrence in the form and content preserved already in transcription. He has argued that by making this form visible in a text and then discerning how it fulfills (or, with special expressive force, fails to fulfill) an "underlying rhetorical form" which native audiences come to expect, close literary readings become more available to nonnatives (Hymes 1980, personal communication). In doing this, he brings to bear his wide experience in analyzing and interpreting these phenomena in native texts from throughout North America.

Areal patterns in the structure of discourse

Attention to areal patterns in Native American languages has focused on features of grammar conventionally conceived, in particular features of phonology, morphology, and to a lesser extent syntax. (See the history and survey in Sherzer 1976.) The papers in this book suggest features of discourse and performance that also display interesting areal patterning. One promising feature that has been discussed is the appearance of numerical constraints on narrative structure based on pattern numbers other than three (Jacobs 1959). For Native America, Hymes (1980) holds that underlying rhetorical form will be based on groups of threes and fives or of twos and fours. Threes and fives turn up in Sahaptin (V. Hymes this volume) and Chinookan (D. Hymes 1981), both spoken in the vicinity of the Columbia River, and far to the north in Central Alaskan Yupik Eskimo (Woodbury this volume). D. Hymes (1980) finds twos and fours in Takelma in Oregon, as well as in Karok in northern California, Zuni in New Mexico, and in Tonkawa in Texas (this volume); for Athabaskan, Scollon (1979) finds them in Chipewyan (interior northwestern Canada) and Tanacross (interior Alaska), and Witherspoon (1977) in Navajo. Thus both patterns are widely attested. A third pattern is discussed for Quiché Mayan by Tedlock (this volume), where couplets and sometimes triplets are prominent. Couplets have frequently been noted in other Mayan groups (cf. Edmonson 1973) and elsewhere in Mesoamerica (Garibay K. 1953). We may further note areal differences in the way and degree to which such constraints are employed: Tedlock finds couplets and triplets in modern Quiché more so in chanting than in narrative, and Woodbury indicates that the multilayered numerical constraints in the text he presents are not apparent in most other texts of its genre.

A second feature of areal interest concerns the range of genres reported in North America. There is little discussion in the literature of metrically counted forms of verse that is spoken rather than sung or chanted, as would be covered by the European folk notion of "poetry"; Tedlock (in press:34) cites Edmonson 1971:99 as observing a lack of versification or meter in Native American song texts, but goes on to suggest that the metrics may be complex and variable from line to line rather than fixed. Our relative lack of knowledge of such patterns may be due to the fact that until recently phonologists have analyzed prosody in Native American languages in terms of length and stress rather than in terms of real-time metrical units such as the "foot" or "beat," which insightfully characterize and organize many prosodic phenomena (Hayes 1981; Liberman 1975; Prince 1983). This, along with an awareness of such formal features as adverbial particle placement and of native rhetorical organization as attested in narrative may prove a prerequisite to a fuller understanding of rhythm, meter, and their relation to larger structures in Native American song texts.

An entirely different sort of areal feature noted by several scholars is the existence of dialogic performances in a region stretching from the Mayan area to tropical-forest South America (see Sherzer 1983:196–200).

In interpreting such widespread features, the greatest challenge is to discriminate between those that diffused as a result of prehistoric patterns of contact and communication and those which, owing to the general nature of language and of discourse, may be likely to arise in different places independently. Thus, though we may suspect diffusion in the cases of constraints based on very specific pattern-number configurations, we would suspect that pause phrasing is simply a general fact of discourse and language use. To get real answers, however, we need much more detailed reconstruction of prehistoric contact, together with improved theories of discourse structure in language generally. We hope that the papers here may make a modest contribution in this direction.

On terminology

In addition to discovering particular features of Native American oral discourse, the papers in this book also contribute to the development of the terms and concepts that are crucial for future research. Central among these are such general notions as "discourse," "narrative," "structure" and "structuring," "poetics," "rhetoric," and "verbal art." These terms are very difficult to define precisely, often because they are used in rather different ways by different individuals. "Discourse" has increasingly become the general term for a level of language structure and use within which grammar is one important structural component. It is medium- and genre-neutral, can be oral or written, can be approached in textual or social interactional terms, and can be brief like a greeting or lengthy like a novel. "Narrative" is a form of discourse, no doubt universal, which involves the recounting of a series of events. In the study of oral performance, it is sometimes useful to make a distinction between discourse or narrative "structure" and discourse or narrative "structuring" (see Sherzer's paper, where it plays a very important role). "Structure" concerns the organization of a particular text into units of various kinds. "Structuring" is a process, the way in which narrators and other performers of discourse draw on the various resources available to them within their linguistic, social, and cultural tradition and create their own personal texts. The three concepts "poetics," "rhetoric," and "verbal art" are particularly difficult to distinguish, especially given the ways they have come to be used. For the most part, the authors of this volume equate the broad, formal organization of discourse, especially when used to meet aesthetic or dramatic ends, as its "poetics." More problematic is the term "poetry." On the one hand, it may be confined narrowly to a set of Old World genres and their close analogs elsewhere. But as Jakobson (1960) pointed out, "poetics" as a component of language may be present in oral as well as written forms, in colloquial and conversational speech as well as in formal and ritual language. Recently, as the poetics of North American narrative has become better known, some have extended the term "poetry" to it as well. In this volume, D. Hymes, Tedlock, and Sherzer operate with a definition of poetry as discourse that is organized in terms of some notion of "line." "Rhetoric" focuses on the strategic function of discourse in persuasion, placed in specific and appropriate social and cultural contexts. "Verbal art" is a community's own conception of what in language use is aesthetically or rhetorically pleasing, the forms and processes that members of the community label or otherwise demonstrate they consider to be verbally artistic. According to this definition, like that of "poetics," verbal art can occur anywhere, from informal and everyday to formal and ritual discourse, and artistic forms, such as narratives, can be embedded in other forms, such as conversation, which in and of themselves might not be considered artistic.

Oral and written discourse

The texts presented on the pages of this book are all oral. In the process of this seemingly contradictory transformation – the writing down and the publication of orally performed discourse – all of the literary and scientific content of this work is brought to bear in one place. In recognizing the close relationship among transcription, analysis, and theory, the study of Native American oral discourse relates to issues that have been raised in other areas where precise transcription has been a necessary prerequisite to theory, such as language acquisition (Ervin-Tripp 1973; Ochs 1979) and conversational analysis (Sacks, Schegloff, and Jefferson 1974). Furthermore, by paying attention to the relationship not only among transcription, analysis, and theory but also between translation and representation on a printed page, we come to appreciate the nature, complexity, variety, and richness of this verbal art. For Native Americans are not and were not only memorizers of texts, acting as human analogs to the printed page. Quite the contrary. The performances recorded and translated in these pages are as much illustrations of the diversity of individual creative voices as they are representatives of maintained tradition; indeed, continued creative transformation is itself a part of the traditions that constitute Native American verbal art.

On the part of students of American literature, there has been growing recognition of the literary value of Native American discourse: See especially Kroeber (1981), Ramsey (1983), Rothenberg and Quasha (1974), and Swann (1983). What all of the authors presented here argue for is an appreciation of that discourse rooted in an understanding of its linguistic, rhetorical, and cultural features in all of their complexity.

Nor is Native American discourse dull, boring, and repetitive, although such features have sometimes been attributed to it by scholars and others not aware of its poetic and rhetorical organization, and of its meaning and significance in the cultural matrices in which it has developed and is performed. Since this organization is oral, it is necessary to present it in a written form which reveals the oral perception that lies behind it and which, to the greatest extent possible, preserves the ties to context present in the original oral performance.

Accordingly, the papers in this book stand as a critique of some statements that have been made in recent years proposing an oral/written distinction. (See for example Goody 1977; Ong 1982; Tannen 1982.) From our point of view, these statements do not come to terms with the nature of oral discourse, but tend rather to take written discourse as a model and then view oral discourse as less complicated, less advanced, and seemingly deficient in relation to the written texts of literate, technological societies. Serious attention to the nature of oral performance in relation to social and cultural context and to the relationship among transcription, representation, translation, and analysis reveals that there is no simple dichotomy between oral and written discourse, between nonliterate and literate societies. Rather there is considerable and quite interesting continuity between the oral and the written, showing diversity within each: There are oral genres in Native America that have such "written" properties as fixed text, "planning," and abstraction from context, and written genres in European-based societies having such "oral" properties as spontaneity and "repair," scansion into pause phrases, and context-dependent interpretability.

The papers in this book provide an empirical basis for a quite different view, one that describes oral performance and oral texts on their own terms. Critically useful in this have been a wide range of formal features of sound and of syntactic form, including those noted earlier for their role in organizing discourse into different kinds of hierarchical units and in so doing creating complex and sometimes discordant oral rhythms. And, the use of basic features of the voice is totally unique to the creation of oral text, manifesting itself in the use of pauses, pitch, and tempo, and the imitation of human and nonhuman voices and noises. Such techniques embed cultural symbolism and meaning directly in the sound patterns of language.

Understanding the nature of oral discourse requires an examination and analysis of the ways in which individuals employ these features and others, the varied and complicated ways they structure their performances. These features do not occur everywhere in the same way. Rather, they provide a set of resources for performance and are drawn on in the structuring of discourse in various ways in different societies, in different traditions, in different contexts within the same society and tradition, and possibly in distinct ways by performers or by the same performer in different contexts. It is by studying the ways in which the different properties and features of oral discourse relate to one another, intersect one another, and play off against one another that we can come to terms with the true complexity of this discourse. Proceeding in this way provides us with a quite different view of oral discourse than does the comparison of oral and written discourse along a simple set of dimensions based on standardized written languages.

One consequence of this approach is that work must focus on the native-language original rather than on translations. Even the best translator will not be able to mirror the structural features of the original in a translation and still preserve its meaning in all of its delicacy. Because of this, it is necessary to develop a full understanding of the linguistic devices available in the native language for conveying meaning even though in many cases such understanding is still the object of the most advanced linguistic research into the language. Another consequence of this approach is that the native context for interpretation is actively sought. Although the notion of a literature with universal appeal and relevance is attractive, our more immediate allegiance as anthropologists, folklorists, linguists, and students of ethnopoetics is to understand how this work is used, interpreted, and appreciated by insiders to the cultures from which it comes. In our view it is precisely this kind of understanding of the work that will clarify to outsiders its relevance and contribution to the broader philosophical, ethical, and aesthetic questions facing humankind.

Implications and relevance

The work represented in the papers in this book is significant for a number of reasons. One way to view this significance is in terms of its extraordinary disciplinary breadth: Taking language, text, and discourse as starting point, the authors draw from and add to linguistics, anthropology, folklore, and literary criticism, as well as in some cases musicology. The complexity, richness, and artistry of the texts they discuss is in part reflected in the combination of disciplines and approaches required in order adequately to come to terms with them.

As already noted, this work adds to a growing interest in and recognition of the importance of discourse in linguistics. It offers a form-based approach complementing mainstream work in the better-studied areas of phonology and syntax. Most important, it provides a useful framework in which to study the discourse functions of many aspects of phonology, syntax, and lexicon in addition to their better-known phrase- and sentence-level functions. And the functions of some features, such as phonological phrasing and ubiquitous particles typically glossed as "now," "well," and "of course," are almost entirely obscure without consideration of discourse.

With regard to anthropology, these papers very much reflect the continuing interest in the relationship among language, culture, society, and the individual, which has been salient in American anthropology, but at the same time they radically recast the nature of this relationship. One set of views of the language–culture relationship, growing out of the work of Boas, Sapir, and Whorf and reaching a height of popularity in the 1940s and 1950s, tries to establish the relationship by seeking correspondences between language and culture (see Friedrich 1979, 1986 and Silverstein 1979 for recent discussions). In the period of the 1960s interest in the language–culture relationship often focused on the content of the lexicon, as well as the application of then-current linguistic models in the study of cultural pattern, leading to a school of cultural anthropology labeling itself "ethnosemantics," "ethnoscience," or "cognitive anthropology" (Casson 1981; Tyler 1969). In the 1970s still another approach to the language–culture relationship came to the fore, an approach known as "ethnography of speaking" or "ethnography of communication" that studies language use in social and cultural contexts and has been largely cross-culturally relativistic in scope (Bauman and Sherzer 1974). Whereas the work represented in this book in some ways develops out of all of these earlier approaches, its special characteristic is that it constitutes an approach to the language–culture–society–individual relationship centered in text and discourse, the broadest and most comprehensive level of linguistic form, content, and use. That is, it sees the locus of the relationship in the structuring of discourse, in which individuals draw on resources provided by grammar, cultural symbolism, and shared beliefs and experiences and create or effect meaningful texts, whether these be narrations, conversations, or magical chants. It therefore carries into discourse inquiry into traditional anthropological issues, taking discourse to be the richest point of intersection of language and culture.

With regard to folklore in particular and the study of oral literature more generally, the papers in this volume contribute texts and analyses based on and steeped in actual performances by actual individuals in actual contexts. The authors all share a concern with the best ways to transcribe, represent, and translate this oral discourse, to build bridges between the original performers and current readers, between the artistic tradition of Sahaptin, Eskimo, Quiché, Tonkawa, and Kuna, and an English-speaking audience. More broadly, the papers develop linguistic methods and techniques of great potential value for folklorists, symbolic anthropologists, literary scholars, and others whose scientific goals critically depend on the interpretation of signs, symbols, and texts. These ways of analyzing discourse yield insight into aspects of oral message form and meaning which usually are inaccessible or pass unnoticed.

In turn, the authors draw on some of the methods and insights of literary critics, insisting on the need for a literary imagination in conjunction with careful and detailed linguistic analyses of verbally artistic discourse. But in addition they contribute to the literature of the world a body of texts of great literary value, a value that has often not been appreciated. The reasons for this lack of appreciation are many – the oral rather than written performance of these texts, the low social, economic, and political status accorded by outsiders to the groups of people involved, the need for cultural contextualization in order to understand symbolic and other meanings. But the types of presentations, translations, and analyses offered here bring out the complicated, rich, and truly literary value of these quite diverse texts. These papers also make an important contribution to questions of translation in that they take most seriously the problems involved in representing oral performances as written texts and in putting into published English the diverse oral traditions of Native America.

A most practical relevance of this line of research is to the publication of Native American texts in their original languages – generally with English translations included – for use in Native American communities, as part of bilingual education and child and adult literacy programs, as well as for general appreciation. This is extremely important in the face of the universalization of a few Western European languages throughout the New World, aided often by "bilingual education" of which the goal is too often to replace rather than reinforce young people's ancestral language. A number of publications prepared for – and in many cases by – native speakers using line-and-verse-type formats have already appeared, including Zepeda 1982 in Pima-Papago, Hinton and Watahomigie 1984 in a selection of Yuman languages, and from Alaska Dauenhauer 1973 and Williams and Leer 1978 in Tlingit, Krauss 1982 in Eyak (now an extinct language), Paul 1980 in Tanacross, Herbert 1982 in Gwich'in (Kutchin), Jones 1982 in Koyukon, and Morrow et al. 1980–2 and Woodbury 1984 in Central Alaskan Yupik Eskimo. Because they accurately reflect the speech patterns of original narrators and hence preserve aspects of linguistic structure that may be lost or buried in block-form renditions, these presentations have rapidly gained popularity with native readers, editors, and transcribers. At the same time, the new linguistic and literary perspectives of Native Americans engaged in this work both enlighten and reorient the approaches of the nonnative students who have struggled to come to terms with languages and literatures that are foreign to them.

Finally, these papers contribute in a unique and crucial way to the understanding and appreciation of Native American languages, cultures, societies, and literatures, for the texts in this book, as carefully analyzed and faithfully represented and translated on printed pages, enable individual voices to speak out, to be heard, to be read, and, we hope, to come into contact with an audience they would not otherwise have reached.

Notes

The editors wish to thank Dell Hymes for his extensive commentary on a draft of this introduction, in which many of his suggestions and interpretations have been incorporated.

1   Two conferences held at the University of Texas at Austin reflect this development. The first, held in April 1982, dealt with issues in Native American discourse in general. The second, in March 1984, concentrated on the discourse of Native South America.

References

Bauman, R. and Sherzer, J., eds. 1974. *Explorations in the ethnography of speaking.* Cambridge: Cambridge University Press.

Beaugrande, R. de and Dressler, W. 1981. *Introduction to text linguistics.* London: Longman Group.

Bright, W. 1979. A Karok myth in "measured verse": the translation of a performance. *Journal of California and Great Basin Anthropology* 1:117–123.

Casson, R. W., ed. 1981. *Language, culture, and cognition: anthropological perspectives.* New York: Macmillan.

Dauenhauer, R., ed. 1973. [Susie James, Sít' Ḵaa Káx̱ Kana.áa: Glacier Bay History; Frank Johnson, Dukt'ootl'/Strong Man; Tom Peter, X̱óotax̱ X̱'ayakuwdligadee Shaawát/Bear Husband; Robert Zuboff, Ḵudatan Kahídee/Salmon Box; Robert Zuboff, Táax'aa Shaadaax' X̱'éidax̱ sh Kalneek/Mosquito.] Fairbanks: Alaska Native Language Center, and Anchorage: Tlingit Readers, Inc.

Edmonson, M. S. 1971. *Lore: an introduction to the science of folklore and literature.* New York: Holt, Rinehart and Winston.

Edmonson, M. S., ed. 1973. *Meaning in Mayan languages.* The Hague: Mouton.

Ervin-Tripp, S. 1973. *Language acquisition and communicative choice.* Stanford: Stanford University Press.

Friedrich, P. 1979. Poetic language and the imagination: a reformulation of the Sapir hypothesis. In Friedrich, *Language, context, and the imagination.* Stanford: Stanford University Press, pp. 441–512.

1986. *The language parallax: linguistic relativism and poetic indeterminacy.* Austin: University of Texas Press.

Garibay K., Angel María. 1953. *Historia de la literatura náhuatl.* 2 vols. Mexico City: Porrua.

Goody, J. 1977. *The domestication of the savage mind.* Cambridge: Cambridge University Press.

Gumperz, J. J. 1982. *Discourse strategies.* Cambridge: Cambridge University Press.

Halliday, M. A. K. 1984. *A short introduction to functional grammar.* London: Arnold.

Hayes, B. 1981. *A metrical theory of stress rules.* Bloomington: Indiana University Linguistics Club.

Herbert, B. 1982. *Shandaa: in my lifetime*, ed. B. Pfisterer and J. McGary. Fairbanks: Alaska Native Language Center.

Hinton, L. and Watahomigie, L., eds. 1984. *Spirit Mountain: an anthology of Yuman story and song.* Tucson: University of Arizona Press.

Hymes, D. 1977. Discovering oral performance and measured verse in American Indian narrative. *New Literary History* 8:431–457.

1980. Particle, pause, and pattern in American Indian narrative verse. *American Indian Culture and Research Journal* 4(4):7–51.

1981. *"In vain I tried to tell you": essays in Native American ethnopoetics.* Philadelphia: University of Pennsylvania Press.

1985. Language, memory, and selective performance: Cultee's "Salmon's Myth" as twice told to Boas. *Journal of American Folklore* 98(390): 391–434.

Jacobs, M. 1959. *The content and style of an oral literature.* Viking Fund Publications in Anthropology 26. Chicago: University of Chicago Press.

Jakobson, R. 1960. Concluding statement: linguistics and poetics. In T. A. Sebeok, ed., *Style in language.* Cambridge: MIT Press, pp. 350–377.

1968. Poetry of grammar and grammar of poetry. *Lingua* 21:597–609.

Jones, E., ed. 1982. *Chief Henry yugh noholnigee: stories Chief Henry told.* Fairbanks: Alaska Native Language Center.

Krauss, M. E., ed. 1982. *In honor of Eyak: the art of Anna Nelson Harry.* Fairbanks: Alaska Native Language Center.

Kroeber, K., ed. 1981. *Traditional American Indian literatures: texts and interpretations.* Lincoln: University of Nebraska Press.

Labov, W. and Fanshel, D. 1977. *Therapeutic discourse.* New York: Academic Press.

Levinson, S. C. 1983. *Pragmatics*. Cambridge: Cambridge University Press.

Liberman, M. Y. 1975. The intonational system of English. Doctoral dissertation, Massachusetts Institute of Technology. Reprinted 1977, Bloomington: Indiana University Linguistics Club.

Lord, A. B. 1960. *The singer of tales*. Cambridge: Harvard University Press.

McLendon, S. 1982. Meaning, rhetorical structure, and discourse organization in myth. In D. Tannen, ed., *Analyzing discourse: text and talk*. Georgetown University Round Table on Language and Linguistics 1981. Washington, D.C.: Georgetown University Press, pp. 284–305.

Morrow, Phyllis, Mather, Elsie, et al., eds. 1980–2. *Yupiit Akiugit*. Bethel, Alaska: Yugtun Qaneryaramek Calivik. [Monthly periodical.]

Ochs, E. 1979. Transcription as theory. In E. Ochs and B. Schieffelin, eds., *Developmental pragmatics*. New York: Academic Press, pp. 43–72.

Ong, W. J. 1982. *Orality and literacy: the technologizing of the word*. London and New York: Methuen.

Paul, Gaither. 1980. *Stories for my grandchildren*, ed. Ron Scollon. Fairbanks: Alaska Native Language Center.

Prince, A. S. 1983. Relating to the grid. *Linguistic Inquiry* 14:19–100.

Ramsey, Jarold. 1983. Reading the fire: essays in the traditional Indian literatures of the Far West. Lincoln: University of Nebraska Press.

Rothenberg, J. and Quasha, G. 1974. *America, a prophecy*. New York: Random House.

Sacks, H., Schegloff, E. A., and Jefferson, G. 1974. A simplest systematics for the organization of turn-taking in conversation. *Language* 50(4):696–735.

Scollon, R. 1979. The role of audience in the structure of Athabaskan oral performances. Paper presented at the 43rd International Congress of Americanists, Vancouver.

Sherzer, J. 1976. *An areal-typological study of American Indian languages north of Mexico*. Amsterdam: North Holland.

1983. *Kuna ways of speaking: an ethnographic perspective*. Austin: University of Texas Press.

Silverstein, M. 1979. Language structure and linguistic ideology. In P. R. Clyne et al., eds., *The elements: a parasession on linguistic units and levels*. Chicago: Chicago Linguistic Society, pp. 193–247.

Swann, B., ed. 1983. *Smoothing the ground: essays on Native American oral literature*. Berkeley and Los Angeles: University of California Press.

Tannen, D. 1982. Oral and literate strategies in spoken and written narratives. *Language* 58:1–21.

Tannen, D., ed. 1984. *Coherence in spoken and written discourse*. Norwood, N.J.: Ablex.

Tedlock, D. 1977. Toward an oral poetics. *New Literary History* 8:507–519.

1983. *The spoken word and the work of interpretation*. Philadelphia: University of Pennsylvania Press.

In press. Verbal art. In W. C. Sturtevant, ed., *Handbook of North American Indians*, vol. 1, *Introduction*. Washington, D.C.: Smithsonian Institution.

Tyler, S. A., ed. 1969. *Cognitive anthropology*. New York: Holt, Rinehart and Winston.

Williams, W. and Leer, J. 1978. *Tongass texts*. Fairbanks: Alaska Native Language Center.

Witherspoon, G. 1977. *Language and art in the Navajo universe*. Ann Arbor: University of Michigan Press.

Woodbury, A. C., ed. 1984. *Cev'armiut qanemciit qulirait=llu· Eskimo stories from Chevak, Alaska*. Fairbanks: Alaska Native Language Center.

    1985. The functions of rhetorical structure: a study of Central Alaskan Yupik Eskimo discourse. *Language in Society* 14(2):153–190.

Zepeda, Ofelia, ed. 1982. *Mat hekid o ju:/When it rains: Pima and Papago poetry*. Sun Tracks: An American Indian Literary series 7. Tucson: University of Arizona, Dept. of English.

2

TONKAWA POETICS: JOHN RUSH BUFFALO'S "COYOTE AND EAGLE'S DAUGHTER"

Dell Hymes

Introduction

The person to whom this essay is dedicated, Harry Hoijer, entered anthropology by devoting himself to the recording and analysis of a near-extinct language. Throughout his career he stood for painstaking care in the description, classification, and interpretation of the languages of native North America, and for the interdependence of language and the rest of culture. What seemed evident to his generation has seemed less evident, even invisible, to many since. The excitement of formal models and what has come to be called "theoretical" linguistics, and the anxiety about language that cultural anthropologists tend to share with other products of American culture, have made linguistic work seem quite separate, except as a source of conceptual metaphor. That it is hard to understand what people do if one does not know what they say; that records of what people say and can say are a natural part of study of their way of life; that linguistics ought to be, for anthropologists, first and foremost a way of coping with language as part of ways of life; that the techniques for coping with language are part of cultural anthropology, not of some other, esoteric discipline; these things tend to be forgotten, uncomfortable. Monoglottic ineptitude and theoretical snobbery, as between cultural anthropologists and academic linguistics, allow much of anthropology and linguistics both to fail. The anthropology fails to live up to the standard advocated by Boas, Lowie, and others, of taking the cultures it studies as seriously as objects of scholarship as we take the high cultures of classical antiquity, modern Europe, China, Japan, and India. The linguistics elaborates formal models that answer to needs for bookkeeping and simplification of manipulable data, rather than to the actualities of language as a means of human life and personal identity.

Old texts and grammars might seem merely an incipient stage of this separation, forbidding in their unfamiliar technical garb, *disjecta membra* of what was once living tradition (among Native Americans and among those who sought them out). And it is indeed the case that the study of Native American languages has yet to take its materials seriously enough, and make them its first concern. The bibliographies of the languages grow, but there is

17

hardly to be found anywhere a comprehensive, cogent presentation of what is known about a language, so that what is known can be used by anthropologists, folklorists, even just other linguists. There are no handbooks that interpret, reconcile, codify the varying orthographies, vocabularies, grammatical discussions that make what is collectively known a means to further knowledge.

The situation is worse even than this. It now appears that we have misled ourselves as to the myths and tales we have thought long known. We have allowed to stand a perpetration of the cardinal sin, the distortion of another cultural reality through imposition of categories of our own. We have thought that Native American myths and tales are prose and have printed them as such.

As the work in this volume amply attests, the fact of the matter now seems otherwise. Dennis Tedlock (1972, 1983, this volume) has used criteria of pause and intonation to present Zuni narratives in lines. Attention to neglected linguistic features, especially the initial particles that often begin sentences in Native American discourse, has begun to disclose patterns in which such particles take part, patterns that show the texts to be organized in lines and verses by grammatical means (for Zuni, see Hymes 1982). Barre Toelken and Tacheeni Scott (1981) have found patterning of a similar sort in a Navajo myth. Sally McLendon has found something of the sort in Eastern Pomo, William Bright in Karok (see McLendon 1982, Bright 1984, Hymes 1980b, 1985b), both languages of California; and I have found it in texts in Hupa, Klamath, Chasta Costa, Takelma (see Hymes 1980b, ms.), Wiyot, and Yurok, languages, like Karok, of northwestern California and southern Oregon. M. Dale Kinkade (1983, 1984, 1985, in press) has demonstrated the presence of such patterns in Chehalis and Cowlitz Salish, languages of southwestern Washington; Judith Berman (1986) has done so for the texts obtained by Boas in Kwakw'ala (British Columbia); and Anthony Woodbury (1985, this volume) for Central Alaskan Yupik Eskimo. Henry Zenk, Robert Moore, and I have found such patterning in Chinook Jargon from various sources (Hymes and Zenk, in press, Zenk and Moore 1983). Several students at the University of Pennsylvania have begun to work out such patterning in other languages (Cree [Deborah Blincoe], Hopi [Susan Fiering], Ojibwa [Ridie Wilson Ghezzi]). It is present in Coos, Alsea, and Tillamook, languages of the Oregon coast, and Kalapuya (see Hymes 1979, 1981b, in press) of the Willamette valley; in Bella Coola (Hymes 1983b), Nootka, and Tsimshian (Dunn 1984), languages, like Kwakiutl, of British Columbia; in Nez Perce and Kutenai, languages of Idaho; in Winnebago, a Siouan language of the midwest (I have analyzed further a text presented by Miner [1982], and Kathleen Danker has analyzed original tape recordings). Donald Bahr has shown the presence of a related kind of patterning in Pima–Papago ritual oratory (1975). The scope of occurrence is no doubt wider, since similar principles are at work in Saramaccan narratives from Suriname (work of Richard and Sally Price), Brazilian Portuguese,

Appalachian English (work of Virginia Hymes), Irish English (work of Henry Glassie), and elsewhere.

My own work has been first of all with texts in the several Chinookan dialects: Wasco/Wishram, Clackamas, Kathlamet, (Shoalwater) Chinook. Some papers resulting from this work are the most detailed presentations so far of such analysis (Hymes 1976, 1977, 1980a [see now 1981a], 1983a, and the Kathlamet Sun myth in Hymes ms.), and the findings there inform the approach here. Over the last several years the Chinookan work has been undertaken in collaboration with the poet and typographer Charles Bigelow, with a view to a book representative of the art of three principal Chinookan narrators, presenting that art in a typeface and format especially designed for the purpose.

The implications of such works, as well as of the Tonkawa text presented here, are far reaching. On the one hand, all the collections that are now in print must be redone. They do not show the structure of the texts they present – a realized structure of poetics, rhetoric, and performance, independent of relations of content (incident and event), encompassing and giving shape to content (see Hymes 1985a). On the other hand, old collections that have seemed of little current interest promise new rewards. There are new reasons for mastering the orthographies and grammatical features. Hidden within the margin-to-margin printed lines are poems, waiting to be seen for the first time. With all these collections we are at a stage corresponding to that at which the Exeter book was known to contain an Old English text called "beowulf," but at which it was not yet known that the text concealed an organization into alliterative verse. Native American texts, so far as we know, do not conceal alliterative verse, but they do contain patterns of organization into verse that often enough have a power, poignancy, or humor of their own.

So far the implications might be taken as limited to those who enjoy or study narrative. There is a further implication as well. Patterns of discourse of this kind are at one and the same time linguistic and cultural. The distinction is without a difference. The means are linguistic, what is patterned in language; yet the patterning is not part of a grammar, but of an event, a performance, of which we have some record. The patterns are uses of cultural (and personal) styles to a complex purpose, at once aesthetic, moral, and informational. Discovery of the patterns makes possible a surer grasp of the aesthetic, moral, and informational intentions that a performance record contains. Dulling repetition and obscure sequence may be discovered to be instead proportion and point.

In sum, insofar as authentic narratives are thought relevant to the understanding of Native American cultures, there is a great body of work to be done before the narratives can be authentically seen. It makes no sense to ask if this work is linguistics, cultural anthropology, folklore, or something else. It cannot be done without some command of linguistics, but it cannot be done without some command of Native American traditions, some sense of the voices to be imagined behind the words. A dash of poetry is helpful, too. The skills needed to interpret the texts must match the skills that made them. Whoever does the work, whatever they choose to call it, the results will be a vital accession to understanding of Native American ways of life, an accession with bearing on general understanding of the place of language and narrative in human culture.

The format for presenting narrative texts in terms of their verse structure has to be invented, just as the conventions for presenting the texts of the Bible in terms of verses, and Shakespeare in terms of scenes, have had to be invented. The conventions adopted here are the result of experience mainly with Chinookan texts. A matrix encompassing the maximum number of distinctions, levels, that need to be recognized has seven terms: part, act, scene, stanza, verse, versicle, line. (See Hymes 1981a for detailed discussion.)

Often enough, as John Bierhorst and Barre Toelken have observed, North American narratives have two major *parts*. The Tonkawa myth has a coming, followed by a going. Parts are indicated here with capital letters in parentheses, e.g. (PART ONE).

A second level is that of *acts* and *scenes*. The major sections within parts can be called "acts," in recognition of the dramatic nature of myth performance. Melville Jacobs wrote of Clackamas myths with dramatic terminology, and it appropriately fits the "dramatistic" perspective toward languages of Kenneth Burke, a perspective that has played an important part in my own thinking. Sometimes, but not always, it is necessary to recognize scenes within acts. Both units usually coincide with shifts in setting, participants, events, or the like. Pattern and proportion in the grouping of stanzas, the next lower level, however, is a key consideration as well. Acts are indicated here with majuscule Roman numerals, e.g. I, and scenes are indicated with minuscule Roman numerals, e.g. *i*.

Stanzas are groupings of verses, usually in accord with patterns of both overt (numerical) and implicit (rhetorical) form. Stanzas are indicated here with capital letters, e.g. A.

Verses are very much the heart of the matter. Where overt initial markers distinguish units, it is usually verses that they distinguish, as in Takelma and Tonkawa, and in the Wishram Chinook narratives of Louis Simpson. Initial markers are not always present. In the Clackamas Chinook narratives of Victoria Howard there are sometimes markers, but not always. The Clackamas texts do show the same kinds of underlying rhetorical relationships among lines and larger units as those overtly marked by pairs of initial particles in Wishram. The same kind of local effects and small-scale units occur. The implicit logic of organization, of rhetorical coherence, is the same, a tripartite scheme that I have labeled Onset, Ongoing, Outcome (see Hymes 1976, 1977). Thus, when Coyote goes along at the beginning of a text, he is likely to "go, go along, get there." When a deserted boy first hears something that will help him survive (the noise of a bit of fire set aside by his grandmothers), he turns his eyes, he looks, he dries his tears. When, successful, he is about to be revenged on those who deserted him, he turns, he looks, he sees (many people coming across in a canoe). And so on.

The Chinookan pattern number is five, and very often a five-part sequence shows two intersecting uses of the three-part rhetorical pattern. The outcome of the first sequence is simultaneously the onset of the second.

I cannot stress too strongly that there is no mechanical way to discover the verses of a text. Initial particles, and other recurrent markers, may provide a segmentation of much of it; some sections may fall into clear patterns; but the organization of the whole will have to be thought through. No text I have seen suggests that the original performers were simply filling in a pattern, analogous to the filling of a fixed number of lines and a prescribed rhyme scheme in the writing of a Petrarchan or Shakespearean sonnet. To be sure, the performers were using formal patterning, and sometimes one can detect a slip and recovery in its use (Hymes 1976:sect. 4.2). Commonly in Chinookan the pattern is so ingrained that it informs casual texts and even English conversation among older people. Hiram Smith, one of the last speakers of Wasco, may say things such as this remark in the course of a restaurant conversation about high prices in grocery stores: "What can you do? You buy, you pay, and you get out."

But the narrators are using formal patterning to rhetorical ends, and often enough a formal pattern can be recognized only by recognizing the underlying rhetorical form that it implements. A line or a verse may fit, but yet may fit in more than one way. Thinking through the text in terms of its implicit rhetorical form can provide a solution. Indeed, no analysis is satisfactory, I think, until one can read and hear the result in terms of such underlying form.

Verses are groupings of *lines*. Just as initial markers, when present, go far toward segmenting a text into verses, so predications, verbs, go far toward segmenting a text into lines. Again, not wholly so. Pattern and proportion and local effect often enough indicate that a phrase or particle other than a verb phrase has status as a line. Sometimes, as often in Chinookan and Sahaptin, lines themselves fit the pattern numbers (three and five in these cases) in a text. In general, however, the numbering of lines is not fixed. Quite the contrary: It is the power of verse markers to come now rapidly, line after line, or to come now slowly, several lines with each, that is a vital factor in the pacing and shaping of a text. A narrative may move rapidly through a scene, a verse marker to each new predicate, or pause for elaboration, filling a verse with a catalog.

Versicle is an obscure term that is useful for designating small groupings of lines within a verse. Sometimes one finds pairings of lines within a verse.

Sometimes one finds pairings of lines or phrases within the scope of a verse marker. The pairs of lines (25–30) within Coyote's preparation of a fire-hardened piece of wood in the Tonkawa myth may appear to be such.

The heart of the matter, as has been said, is in the identification of verses. When a narrative is organized by initial particles, these particles identify verses by their presence, and stanzas by their grouping. The larger units, acts and scenes, are larger groupings of the stanzas; the lines are partly derivative constituents of the verses. When a narrative is organized without regular use of initial particles, the interdependence of lines and underlying rhetorical form comes to the fore. The form/meaning covariation that is the key to analysis is between groups of lines and rhetorical form directly.

I can attempt to summarize the experience of such analysis so far in definitional style in the following way.

Native American narratives, those at least that stem from valid perform-ances, are organized in terms of lines, verses, and stanzas. The grouping of lines into verses, and of verses into stanzas, tends to follow, but not exclusively, the pattern numbers of the culture. Verses are often, but not always, overtly marked by the recurrence of a small set of initial elements. Verses appear always to be grouped in terms of a covert pattern of rhetorical cohesion. Such a pattern appears to be congruent with the pattern numbers of the culture, depending upon pairs and sets of pairs in cultures in which the pattern number is four, and upon threes and fives in cultures in which the pattern number is five.

It is important to notice that the pair of pattern numbers, whether three and five, as in Chinookan, or two and four, as in Tonkawa, does not exhaust the kinds of relationship within a text. Some portions of a narrative may show intrinsic patterning of their own, distinct from the general schema (see Hymes 1983a, 1985b). The scheme, which may variously be called a pattern of rhetorical cohesion, a narrative analysis of experience, a logical narrative action, bespeaks a conventional form of thought and convincing speech. The segment of six lines in which Coyote prepares to fight the dangerous being is an instance. It stands as a unit by itself within the two- and four-part patterning that surrounds it. (Perhaps it is echoed by the combination of four- and two-line units, totaling six, that follows [lines 30–3, 34–5].)

Moreover, a contrasting principle of relationship may have a subordinate role in a narrator's tradition or style. Thus, in Chinookan, the fundamental principle of three- and five-part relationships is sometimes found to comprise pairs of lines or turns at talk. Such pairs fit within the three- and five-part ground plan; there may, for instance, be a stanza with ten turns at talk, grouped in five pairs, or a stanza of three verses, each verse consisting of two lines. Such use of pairing seems to involve an intensification or heightening.

In this Tonkawa text, the ground plan of two- and four-part alternation sometimes comprises a relationship of three against one. This is true of the four pairs of stanzas that make up Act IV at the conclusion of Part One. In each case, the (a) verse has three lines, the (b) verse one. The same relationship appears again in the concluding Act VIII of Part Two and in the myth as a whole, if in less concentrated a way: See VIII *ii* C (lines 170–3) and *iv* C (203–6). All these instances could be taken to involve a local peripety of the action: Coyote's restoration of the people; Coyote's acceptance of being commanded by his wife's emissary; the wife's departure with her parents.

Again, in what appear to be two focal acts, VI and VIII, certain stanzas contain three verses. VI *ii* D and *iv* G are alike in containing actions of Coyote that offend his wife, and so contribute to the outcome of the act (her departure). In Act VIII the last three stanzas (BCD) of scene *i* have each three verses. These stanzas contain essentially the same content as the corresponding stanzas of Act IV, but here the content is marked for an additional verse by an additional initial anaphoric particle. The clear contrast in treatment as between the two acts suggests an intentional pointing up of the contrast in outcome. So does the doubling of the action. In VI the wife's pursuit has two stanzas, each with two turns of speech, the second of which introduces water, topic of the next scene. In VIII the pursuit has four stanzas, each with two turns of speech, and all are devoted incrementally to the pursuit.

All this suggests that in Tonkawa, at least in Tonkawa as deployed by John Rush Buffalo, three-part relationships, working within the general two- and four-part frame, foreground material especially pertinent to the outcome of a story. Verse form itself arouses expectations, as between Act IV, in which the wife leaves Coyote, but will come after him again, and Act VIII, in which she conducts herself differently and will leave him for good.

Tonkawa: retrospect and prospect

Harry Hoijer's dissertation at the University of Chicago under Edward Sapir was based on his own fieldwork with the surviving speakers of the Tonkawa language of Texas. This research found fruit first in a grammar, his dissertation, published in revised form in the third and last volume (1933) of the *Handbook of American Indian Languages* instituted by Boas. This was followed by a grammatical sketch in a set of typological sketches (1946), a Tonkawa-to-English analytical dictionary (1949b), and the texts from which this myth is taken (1972). The first part of the same text was used as the subject of analysis at the end of the published grammar, so that we have Hoijer's English equivalents and comments at separate stages of his career and work with the language: the new adherent to the Boas tradition and the onset of structural linguistics, the settled scholar emerging as senior living figure in American linguistic anthropology.

The work of providing an adequate descriptive base for a little-known language has been rather far from the forefront of linguistic discussion in recent years, although it is perhaps regaining attention now. In the short run there always are more pertinent things to do, although in the long run hardly anything proves more important. It is good to be able to pay tribute once again to Hoijer's contribution to such work (see Hymes 1967) by using it. The feeling is strengthened by encountering the following remark (Bulow and Bulow 1975:58): "A nationally known folkorist recently gave us a copy of Hoijer's *Tonkawa Texts* with a note that reads, in part, 'This is without a doubt the most boring book of stories I have ever read; therefore, it is likely very authentic and will be interesting to you.' " The point of this analysis of a Tonkawa text is to show that the folklorist, and those who quote him, had not actually read the Tonkawa stories. What was read was a document, meant to make text available in linguistically scrupulous form. The literary form of the text, like the literary form of most Native American texts, is not available without further study.

It is a pleasure to present this Tonkawa text also because the authors of the essay just quoted impugn a perspective that Hoijer helped to maintain. They join the uninformed parade that blames Whorf and the perspective of linguistic relativity for something with which neither had anything to do. Hoijer was of course a cautious interpreter of the views of Sapir and Whorf on linguistic relativity, very much in the cautious spirit of Boas, for whom recognition of relativity, both of structure and associated form of thought, went hand in hand with analysis and validity. For an analysis of a language to be valid, it must describe the language in its own terms, *sui generis*, that is, in terms of features and relationships actually present and significant in it. The perspective of linguistic relativity was the perspective of avoiding ethnocentrism. Within this perspective, Sapir gave brilliant suggestions of typological patterns that linked quite different languages, and Whorf divined an underlying plane of form of which specific languages were manifestations. The very generality and rigor of linguistic methodology itself implied fundamental characteristics common to all languages. The perspective of linguistic relativity required that common characteristics be warranted, not imputed; it prescribed respect for the configurations to which individual histories and ways of life had given rise; it delighted in the variety of human language, as creations of the human spirit, much as one may delight in the variety of styles of art and music to which different cultures and periods have given rise. The perspective of linguistic relativity saw itself as defending the underdog against established prejudice, prejudice unfair to most languages of the world either in forcing them into an ethnocentric Procrustean bed, or in stigmatizing them as inferior for differing from an ethnocentric standard of what a language should be.

Perhaps the authors quoted above are right in thinking that some who write about Native American literature use a vulgar notion of linguistic relativity as an excuse for ignoring it, or for damning it with faint praise for its authentic crudity. Perhaps there are some who think that relativity implies that Native

American literature is too alien to understand, so that one can be excused from the attempt. Whorf would have had no patience with such myopia. Linguistics for him was a key to meaning and discovery. The very point of the linguistic tradition of Boas and Sapir, with which he identified himself, was that it was possible to penetrate surface oddity and confusion, disclosing the rich architecture beneath. The rigor of linguistic form was a guide to validity of interpretation, to the probing of meaning, to getting subtle, novel relations of meaning right.

It is just such a perspective that is required if we are to do justice to Native American texts. Of course it is to be assumed that each literature, just as each language, is grounded in what is universal in human life and in the use of verbal means to expressive, reflective ends. But one accepts as well that the literature, like the language, must be allowed its own configuration, its own economy of means and meanings, in effect, its own voice. Spareness, and avoidance of metaphor, for example, may be canons of a lucid, effective style. To assume otherwise, as do the Bulows in their comments on what Stanley Newman and Ann Gayton have said of Yokuts, is not to defend Yokuts, but unwittingly to retreat to the assumptions that let the fustian of James McPherson's *Ossian* stand for primitive poetry to a willingly deceived public two centuries ago. In my own experience, the power of Native American literature seems often to lie, not in decorative elaboration, but in uncanny selection. Images often enough are not recognized as images at first because they are not invented, but chosen. The obscuring of the morning sun by cloud and the involuntary blinking of the chief's eyes in the Kathlamet myth of the Sun (Hymes 1975) seem to me examples of this. Light is knowledge, the partial seeing of the sun at the outset of the myth is the proper balance in human knowledge of the power the sun represents, the blinking is sign that the shining thing now wanted is beyond the knowledge, and control, of the chief. All this is grounded in an identification of light with knowledge that is common to mankind, and expressed in a selection of details so natural to the region and events of the story that the power of the images is not at first noticed. Spareness of surface may reflect poverty of art, but it may also reflect the fact that the text in question fits a canon once stated by Keats (quoted in Booth 1969:26–7): "Poetry should be great and unobtrusive, a thing which enters into one's soul, and does not startle it or amaze it with itself, but with its subject."

In the perspective of Boas, Sapir, Whorf, and Hoijer, difference was emphasized out of respect for the integrity of individually shaped cultures, languages, literatures. Today many seem to find that difference implies inequality, as does the essay that has been quoted. I do not quite know why, but the inversion is real. Where recognition of difference meant recognition of equal right, it now seems to imply denial of equal right. A perspective championed by a German Jew who emigrated to the United States for lack of scientific community in his homeland, who fought all his life against racism, has been branded as racist in public linguistic meetings. I suspect that this new dispensation has to do with the changed relation between dominant and dominated cultures and ethnic groups; in the earlier period the other cultures would still be thought of as separate, there as distinct from here. The world could be imagined as an ethnological map, each culture with its color and boundary amid the whole. Now subordinated groups are here as well as there, caught up in the workings of the subordinating system much more; their members often have the identity of their group of origin, but not its language, or not of its traditional ways of life. The suggestion "You think differently" once could imply the response "Yes, we have our own ways (as good as yours)"; now the suggestion may seem to imply the corollary: "And so we can exclude you from the positions in our society (in which you are inescapably caught up) to which you aspire." All this is conjecture on my part. I can point to the false reinterpretation of the perspective in which Whorf and Hoijer worked, but cannot be sure of the explanation of the shift. I can be sure, however, that our present stage in knowledge of the true nature of Native American literature requires the humble respect for the integrity of alternative configurations and the use of linguistic form as a guide to meaning that the traditional perspective brought to grammar itself. If we are not to be allowed to recognize the difference in the verbal art of Frances Johnson, John Rush Buffalo, Charles Cultee, and others, then we shall in effect be acting as if the only good Indian is a dead Indian, an Indian dead to our minds, and might as well bury their texts with their bodies. We will join the conspiracy to keep ourselves safe from the dangerous knowledge that there was a verbal art in the land in which we live before we came. Much was done to destroy that art and the languages in which it lived, and much still conspires to keep the knowledge of it from us, Indians and others alike. Yet if recognition of the worth of Native American cultures is not part of the vocation of anthropology (and folklore and linguistics) in the United States, what true vocation can be claimed?

We have for dictionary only a Tonkawa-to-English list, but we do have a thorough grammar. Dr. Rudy Troike, once a student of Hoijer, has devoted some time to the language, and the sources for it, and could provide, as I cannot, a full account. Perhaps he will be able to provide an edition of all the Tonkawa texts in the poetic format that they can now be seen to have. To do so would be a deserved tribute to John Rush Buffalo, who appears to have been the key to Hoijer's success in obtaining texts (1972:1). He "had a reputation as an excellent storyteller," Hoijer says, and I hope that the present analysis does some justice to his art. I am less familiar with Tonkawa than with Chinookan in verbal style and device. For the present analysis I claim only that it shows the presence of organization into verse and line in Tonkawa narrative. Something of the aesthetic use of such organization can be glimpsed, but a great deal more is to be learned, both from closer analysis of Tonkawa and from comparison with other southwestern styles.

The title of the myth is that given by Hoijer in the text collection (1972: 19–24, text no. 4). In the grammar of 1933 the analysis of the first part of the text was headed "Coyote and the Monster" (1933:ch. 3, "Text Analysis," pp. 140–8), perhaps to fit the use of only the first part, which does focus on Coyote and the fearsome being. The title of the text collection is better suited to the full myth.

The Tonkawa text occupies 101 lines in twenty-two (numbered) paragraphs in the published collection. Analysis indicates that the text comprises 208 lines, organized in 100 verses. The verses are distributed mostly in twos, sometimes in fours, but sometimes as an isolate or a series of three, among forty-eight stanzas. The stanzas can in turn be grouped into two sets of four acts each (Parts One and Two), with the second and fourth acts of the second set (Part Two) parallel in action, having what appears to be an intermediate level of organization in the form of four scenes each. This structural elaboration suggests that the focus of the telling lies in the contrasted depiction of the relation between the wife and Coyote in these acts (VI, VIII). So does the unusual fact of three verses, not two or four, within a stanza at certain points in these two acts (VI *ii* D, VIII *i* BCD), as mentioned at the end of the first section of this essay. It is noteworthy that this emphasis on the rightness of a woman's point of view comes from a man.

The profile of the verse analysis may be useful as an indication of the structure and a guide to the myth itself, which follows now in Tonkawa and in English. The myth is followed in turn by further discussion of the analysis and of some of the myth's main features.[1]

Profile

Parts/acts		Scenes/stanzas	Verses	Lines	Total
ONE I		A	ab	2, 2 (1–4)	4
		B	a	4 (5–8)	4
		C	ab	2, 3 (9–13)	5
		D	ab	3, 2 (14–8)	5 = 18
	II	A	ab	3, 2 (19–23)	5
		B	a	6 (24–9)	6
		C	ab	4, 2 (30–5)	6
		D	ab	2, 2 (36–9)	4 = 21
	III	A	abcd	1, 2, 1, 1 (40–4)	5
		B	abcd	1, 1, 1, 1 (45–8)	4
		C	ab	3,1 (49–52)	4
		D	ab	1, 3 (53–6)	3 = 16
	IV	A	ab	3, 1 (57–60)	4
		B	ab	3, 1 (61–4)	4
		C	ab	3, 1 (65–8)	4
		D	ab	3, 1 (69–72)	4 = 16
TWO V		A	a	1 (73)	1
		B	ab	2, 3 (74–8)	5

(*Table continues on next page.*)

Profile (cont.)

Parts/acts			Scenes/stanzas	Verses	Lines	Total	
			C	ab	3, 2 (79–83)	5	
			D	ab	1, 2 (84–6)	3	= 14
VI	*i*		A	ab	3, 2 (87–91)	5	
			B	ab	3, 2 (92–6)	5	= 10
	ii		C	ab	2, 4 (97–102)	6	
			D	abc	2, 2, 4 (103–10)	8	= 14
	iii		E	ab	2, 2 (111–4)	4	
			F	ab	2, 2 (115–8)	4	= 8
	iv		G	abc	4, 1, 1 (119–24)	6	
			H	ab	1, 2 (125–7)	3	= 9
VII			A	ab	2, 1 (128–30)	3	
			B	ab	2, 2 (131–4)	4	
			C	ab	2, 1 (135–7)	3	
			D	ab	2, 2 (138–41)	4	= 14
VIII	*i*		A	ab	3, 2 (142–6)	5	
			B	abc	1, 2, 2 (147–51)	5	
			C	abc	1, 2, 2 (152–6)	5	
			D	abc	1, 2, 2 (157–61)	5	= 20
	ii		A	a	4 (162–5)	4	
			B	ab	2, 2 (166–9)	4	
			C	ab	3, 1 (170–3)	4	
			D	ab	2, 1 (174–6)	3	= 15
	iii		A	ab	2, 2 (177–80)	4	
			B	ab	2, 2 (181–4)	4	
			C	ab	2, 2 (185–8)	4	
			D	ab	2, 4 (189–94)	6	= 18
	iv		A	ab	2, 2 (195–8)	4	
			B	ab	2, 2 (199–202)	4	
			C	ab	3, 1 (203–6)	4	
	(Close)		D	ab	1, 1 (207–8)	2	= 14

Tonkawa text

(PART ONE) Coyote restores the people

I   [*He discovers an empty camp.*]
A (a)   Ha:csokonayla ha:nanoklakno'o;
          'E:no:la na:to:n'a:y'ik hayconat.
    (b)   Heylapanoklakno'o;
          'E:l'ok na:to:nwa:'a:lak 'a:yay'a:y'ik yacox'ana:naxok ye:laklakno'o
          lak.

B (a)   Ha:csokonayla haklanat,   5
          yacox'ana:naxokwa:y'ik xa:xat;
          holaw'a:y'ik xa:xal'ok,
          yacox'an':yay'a:y'ik ma:kanoklakno'o.

C (a) 'E:kla Ha:csokonayla hakxonat,
       "Hecu: 'e:kwa?" noklakno'o.   10
   (b) 'E:kla kwa:nwa:'a:la,
       "Te:w'an yacox'antanate:la tickan'a:ka kapa:we," noklakno'o.
       "Hecocxo:kla wetoxano'o," noklakno'o.

D (a) 'E:kla Ha:csokonayla,
       "Na:kw ma:kapew," noklakno'o.   15
           "Taxso:l'ok ta:he:sokyawa:ha'a," noklakno'o.
   (b) 'E:kla kwa:nwa:'a:la kaltey'a:y'ik hatxilnata,
       "Ha:csokonayla taxso:l'ok ta:he:sokyawa:toyow no:na'a," noklakno'o.

II   [*He prepares to fight.*]
A (a) "Taxso:l'ok, ta:he:sokyawa:s'ok,
       "Yalxilnapew," noklakno'o Ha:csokonayla.   20
       "Ya:ckexwelpew," noklakno'o.
   (b) 'E:kla,
       "Hehe:'," noklakno'o.

B (a) Ke:sxaya:kwa,
           cakaw'a:y'ik haklanat,   25
       tekalak yaxwkaycet,
           kaxaw nesam'am'ata,
       sokota,
           coxnaklakno'o.

C (a) 'E:t ho:staxso:n hacxot,   30
       kaltey'a:y'ik hatxilnata,
       taxasaycotak yelnata,
       hawa:tak hexsasaklakno'o.
   (b) 'E:ta yantanawaye:w'an yelnata,
       hexsasaklakno'o.   35

D (a) 'E:ta 'ecin'e taxasaklanake:w'an,
       'ecin'e hexsasaklakno'o.
   (b) 'E:ta holaw'a:lak 'acxo:nte:w'an yelnata,
       hexsasaklakno'o.

III   [*He meets the monster.*]
A (a) 'E:kwa kwa:kwanka noho:na:'e:kla, Ha:csokonayla
           hetay'o:klakno'o.   40
   (b) 'E:kwa,
       "We:l'at 'eyte:l!" noklakno'o.
   (c) 'E:kwa hecocxo:kwa:'a:la xokos'a:w'an samox ye:laklakno'o;
   (d) 'Enik kes'acan'a:w'an kaxaw ye:laklakno'o.

B (a) 'E:kla kwa:kwanwa:ka saxwaklakno'o.   45

(b)   'E:kla Ha:csokonayla c'a:peklakno'o.
(c)   'E:kwa wa:tel henkwa:takla;
(d)   Ha:csokonayla ta:he:sokyo:klakno'o hecocxo:kwa:'a:lak.

C (a)   'E:kwa, Ha:csokonayeyka'ay'a:la ha:naxokita,
      hecocxo:kwa:'a:lak hewlet,   50
      ta:he:sokyo:nonlakno'o.
(b)   'E:no:ka, ya:lo:nonlakno'o, hecocso:kwa:'a:lak.

D (a)   'E:ta Ha:csokonayeyka'aywa:ka na:'e:klakno'o.
(b)   'E:kla Ha:csokonayla yacox'ane:w'an tickankapaye'e:lak.
      "Yacox'aneka:tkak tamow neseskapaw!" noklakno'o.   55
      Yacox'anwa:'a:lak losos neseskapaklakno'o.

IV   *[He restores the people.]*
A (a)   'E:nik Ha:csokonayla te:ca'a:y'ik ha:nata,
      yanicicxil'an,
      "Ma:tan 'o:s'ow! Yacox'ante:la nawe:l!" noklakno'o.
(b)   'E:l'ok kapay 'e:noklakno'o.   60

B (a)   'E:kla 'ecin'e ha:nata,
      yancicxilta'an,
      "Hetan'ok 'o:s'ow! Yacox'ante:la nawe:l!" noklakno'o.
(b)   'E:l'ok kapay 'eklakno'o.

C (a)   'E:kla 'ecin'e ha:nata,   65
      henkwa:tan,
      "Hetan'ok 'o:s'ow! Yacox'ante:la nawe:l!" noklakno'o.
(b)   'Ekla kapay 'e:klakno'o.

D (a)   'E:kla holaw'a:lak ha:nata,
      henkwa:tan,   70
      "Hetan'ok 'o:s'ow! Yacox'ante:la nawe:l!" noklakno'o.
(b)   'E:kla tickan'a:la ha:naxok ha:nacicxileklakno'o.

(PART TWO) Coyote goes gambling

V   *[He leaves his wife for another camp.]*
A   'E:kla Ha:csokonaylak kwa:nenoxlak nesta:'e:klakno'o.

B (a)   'E:kla pas'e:no:la kwa:nwa:'a:lak,
      "Yacox'ankalake'e e:k ha:na:tewo's," noklakno'o Ha:csokonayla.
                                                75
(b)   'E:kla kwa:nwa:'a:la,
      "We:l'a!" noklakno'o.
      "Ha:napew!" noklakno'o.

C (a) 'E:kla Ha:csokonayla,
        "Pas'a:pa:'," noklakno'o.   80
        "Ketay hecneta 'e:taha:'," noklakno'o.
   (b) 'E:kla kwa:nwa:'a:la,
        " 'Eyew," noklakno'o.

D (a) 'E:kla Ha:csokonayla ha:naklakno'o.
   (b) 'E:t yacox'ana:naxokwa:y'ik xa:xat.   85
        pas'e:noklakno'o.

VI   [*She follows, but, insulted, goes away.*]
i   [*She follows him.*]
A (a) 'E:nokla, kwa:nwa:'a:la c'el'e:klakno'o;
        xa:xat yacox'ana:naxokwa:y'ik,
        " 'En Ha:csokonayla?" noklakno'o.
   (b) 'E:kla,   90
        "Hel'a:t hetay'o:ka:lweno'," noklakno'o.

B (a) 'E:kla ha:cin'a:y'ik xa:xata,
        yacox'an'a:y'ik hakxonat,
        " 'A:xkak," noklakno'o.
   (b) 'E:kla,   95
        "Kapa:we," noklakno'o.

ii   [*He tells a young man to watch him get water from her.*]
C (a) 'E:kla yakwan'a:lak ta'aneta,
        yakwa:naklakno'o.
   (b) 'E:kwa, hekalwekwa:y'ik we:'is ha:'ako:nosasla,
        " 'O:c!" noklakno'o.   100
        "Ha:csokonay'an ta:'e:kla!" noklakno'o.
        "Te:l xa:ne:l!" noklakno'o.

D (a) 'E:kla Ha:csokonayla ya:cet,
        x'ax'ay'anoklakno'o.
   (b) 'E:kla ha:'ako:nosa'aswa:ka,   105
        "Canenekno'o," no:nonlakno'o.
   (c) 'E:kla Ha:csokonayla,
        " 'O:ko," noklakno'o.
        "Keyaco:s'ow!" noklakno'o.
        " 'A:xkak kenesxana:tonwa'," noklakno'o.   110

iii   [*She refuses his demand to give him water.*]
E (a) 'E:ta kwa:nla 'e:kwa:y'ik xa:xata,
        'eynetxew'aklakno'o.
   (b) 'E:kla kwa:nwa:'a:la Ha:csokonaylak ya:cet,
        "Kecnew!" noklakno'o.

F   (a)   'E:kla Ha:csokonayla,   115
          "Kenesxanew!" noklakno'o.
    (b)   'E:kla kwa:nwa:'a:la nesxanapeta,
          ha:naklakno'o.

iv   [*Young men keep him up and she decides to leave him.*]
G   (a)   'O:'okwa xa:xat kwa:nwa:'a:lak,
          ta:he:pano:kwa, ha:'ako:nosa'aska: 120
          "Ha:csokonaylak nescoxnapenon 'o:'awa:tak," no:nonlakno'o.
          "Kwa:n'a:lak ho:'oxo:non," no:nonlakno'o.

    (b)   'E:ta 'o:'o:kla ta:he:malo:nonlakno'o;
    (c)   'E:t nescoxnape:kwa taxso:klakno'o, Ha:csokonaylak.

H   (a)   'E:kla kwa:nwa:'a:la xaclo:klakno'o;   125
    (b)   'E:t
          "Ha:na:tewo's," noklakno'o.

VII   [*He goes north to gamble.*]
A   (a)   'E:kla Ha:csokonayla,
          "'Acso:ne:w'an ka:lwena:ha'a," noklakno'o;
    (b)   'E:t ha:naklakno'o, Ha:csokonayla.   130

B   (a)   'E:t yacox'ana:naxoka:y'ik xa:xata,
          "'Acxo:ne:w'an ka:lwa:nacek," noklakno'o.
    (b)   'E:ta ha:nat,
          yacox'ana:naxoka:y'ik xa:xaklakno'o.

C   (a)   'E:t taxso:kla,   135
          "'Acxo:ne:w'an ka:lwa:nasek," noklakno'o Ha:csokonayla.
    (b)   Taxsokla ha:naklakno'o.

D   (a)   Yacox'ana:naxoka:y'ik xa:xat,
          hetay'o:ka:lwenoklakno'o.
    (b)   'E:kwa, kwa:nwa:'a:la,   140
          "Ha:csokonaylak c'el'eya:ton'es," noklakno'o.

VIII   [*She follows, but insulted, leaves him.*]
i   [*She follows him.*]
A   (a)   'E:t c'el'e:klakno'o;
          yacox'ana:naxoka:y'ik xa:xat,
          "'En Ha:csokonayla?" noklakno'o.
    (b)   'E:kla,   145
          "'Acxawtake:w'an ka:lwa:no'o," noklakno'o.

B   (a)   'E:kla kwa:nwa:'a:la c'el'e:klakno'o.
    (b)   'E:t 'ecin'e yacox'ana:naxoka:y'ik xa:xat,
          "'En Ha:csokonayla?" noklakno'o.

   (c) 'E:kla,   150
      " 'Acxawtake:w'an ka:lwa:no'o," noklakno'o.

C (a) 'E:kla kwa:nwa:'a:la c'el'e:klakno'o.
  (b) 'E:t yacox'ana:nxoka:y'ik xa:xat,
      " 'En Ha:csokonayla?" noklakno'o.
  (c) 'E:kla,   155
      "Acxawtake:w'an ka:lwa:no'o", noklakno'o.

D (a) 'E:kla kwa:nwa:'a:la c'el'e:klakno'o.
  (b) 'E:t yacox'ana:naxoka:y'ik xa:xat,
      " 'En Ha:csokonayla?" noklakno'o.
  (c) 'E:kla,   160
      "Te:ca ka:weno'," noklakno'o.

ii   [*She has a young man summon him.*]
A (a) 'E:kla,
      "Xa:xat,
      "Hepakew,
      " ' 'E:taw!' " noklakno'o.   165

B (a) 'E:kla, xa:xat,
      "Kwa:na:xenla yamka:no'," noklakno'o.
  (b) 'E:kla Ha:csokonayla,
      "To:nano:nwan'ey," noklakno'o.

C (a) 'E:kla,   170
      "Wa:xes no's," noklakno'o;
      "Na:kw 'e:taw!" noklakno'o.
  (b) 'E:kla Ha:csokonayla tasa'e:klakno'o.

D (a) Xatxanes'eklakno'o yacox'an'a:y'ik;
      "Te:ca 'e:no'," noklakno'o.   175
  (b) 'E:kla Ha:csokonayla hel'eyakxonaklakno'o.

iii   [*He refuses her command to come in.*]
A (a) 'E:kla kwa:nwa:'a:la,
      "Hakxotaw!" noklakno'o.
  (b) 'E:kla Ha:csokonayla hakxonapeta,
      x'ax'ayanoklakno'o.   180

B (a) 'E:kla 'ecin'e,
      "Hakxotaw!" noklakno'o.
  (b) 'E:kla Ha:csokonayla hakxonapeta,
      x'ax'ay'anoklakno'o.

C (a) 'E:kla 'ecin'e kwa:nwa:'a:la,   185
      "Hakxotaw!" noklakno'o.

(b)   'E:kla Ha:csokanayla hakxonapeta,
        x'ax'ay'anoklakno'o.

D (a)   'Ecin'e hel'eyakxonakla,
        "Hakxotaw!" noklakno'o.   190
   (b)   'E:kla Ha:csokonayla x'ax'ay'a:kwa, kwa:nwa:'a:la,
        "Ha:na:to:n'es," noklakno'o;
        "Hececo:n' ," noklakno'o;
        Hatxilnan, yoxnaklakno'o.

iv   [*She is gone for good.*]
A (a)   'E:kla Ha:csokonayla hel'eyakxonat,   195
        " 'En kwa:nkela?" noklakno'o.
   (b)   'E:kla,
        "Ha:no' ," noklakno'o.

B (a)   'E:kla Ha:csokonayla yancicxiltanoklakno'o,
        hececo:n.   200
   (b)   'E:kwa, kwa:nwa:'a:la xa:xat,
        "Cano's," noklakno'o.

C (a)   'E:kla 'ewas'a:l'en x'ay'a:l'en,
        "Henox 'e:nokco'," noklakno'o;
        "Na:'e:non," noklakno'o.   205
   (b)   'E:t c'elte:ca wetayuyuxa:naklakno'o.

D (a)   Ko:l'a:takla 'e:noklakno'o.
   (b)   We:tic.

English translation

(PART ONE) Coyote restores the people

I   [*He discovers an empty camp.*]
A (a)   They say Coyote was going along;
        In doing so, he went up a mountain.
   (b)   They say he stood there;
        When he did, they say, there was a large camp at the mountain's
        foot.

B (a)   Coyote went down,   5
        he went to that large camp; and
        when he went to the tipi on the edge,
        there was weeping inside, they say.

C (a) Then Coyote went in,
            "What is it?" they say he said.   10
    (b) Then that woman,
            "Here all the people in this camp are gone," they say she said.
            "A fearsome being destroyed them," they say she said.

D (a) Then Coyote,
            "Now, do not weep," they say he said.   15
            "Tomorrow I shall fight it," they say he said.
    (b) Then that woman went outside, and
            "Coyote says he will fight it tomorrow," they say she said.

II   [*He prepares to fight.*]
A (a) "Tomorrow when I fight it,
            "Do not run away," they say he said, Coyote.   20
            "Watch me closely," they say he said.
    (b) Then,
            "Yes," they say she said.

B (a) When it was evening,
                he went down to the river, and   25
            cutting off a piece of hard wood,
                he burned it black, and
            putting it away,
                he went to sleep, they say.

C (a) And at daybreak, arising,   30
            he went outdoors, and
            sitting to the east,
            he howled loudly, they say.
    (b) And then, sitting to the south,
            he howled, they say.   35

D (a) And then again, to the west,
            again he howled, they say.
    (b) And then, last, sitting to the north,
            he howled, they say.

III   [*He meets the monster.*]
A (a) This done, they say, Coyote joined some women going after
                wood.   40
    (b) As he did,
            "That one is coming!" they say was said.
    (c) As it did, that fearsome being from the waist up, they say,
                was red;
    (d) And there, from the waist down, they say, it was black.

B (a) Then, they say, those women were afraid.   45

(b)   Then, they say, Coyote hid.
(c)   As he did, it came in that direction at a run;
(d)   Coyote fought it, they say, that fearsome being.

C (a)   As he did, a great many Wolves,
         catching that fearsome being,   50
         were fighting it, they say.
   (b)   Doing so, they killed it, they say, that fearsome being.

D (a)   And then, they say, those Wolves left.
   (b)   Then Coyote went toward that camp that had no people.
          "Close all those tipis tight!" they say he said.   55
          All those tipis were closed, they say.

IV   [*He restores the people.*]
A (a)   And then Coyote went off from the place, and,
         galloping,
         "Quick! This camp is on fire!" they say he said.
   (b)   When he did, they say, nothing happened.   60

B (a)   Then again he went off, and,
         coming at a gallop,
         "Hurry! This camp is on fire!" they say he said.
   (b)   When he did, they say, nothing happened.

C (a)   Then again he went off, and,   65
         coming at a run,
         "Hurry! This camp is on fire!" they say he said.
   (b)   Then, they say, nothing happened.

D (a)   Then the last time he went off, and,
         coming at a run,   70
         "Hurry! This camp is on fire!" they say he said.
   (b)   Then, they say, many people ran out.

(PART TWO) Coyote goes gambling

V   [*He leaves his wife for another camp.*]
A   Then, they say, they made Coyote marry a beautiful girl.

B (a)   Then, after staying a while, to that woman,
         "I'll go to the other camp over yonder," they say he said,
         Coyote.   75
   (b)   Then that woman,
          "Oh!" they say she said.
          "Don't go!" they say she said.

C (a) Then Coyote,
    "I won't stay long," they say he said.   80
    "In two days I'll come back," they say he said.
  (b) Then that woman,
    "All right," they say she said.

D (a) Then, they say, Coyote went off.
  (b) And, getting to that large camp,   85
    they say he stayed for a long while.

VI   [*She follows, but, insulted, goes away.*]
i   [*She follows him.*]
A (a) It was then that woman went after them, they say;
    getting to that large camp,
    "And Coyote?" they say she said.
  (b) Then,   90
    "He's joined a bunch of gamblers over there," they say they said.

B (a) Then she got to a place nearby, and
    entering the tipi,
    "Water," they say she said.
  (b) Then,   95
    "There is none," they say they said.

ii   [*He tells a young man to watch him get water from her.*]
C (a) Then she picked up the bucket, and,
    they say, she went to get water.
  (b) As she did so, one young man at the gambling place:–
    "Oh!" they say he said.   100
    "Coyote's wife!" they say he said.
    "She comes this way!" they say he said.

D (a) Then Coyote saw her, and,
    they say, he was laughing.
  (b) Then the young man,   105
    "We heard that you left her," they say they said.
  (c) Then Coyote,
    "No," they say he said.
    "Watch me!" they say he said.
    "She'll give me water to drink," they say he said.   110

iii   [*She refuses his demand to give him water.*]
E (a) And then, getting to where that woman was,
    they say, he touched her.
  (b) Then that woman, seeing Coyote,
    "Leave me!" they say she said.

F (a) Then Coyote,   115
        "Give me water to drink!" they say he said.
   (b) Then, that woman, not giving him water to drink,
        went off, they say.

iv   [*Young men keep him up and she decides to leave him.*]
G (a) When night came he came to that woman,
        and as he talked with her, the young men,   120
        "Let's not let Coyote sleep tonight," they say they were saying.
        "Let's steal that woman," they say they were saying.
   (b) And then that night, they say, they danced with him;
   (c) And, they say, they didn't let him sleep until daylight, Coyote.

H (a) Then, they say, that woman was angry;   125
   (b) And,
        "I'll go," they say she said.

VII   [*He goes north to gamble.*]
A (a) Then Coyote,
        "I'll go to gamble in the north," they say he said;
   (b) And, they say, he went away, Coyote.   130

B (a) And he got to a large camp, and
        "I go to gamble in the north," they say he said.
   (b) And then, going away,
        they say, he got to a large camp.

C (a) And the next day,   135
        "I go to gamble in the north," they say he said, Coyote.
   (b) The next day, they say, he went off.

D (a) Getting to a large camp,
        they say, he joined a bunch of gamblers.
   (b) While he did, that woman,   140
        "I'll go after Coyote," they say she said.

VIII   [*She follows, but insulted, leaves him.*]
i   [*She follows him.*]
A (a) And, they say, she went after him;
        getting to a large camp,
        "And Coyote?" they say she said.
   (b) Then,   145
        "He's gone to gamble in the north," they say they said.

B (a) Then, they say, that woman went after him.
   (b) And again getting to a large camp,
        "And Coyote?" they say she said.

(c) Then,   150
     "He's gone to gamble in the north," they say they said.

C (a) Then, they say, that woman went after him.
   (b) And getting to a large camp,
        "And Coyote?" they say she said.
   (c) Then,   155
        "He's gone to gamble in the north," they say they said.

D (a) Then, they say, that woman went after him.
   (b) And getting to a large camp,
        "And Coyote?" they say she said.
   (c) Then,   160
        "He's gambling here," they say they said.

ii   [*She has a young man summon him.*]
A (a) Then,
        "Go to him, and
        "Tell him,
        "Come!" they say she said.   165

B (a) Then, going to him,
        "Your wife is summoning you," they say he said.
   (b) Then Coyote,
        "You're lying," they say he said.

C (a) Then,   170
        "I speak the truth," they say he said;
        "Now come!" they say he said.
   (b) Then Coyote went with him, they say.

D (a) The two got to the tipi, they say;
        "She is staying here," they say he said.   175
   (b) Then, they say, Coyote peered inside.

iii   [*He refuses her command to come in.*]
A (a) Then that woman,
        "Come in!" they say she said.
   (b) Then Coyote, they say, not going in,
        was laughing.   180

B (a) Then again,
        "Come in!" they say she said.
   (b) Then Coyote, they say, not going in,
        was laughing.

C (a) Then again, that woman,   185
        "Come in!" they say she said.

(b)   Then Coyote, they say, not going in,
       was laughing.

D (a)   Again as he peered in,
       "Come in!" they say she said.   190
  (b)   Then when Coyote laughed, that woman,
       "I shall go away," they say she said;
       "Back," they say she said;
       Going outside, she flew away, they say.

iv   [*She is gone for good.*]
A (a)   Then Coyote peering in,   195
       "And my wife?" they say he said.
  (b)   Then,
       "She has gone away," they say they said.

B (a)   Then, they say, Coyote came running,
       back.   200
  (b)   As he did, that woman was getting home;
       "I left him," they say she said.

C (a)   Then her father and mother,
       "You are doing the right thing," they say they said;
       "Let us go," they say they said.   205
  (b)   And, they say, she flew away with them up into the air;

D (a)   She was an Eagle, they say.
  (b)   So it is.

Discussion of the translation

When one works with a language little known and little studied, such as
Tonkawa, one has a special responsibility. The original publication of a set
of texts is likely to remain the only publication, or the only publication to
which reference can be readily made. Changes in the form of a text, as
originally published, must be explicitly stated and explained. Few will follow
the philological trail involved, but the trail must be clearly marked. Before
proceeding to further discussion of the analysis and the interpretation of the
myth, then, let me discharge that responsibility.

    In this section I explain certain changes in orthography and the translation
of words, while taking into account the existence in this one case of two
different presentations of the text by Hoijer himself. The orthographic changes
are minor, and easily assimilated; they are motivated in part by the presentation
of the text as a kind of poetry. The changes in translation are partly for the
sake of what appears to be greater consistency, partly, again, for the sake of
presentation of the text as something to be read as a kind of poetry in English.

It may be useful to reproduce the first paragraph of Hoijer's presentation of the text in 1972 (sect. 1) in both Tonkawa and English. In the English translation the slash lines separate equivalents of Tonkawa words, and S (as discussed further below) represents the quotative.

> 1. ha:csokonayla ha:nanoklakno?o. ?e:no:la na:to:n?a:y?ik hayconat heylapanoklakno?o. ?e:l?ok na:to:nwa:?a:lak ?a:yay?a:y?ik yacox?-ana:naxok
> ye:laklakno?o lak. ha:csokonayla haklanat yacox?ana:naxokwa:y?ik xa:xat
> holaw?a:y?ik xa:xal?ok yacox?an?yay?a:y?ik ma:kanoklakno?o.

> 1. Coyote / he was walking along, S. He so doing / to a mountain / climbing up / he was standing there, S. When he did so / that mountain afm. / at its foot / a large camp / there was, S / (accus.) Coyote / going down / to that large camp afm. / he arrived and / to the last one / when he arrived / inside a tipi / there was weeping, S.

Here are the details.

The *orthography* used in the full presentation of the text is that of the 1972 publication shown just above, allowing for minor substitutions and stylistic innovations. The two substitutions are a single apostrophe, or close quote, for the top half of a question mark used for the glottal stop in the publication, and the writing of the labiovelars on the line as "xw" and "kw." The stylistic innovation is that of capitalization. The name of the one named actor, Coyote, is capitalized, and capitalization is used at the beginning of sentences and quotations. Because glottal stop lacks a capital form, yet is often word-initial, I have capitalized the following vowel. The tradition in which Hoijer worked was concerned to avoid the imposition of ethnocentric conventions on other languages and their texts, and so both eschewed capitalization in them and organized dictionaries by the phonetic alignment of sounds rather than by the arbitrary order of the Roman alphabet. The trouble with this is that differences among languages and linguists make the "scientific" and "objective" phonetic order arbitrary, too (having to be learned anew with each language), and an obstacle to the use of the material. Avoidance of capitalization simply makes it more difficult for a Western-language audience – the only audience that Tonkawa literature is now likely to have – to recognize new sentences, quotations, actors. We need not fear distortion of the original by use of a bit of familiar frame.

As to philology, Dr. Troike has told me that he has not been able to locate the original notebooks in the library of the American Philosophical Society, where Hoijer's materials were sent. It is to be hoped that they may still be found.

There is a bit of philology in the comparison of the two printed versions of the first part of the text. In the 1933 publication of the first part, as "Coyote and the Monster," there is an interlinear translation and an extensive series of grammatical notes. The English form of the 1933 translation is generally less analytically literal itself. Most noticeable is the fact that the quotative element is rendered in the words "it is said," and the back-reference of certain particle elements is translated with "aforementioned" as a full word in the sentence. In the 1972 publication the quotative is rendered by the abbreviation "S" (see Hoijer 1972:2), and "aforementioned" appears abbreviated as "afm." These differences go together with differences in diction. The second word of the text is rendered "was going along, it is said" in 1933, but as "he was walking along, S" in the 1972 texts. (In the 1972 texts the English equivalent of a word is separated from the equivalent of a preceding or following word by a slash; thus it is possible to have full control over the relation between text and translation, word by word.) The 1972 translation appears to render explicit the presence of an implicit singular subject in the root *ha:-* 'one person moves, goes.' The introduction of "walking" is not discussed (nor are any changes in lexical choice between the two translations). The notes to the *Handbook* text of 1933, and the lexical choices in the interlinear translation there, seem preferable as idiomatic English, and have generally been preferred here. The expression "going along," for example, is fairly well established as an initial phrase characteristic of Coyote in English versions of myths from a number of languages.

To continue with the question of *diction*, which has arisen here: There does not seem to be a consistent basis for the lexical differences between the two versions. In the 1933 translation attention is called to the presence in the text of three locative themes, all beginning with *ha:-* 'one person goes' (p. 142 n. 9); but the translation itself has "ascending," "descending," "going in." That is, the translation does not bring out the parallelism in initial stem, and misses the fact that the series has four members in actuality, the first of the series being the verb "going along" just mentioned. To cite all four:

> *ha:-na-no-* 'one person goes, continuative'
> *ha-idjo-na* 'one person goes, up'
> *ha-gla-na-* 'one person goes, down'
> *ha-gxo-na-* 'one person goes, in'.

(In all the forms, *na-* is directional "away" [from here to there]; "dj" is "c," "g" is "k" in the later orthography.) Neither translation in fact exploits the presence of four grammatically parallel verbs, a number in keeping with the Tonkawa pattern number. If the 1933 translation has "going along," "ascending," "descending," "going in," the 1972 translation has "walking along," "climbing up," "going down," "entered." Recognition of repetition as a key to structure in the form of the texts, as verbal art, makes it desirable to render such patterns insofar as possible.

In the present case one might wish to see a four-part series as defined not by recurrence of stem-initial *ha:-*, but by recurrence of final suffix *-d*, subordinating the verb it accompanies to a following verb. On such an assumption, the verb, *ha:-na-no* 'was going along' would stand apart. The four verbs of the series would be

> *ha-idjo-na-d* 'going up'
> *ha-gla-na-d* 'going down'
> *xa:xad* 'arriving' (analyzed by Hoijer as *xa-ha:-xa-*: "from, to a distance, one person goes, arrival," plus -*d*)
> *ha-gxo-na-d* 'going in'

(The "d" is "t" in the later orthography.)

In either event, one has a four-part series, identifiable by overt formal recurrence. The second series could in fact be identified by occurrence of *ha:-* as well as of -*d*, given its implicit presence in the third verb. I have chosen the set with the initial *ha:-*, because the stem meaning, rather than the subordination of the verb, seems the essential thing here, beginning with the first instance; and because the implicit *ha:-* actually occurs twice, first as shown, then two words later as *xa:xal'ok* 'as he arrived' (from *xa-ha:l-ok*, -*l-ok* being the third person form of the subordinating suffix *ok* 'when, while, as').

English suppletion (go: went) prevents exact repetition, but the "to" of "went to" can be let stand for the sense of "arrival" in the *xa-(ha:-)* forms to bring them into the series. There are two levels, however: that of the four stanzas, which can be summarized as "he went up; he went down; he went in; she went out," and that of verbs having to do with movement. There are eight in Act I. Seven use *ha:-*, and one *he-y(a)lapa* 'to stand up, stop moving'. Seven are by Coyote (going along, went up, stood up; went down, went to, went to; went in), and one by the woman (went out). All this seems to frame the last of the series, the woman's announcement to the (presumably slain) camp.

The principle of repetition in English of what is repeated in Tonkawa is followed in choice of diction wherever possible. Thus, in Act IV, when Coyote restores the people, he comes at the camp with one stem the first two times, and another stem the second two times. The second stem suggests no translation but "run" (*henkwa:-*), but the first is associated with the running of horses (*yanciexile-*) as well as running in general, so far as the dictionary indicates. Since Webster's Second says that a gallop, when much quickened, is called a run, "gallop," then "run," seems apt here, conveying both distinction and sequence.

I have departed from literal respect for the Tonkawa order in the case of the quotative element, or "narrative enclitic" (Hoijer 1972:7). Literal respect for order would have the first stanza and four lines, for example, as follows:

> Coyote was going along, it is said;
> In doing so, he went up a mountain,

> He was standing there, it is said;
> When he did, there was a large camp at the mountain's foot, it is said.

The translation presented here has instead:

> They say Coyote was going along;
> In doing so, he went up a mountain.
> They say he was standing there;
> When he did, they say, there was a large camp at the mountain's foot.

In general, the present translation retains the quotative at the end of a line when it occurs with the verb of saying, and occasionally elsewhere as part of an apparent pattern (lines 55–6, for example). When the quotative occurs without the verb of saying, it is put after the initial particle, or occasionally initially or medially. An intuitive sense of readability in English has governed. Thus, "they say" is final in I B and II B, because in both stanzas an earlier position would seem too obtrusive, to make too much of the possibility of reading the phrase for information, rather than as formal marker of traditional narrative. The placement of the phrase earlier in other cases seems to me to serve the same concern. Others must judge the success of this experiment. It seems wrong to omit any English equivalent (as did Hoijer's abbreviation "S"). The usual "it is said" seems overly formal; "they say" comes as close as anything in English to the presumed effect of the narrative enclitic in the original. The effort here, then, is to be true to the effect. In this one case, variation rather than faithful order seems required. It remains the case, as the Tonkawa text shows, that the original Tonkawa effect was that of a recurrent punctuation, a sentence-ending eddy, as it were, rippling through the narrative.

Let me provide here some notes from Hoijer's two treatments of the text that clarify some of the choices of English words.

In line 4 and subsequently "a large camp" is literally a place of "many tipis." The word for camp (third in line 4) contains the same stem as the word translated "tipi" (first word in line 7). In line 7 the expression "he went to the tipi on the edge" is an effort to capture the import of the Tonkawa expression "he arrived to the last one." The tent is last from the standpoint of a Tonkawa encampment, last, that is, in reference to the center of the encampment. So far as Coyote is concerned, the tipi is the first he reaches.

In line 11 the woman is designated "that woman" because the word is marked as "aforementioned" in Tonkawa. The weeping in line 8 was hers, and thus she is already present in the story. Conversely, the syntactic relationship can be taken as retrospectively identifying the source of the weeping.

In line 26 "hard wood" translates a name of a wood that was hard but not certainly identified. Hoijer reports that John Rush Buffalo explained that the wood was formerly used to make bows, and that it is possible, but not known, that the reference is to ash.

In lines 30–9 the terms for the four directions are literally: "east" = "sun rising"; "west" = "sun setting"; "north" = "north wind blows"; "south" = "long wind," in reference to the constant south wind that blows during the summer.

It remains to be mentioned that *punctuation* does not follow the published texts, but is made to accord with the analysis of verses and lines that depend in important part on the pattern of rhetorical cohesion discovered in the text. In general, indeed, we would do better by oral narrative if we could punctuate and read punctuation rhetorically, rather than "logically." (See discussion of the dilemma involved for a contemporary publication of Shakespeare's sonnets in Booth 1969: xiii–xiv.)

Discussion of the analysis

Lines and verses

The greater part of the verses of the Tonkawa text are signposted, and the greater part of the organization of the narrative can be blocked out, once the verse-making function of the signs is recognized. Like Takelma, Tonkawa has sentence-initial particles and syntactic suffixes. The interaction between the two is the most striking feature of Tonkawa discourse structure. Hoijer himself wrote a special article on the interaction (1949a), saying that in writing the grammar and sketch of the language (1933, 1946) he had not properly understood the suffixes. Briefly put, a construction with more than one verb places the principal verb at the end, where, if it is in the third person in the narrative, it will typically have a quotative suffix. (Cf. the partial correlation in Takelma between the third person in verbs of saying and the element -*hi'*.) The preceding, subsidiary, verbs will each have a syntactic suffix, linking the parts of the sequence.

The syntactic suffixes also occur as second elements of the sentence because initial particles consist of an initial theme '*e:* followed by one or more suffixes. Unlike the forward-punctuating initial particles of Takelma and Chinookan, the Tonkawa initial particles look backward as well. They serve as anaphoric substitutes whose antecedents are the immediately preceding constructions. As Hoijer summarizes (1949a:55), "These anaphoric particles link independent syntactic constructions in much the same way as the syntactic suffixes link the subsidiary and principal verb expressions of a complex syntactic construction." Hoijer was aware of a discourse role for these elements. Noting that the initial construction of a text usually lacked an anaphoric particle, while most of those following required one, he observed (ibid.): "In other words, the 'sentences' of a Tonkawa text are united, not only by their occurrence in a connected narrative, but also by specific syntactic elements (i.e., the anaphoric particles) which, in a sense, summarize the preceding action and relate it, in each instance, to the action which follows." And he concluded by relating these facts to the nature of oral tradition (ibid.):

> It is not improbable that this cumbersome syntactic device results from the fact that Tonkawa texts are transmitted orally rather than in written form. Though complete data are lacking, it is possible that devices similar to the Tonkawa anaphoric particle may be found in most, if not all, the languages of preliterate peoples. And it is also worth noting that speakers of English, particularly if they are illiterate, very often begin each sentence of a long utterance with a conjunction or introductory particle like "and," "then," "now," or "well." Speech, unlike writing, appears to require a more or less continuous emphasis on the interconnectedness of the independent syntactic constructions which make up a long utterance.

It is now possible to show that the syntactic device serves not only to connect, but also to shape. Individual particles connect. Sets of particles shape. Or rather, sets of particles are the means employed to shape stanzas.

As with other Native American literature, formal markers do not alone suffice to reveal form. The other side of the verbal sign, in this case the literary sign, meaning, has to be taken into account. There is an implicit logic of narrative action, or principle of rhetorical cohesion. Indeed, the realization of its force was a memorable experience to me. I had blocked out the text pretty well, having recognized the verse-making role of the particles, before flying to Los Angeles for my presentation in the series of lectures honoring Hoijer. Uncertainty as to several divisions and groupings made me feel able to offer copies of the rough analysis only as showing the presence in Tonkawa of the verse patterning. No more. On the plane I went through the text once more, observing a hypothesis as to rhetorical cohesion, and almost every uncertainty vanished. Major set pieces, such as Coyote's restoration of the people and the wife's second search for Coyote, fell into form, into firm, convincing shape.

The difficulty had been, as always in such analysis, that the principle of grouping of verses may allow for more than one particular grouping. An external sense of narrative logic may misplace an end or a beginning: A limited hypothesis as to the formal organization may amputate actual narrative patterns. So much of the first portion of the story groups verses in terms of pairs that I had tried to carry pairing throughout. That led, among other things, to organizing lines 45–59 by pairs of initial particles alone: (45, 46) and (47–8, 49–51) as two sets of pairs; then (52, 53) and (54–55–56), (57–58–59), as another two sets of pairs. The result, of course, is to destroy the integrity of the next scene. In its four repetitions of Coyote running there are four outcomes: Nothing happened (three times), many people ran out (fourth time). Parallelism of position, final position, is the means of conveying the effect. Furthermore, the four lines of the four stanzas in the present version fit a recurrent four-part narrative schema (to be discussed below).

In this particular case, recognition of the schema was a key, pointing to the need to recognize line 48 as coordinate in its stanza as a verse. It lacks an initial particle, but it does begin with the name Coyote. Now in lines 5–8 the only possible initial marker is Coyote's name; yet the relation of the lines to the clearly marked stanzas on either side, and the internal logic of the lines themselves, show it to be indeed a stanza. It seems, then, that Coyote's name, by default or design, may occasionally initiate a verse in Tonkawa.

Again, in the first scene of Act VIII, in which Coyote's wife follows him a second time, there is a clear pattern. It is such regular repetitions of a pattern as this, indeed, on which one should most rely in breaking the code of a new case. The wife goes after him, gets to a camp, asks for him, receives an answer. Four parts, four times. The clarity of the internal organization of the scene requires setting the preceding verse apart, where it is needed, indeed, to complete the eight verses of the preceding scene. Most significant of all, this clear four-part logic involves not two, but three, initial particles.

There is no escape from it. A determination to stick to pairs of particles, no matter what, would wreck the integrity of the scene. The scene has a coherence that uses particles, but not in twos. One is forced to the insight that John Rush Buffalo had more than one particle-using schema in his arsenal. Sometimes two make a stanza, but sometimes three. Even though the number of Tonkawa texts preserved to us through Hoijer's effort is not large, it may be possible to detect kinds of meaning, kinds of effect, kinds of intention, that covary with the organization of stanzas in sets with two particles, on the one hand, and sets with three particles on the other.[2]

Other formal devices also appear in this text, set out by their surroundings. Lines 24–9 form a distinct unit. There appears to be no way to fit the structure of the unit, except to recognize it as a sequence of six lines. The preceding conversation and the following ritual action at daybreak are separate. There is no basis for just two pairs or sets of pairs within the six lines. (I have found a case of the weaving of ten lines in an internally intricate sequence in the Clackamas Chinook myth "Gitskux and His Older Brother," as told by Virginia Howard, where again the usual numerical groupings of the literature do not obtain (Hymes 1983).) Both cases, Tonkawa and Clackamas, do not at all seem failure of pattern, but difference of pattern. In sum, it appears that Native American narrators might sometimes work directly with lines as units to shape into a whole of its own, apart from usual markers and patterns. There is a warning and an opportunity here, a warning not to impose newly discovered pattern too far, and an opportunity to understand individual subtleties of design.

The next two stanzas (II CD, lines 30–9) may seem overimposition of pattern. The four directions make up a four-part sequence that might be taken as a single whole. I take the double use of "again" with the third howling (lines 36–7) as an indication that there are in fact two parts within the whole. In many other traditions, indeed, "again" signals relevant units of repetition; here in the third howling it signals the direction (west) and the act (howling). There is no "again" with the second howling, only with the third; and the fourth howling has "last." The third and fourth howlings thus seem marked together as a repeated pair. Notice that the pairing of directions can be taken as having a certain sense: first sunrise and summer (east, south), then sunset and north wind; in other words, light and warmth, then darkness and cold. Whether Coyote is following an accepted Tonkawa ritual order, or perverting one, I do not know. The latter would not be surprising, since we are to understand Coyote here as putting on a front that he will not maintain. When the monster comes, he hides, fights it only because it comes to him, and apparently takes credit for killing due to the wolves, who conveniently do not stay. All this after he had enjoined upon the woman the necessity of not running away, but watching him, as here, closely. (Hoijer gives Coyote too much credit, I fear, in the note in which he says he "is a hero who conquers the fearsome one" in the first part of the tale (1972:101 n. 4.7). As monster slayer here, as singer in Takelma, Coyote does it only half right.)

In sum, there are several different patterns of grouping lines and verses in this text. Paired verses predominate, there being thirty-three such stanzas. Doubled pairs occur in three stanzas (III ABC); trios in five (VI, DG; VIII BCD). There are four stanzas without internal division into more than one verse (I B, II B, V A, VIII *ii* A), three when Coyote enters new relationships with women, the other perhaps with ritual power.

The identification of verses, and of sets of verses, is the most certain feature of the analysis. A certain portion of the identification of lines is arbitrary, in that verbs of saying, following quoted speech, have been treated as part of the same line, rather than being given a separate line, as I have done in analyses of Chinookan and Takelma. Were the practices to be followed in Tonkawa, this text would increase in number of lines by sixty-one. It is notable, by the way, that quoted speech is concentrated in the second part, the part in which Coyote goes away and finally loses his wife. There are ten verbs of saying in Part One and fifty-one such verbs in Part Two. This difference depends of course in part on the greater length of Part Two, but the elaboration of action through direct speech in Part Two was also an option that the narrator need not have taken. The first part seems clearly of some fun itself, but a preparation for the greater fun of the second part.

My sense of the text has led me to think that the verbs of saying in a scene such as the first of VIII are an appendage that punctuates, rather than a distinct element in the rhythm. I feel the quoted speech and the verb of saying as a unit, coordinate with the preceding and following units. In Takelma, on the other hand, there are instances in which the report of saying seems used itself as a coordinate element. Further verse analysis of Tonkawa may confirm or supersede this sense. But to repeat, while the number of verses is mostly directly determined by the number of particles, the number of lines is partly determined by the judgment just discussed.

Rhetorical coherence

The frequent pairing of verses in stanzas indicates that the underlying rhetorical schema involves pairing and multiples of two. As we have seen, however, the relation between stanzas and pairs is not automatic. A sense of pairing, of initiation and outcome as complementary parts, is indeed easiest to obtain at the larger levels of organization. The myth has two major parts, in one of which Coyote comes, in effect, and in the other of which he goes. The first results in his gaining a wife, the second in his losing her.

The acts within parts show a similar logic. In I Coyote discovers the empty camp and its cause, in II he prepares to do something about it. In III he is involved in fighting the monster, in IV the demise of the monster makes possible restoration of the people. Acts I and II go together as preparation overall, III and IV go together as outcome overall. This two-level relationship recurs in the myth. Put schematically, using "I" for initiation, and "O" for outcome:

I
    I
O
       I
I
    O
O

With regard to Part One, it stands as initiation to Part Two. Within it (I, II) stand as initiation to the outcome of (III, IV). And within each pair of acts, the first stands as initiation to the outcome of the second. It has seemed too much in the way of superstructure to introduce a level, labeled and counted, between the acts and the parts. The logical rhythm, as it were, is present nevertheless.

The same relationships hold in Part Two, except that the rightmost symbol in a diagram for it would be O (outcome to Part One).

Similar relations appear with acts. In I, for example, the first two stanzas (A, B) bring Coyote to the tipi; the second two discover through conversation the problem and produce his resolve. In A Coyote perceives the camp, in B he gets to it and perceives the weeping. In C Coyote learns of the monster, in D he states his resolve (confirmed by repetition in the form of a public announcement, presumably to the lingering souls of the people later revived, who have not been wholly and permanently killed, but perhaps to the women who go after wood in III. The latter would imply that the destruction of the people means effectively the destruction of the men of the camp).

Again in II the first two stanzas give Coyote's preparations on the same day, both immediate instructions to the woman (A) and evening preparation of a weapon (B); and then give his ritual preparations on the next day, howling to east and south (C) and again to west and north (D). The initiation/outcome relationship can be seen between (A) and (B), and between (C) and (D), respectively.

Such relations hold throughout the myth, sometimes clearly sometimes loosely, at the levels of relations among stanzas and within stanzas.

When we focus attention on the relations within stanzas, however, a richer, more complex aspect of the organization of verses and lines appears. Tonkawa appears to make use of a certain number of specific patterns, relating actions in terms more specific than those of initiation and outcome. One of these patterns appears to show an areal affiliation with a discovery made by Donald Bahr in the study of Pima–Papago ritual oratory (1975). Bahr has discovered that a set of ritual texts consistently show organization into a sequence of four parts. Departure, Travel, Arrival, Do (X) (p. 13). Thus,

> Elder Brother set out,
> traveled,
> reached the mountain,
> and climbed it.

This pattern might seem a Pima–Papago instantiation of a human schema expressed by Cleanth Brooks and Robert Penn Warren in their *Modern Rhetoric* (1949) as the familiar "exposition, complication, climax, denouement" (p. 312). But it is indeed more specific, and connected with the importance of traveling motion in the imaginative art of the Native American Southwest.

The first two stanzas of "Coyote and Eagle's Daughter" fit this schema with very little modification. Abbreviating Bahr's discovery as D T Arr X, one can see it in Coyote going along (D), going up a mountain (T), standing there (at the top) (Arr), and finding a large camp at the foot. That the sequence ends on a perception is familiar in Chinookan and Takelma, and may be quite widespread in Native American literature. Again, in stanza B one can see the schema in Coyote going down, getting to the camp, getting to the tipi, hearing weeping. Again, the outcome is a perception.

The next two stanzas do not fit this pattern. In essence, they are built around alternating turns of speech. The difference between this myth and Bahr's texts is not surprising, since the Pima–Papago ritual oratory analyzed by Bahr is entirely in the third person. A genre with dramatic action can be expected to include schemes of action suited to its nature.

It remains that some stanzas involving speech in this text do fit a modified form of Bahr's schema. In IV Coyote goes off first in each of the four stanzas (D); he then comes galloping or running (T); he exclaims on what must be his implicit arrival (Arr, Quoted speech); and there is an outcome, nothing three times, restoration of the people the fourth (X).

Again, when Coyote's wife goes after him, she goes (D), gets to a camp or tipi (Arr), asks for Coyote ("O"), and receives an answer ("A"). This pattern seems a modification of the one discovered by Bahr, sharing the same proportions, in that a sequence of three actions on the part of the first participant leads up to what is done by the other, the response. The same pattern governs the four stanzas of scene *i* of VIII. A variant appears to hold in VIII *iii* A.

Notice that the four-part schema holds throughout the first scene of VIII, although the first stanza has two initial particles and the remaining three stanzas each have three. This scene is the clearest demonstration that content form, as it were, governs expression form in this literature. The requirements of the rhetorical schema are met consistently, but the disposition of syntactic markers varies.

Most of the other stanzas in this myth show variants of a two-part relationship. We have noted pairs of turns at speech, which recur in I C, I D, II A, V B, V C, VI *i* AB, *ii* D, VIII *i* ABCD, *ii* B, and *iv* A. An action, followed by another's speech, occurs in VI *ii* C, *iv* G, VII D, and VIII *iv* B. (The initial action is observed by the speaker in VI *ii* C and VI *iv* G, but is correlative across different locations in VII D and VIII *iv* B.) Speech, followed by another's actions, occurs in VI *iii* F, VIII *ii* CD, VIII *iii* ABC. (The concentration of this latter kind of pairing at this point in the story is significant for the changed relationship between Coyote and his wife.)

A reported attitude, followed by the same person's speech, occurs in VI *iv* H; speech followed by an action of the same person occurs in VII ABC and VIII *iv* C. Two actions of the same person occur in II C and D, and two turns at talk plus an action of the same person in VIII *iii* D.

Finally, a single initiatory turn at speech appears to constitute a stanza in VIII *ii* A, though it sets in train a series of pairs of turns at talk between two others. It is the last one-verse stanza, the only one with speech, and a reversal in the relationship between Coyote and his wife.

These different patterns tend to bunch, each in part of the narrative to which it is adapted, and perhaps there is no principle to be inferred beyond the general disposition to pair actions or speech, by the same or two participants, within a stanza.

One suggestion of a further kind of pattern within stanzas lies in the alternation in number of lines allotted to each speaker, when two stanzas are devoted to speech between the same two parties. In I C Coyote has one line, the woman two lines in response; then in I D Coyote has two lines, the woman one. The same thing recurs in V, where Coyote has one line, his wife two in B; then in C Coyote has two lines, the wife one.

Another pattern may appear in the elaboration of quoted lines in the last verses of VI *ii* C and D. The effect is to devote four lines to what may be intended as a culminating sequence, locally at least. In C a young man is mentioned, then has three lines to remark on Coyote's wife. In D Coyote is named, then has three lines to assert his relationship and control over the wife. These two apparent patterns should be tested in the other Tonkawa narratives.

Further study of Tonkawa and of other southwestern Native American literatures may disclose much more. For the present, the most striking finding is the similarity between the Pima–Papago pattern in ritual oratory and the patterning of certain stanzas in this Tonkawa myth.

Assumptions and conventions of the myth

Several features of the myth have been mentioned in the preceding section, but some additional comments seem desirable.

Assumptions about actors

Coyote is the principal actor of the Tonkawa "night stories" that have been preserved, as has been noted. In this myth he is a Coyote of the same character as in other Native American literatures. He enters as the myth begins, going along; vaunts his courage, but quails in the event. The preparation of a piece of hard wood and the howling to the four directions no doubt were interpreted by Tonkawa in terms of normal cultural practices. We can reasonably guess that they are not direct reflections of culture, but at least tinged with parody. Perhaps a piece of hard wood, burned black, is a poor deputy for the weapon a true hero would have; perhaps Coyote howls to the four directions where a true hero would invoke or sing. To say that Coyote joined some women going after wood is perhaps to indicate that, boast and preparation aside, his mind now turned to whatever dalliance might be at hand. A serious man might not have accompanied women on a humble task. This one line (40), I suspect, is a comic touch, undercutting the preparations that have just preceded, and putting Coyote in a mood and situation quite unprepared for the monster.

The text shows Coyote to be no protector, not only afraid, as are the women, but hiding. His fighting is forced upon him; the monster comes right to him at a run, and he fights in spite of himself. Nothing daunted, as soon as the real slayers of the dangerous being have left, Coyote peremptorily takes charge.

The reviving of slain persons is a common element of native American myths. A hero, or even Coyote, is often able to restore people, by leaping over them a ritual number of times or by some other means. Coyote's method here again seems a parody of respected practice. There is nothing of dignity or spiritual power. The people are finally brought out of their tipis by a fraudulent threat of fire, rather as if they had been malingering, or needed to be frightened out of their deaths as out of an attack of hiccups. As so often, Coyote is the agency of a good result, but on his own terms, that is, in terms of his perduring character. Thus the sequel is not an abrupt reversal, but a further manifestation of the same character. At the end of some Chinookan myths, when Coyote is given a woman in reward for some humorously accomplished good, he says, "What do I want with a woman? I am just traveling along," and off he goes. His eagerness for women is matched by his inability to stay with any. So also here. His preference here for gambling over women is an element of a myth of the Kalapuya of the Willamette valley in Oregon (Jacobs 1945:205ff) and no doubt elsewhere.

In all these respects, then, what we have in this Tonkawa myth is the fashioning in Tonkawa idiom and setting of a widely known figure in the Native American *commedia dell'arte*. The falsified promise in V; the falsified boast about his wife in VI, together with the inability to resist the young men's dancing; the persistence in traveling again to gamble in VII; the inability to take the wife seriously in VIII; and the expression of surprise at an outcome that has been prepared for many verses, when she does leave him, are all extensions of this character. He runs again, but this time in vain. At the end of Part One his kind of running could restore people, but now it cannot restore a wife. The implicit verdict of the normative culture is put into words in the mouths of the wife's father and mother: "You are doing the right thing."

Of the wife, we are told only at the end that she is an Eagle, an identification that fits her character and autonomy. An Eagle is admirable to behold, strong, and so far as I know, noble in myths. As a faithful wife, she wishes him to stay rather than go; she follows him twice when he does not return; but she is also a noble wife and does not accept affront. In VI Coyote's boast that the wife will give him water apparently reflects a Tonkawa custom. Hoijer notes that here and in another myth (see 1972:99 n. 2.2, and 101 nn. 4.5, 4.6) for a woman to give water to a man is to indicate that he is her husband. Such a means of symbolization of relationship in turn may reflect the Texas environment of the Tonkawa, water being scarce enough to be precious. Thirst and a need to go to find water in a spring or the like, however, figure also in myths of the Chinookan, Sahaptin, and Salishan peoples of the Pacific Northwest, as a way of getting enemies to springs where they can be killed. We may have here simply a reflection of the general fact that water had to be obtained where one could find it naturally or could store it.

The woman refuses Coyote water, even though she had followed him. The reason presumably is that he has exposed her to ridicule, as Hoijer notes (1972:101 n. 4.7). Indeed, the specific fact appears to be his own ridicule. The young men observe her and think he had left her, so are surprised; it is Coyote who laughs (lines 103–4). Again, it is in direct response to his repeated laughing, instead of heeding her command to enter, that she leaves for good (VIII *iii*). The verse analysis brings this out in its placement of the laughing at the end of stanzas B, C, and D in the latter scene. (His laughing in VI *ii* could have been assigned to the end of stanza C, rather than to the beginning of stanza D; but in this scene he is not directly with his wife, so that the placement is not so much to the point, not the immediate reason for the outcome; and the three lines of speech at the end of C b and D c seem parallel.)

That she refuses Coyote water apparently does not mean that she has decided to end the relationship permanently, as of scene *iii* in VI. Separation, rather than divorce, would seem the right analogy. It is only when he does not stay with her at night, renewing the marital relationship, but lets the young men who want to steal her take him away to dance all night that she is said to become angry and to say, "I'll go." The going is left implicit, as if saving the statement of going for the going for good of the last scene, a nice touch. At the end of VI we have the woman's character, not yet in so many words divorce. Perhaps her intention is overtaken by Coyote's announcement of intention to go gamble in the north in the next scene. She is a loyal wife indeed, overlooking virtual desertion of her camp, laughter, desertion of her bed, to follow him again. But this time she asserts her position; he is to come to her.

Notice the neat reversal as between VI and VIII, which I have tried to indicate in the scene headings. In VI he tells a young man to watch him assert his position by getting water from her (*ii*); in the corresponding scene of VIII, she has a young man summon him. In VI he refuses his demand to give him water; in the corresponding scene of VIII (*iii*), he refuses her command to come in. In other words, in the first context of his having left and her having followed, he takes the role of the one with the rights of the relationship, but she refuses to act as if nothing had happened. Her refusing water and yet letting him come to her at night and talk to her presumably reflect a concern to have the balance of the relationship righted. In the second context of his having left and her having followed, she now takes the role of the one with the rights of the relationship. The reversal seems a statement of one last chance. He must come to her at her summons if the balance of the relationship is to be restored. That is in character for Eagle's daughter.

There is another Tonkawa story in which Coyote gains Eagle's daughter by killing the young man she prefers (Rabbit) and then both kills her and uses half her body in a necrophilic manner. Hoijer notes the exceptional nature of the story in this evil role of Coyote (1972:1 and 100 n. 3.18). The woman is strong and proper while alive and, according to John Rush Buffalo, is very beautiful precisely because she is Eagle's daughter (1972:100 n. 3.1). As for Coyote, he is still comic as well in the story, pretending to be constantly bitten by ants so that the other two cannot sleep (the woman having assigned him a place to sleep separate from herself and the young man); cheating in a contest of staying under water that she had proposed to determine who will marry the woman, and then in anger killing the other man; killing the woman he has been trying to get in shooting arrows at her (he weeps at the consequences); and being beaten, and defecating all around as he runs off at the end.

Both stories seem to me to assume the same thing: Coyote cannot be the husband of a woman like Eagle's daughter. (Some Navajo Chantway myths enact the same theme.) In the story analyzed here he loses her because he is such a ne'er-do-well. In the story with Rabbit he is not so much an evil miscreant as bungling and obsessed. It is not surprising that Coyote kills Rabbit, even if it is by welshing in anger in a contest he has himself proposed. The point is that once Coyote has Eagle's daughter to himself, he stupidly causes her death. He cannot even keep her sexually as a corpse, but is discovered and sent packing in shame. The two stories together, then, seem to explore the same theme, one in comic vein throughout, the other in a humor that can only be called black.

Such complementary explorations of common characters and themes seem to recur in Native American literature in a way rather analogous to such an aspect of English literature as the novels of Trollope (see Kincaid 1977; Tracy 1978).

Additional aspects of the character of Coyote for the Tonkawa are reported by Hoijer on the basis of remarks of John Rush Buffalo (1972:introduction). The Tonkawa divided stories into two broad categories, Night Stories of the time before human beings, and Old Stories. Coyote is the principal actor in all but five of the nineteen Night Stories obtained. While often gullible, he also brings both fire and the buffalo, and was, according to John Rush Buffalo, "a kind of divinity" (p. 1):

> His name, ha:Csokonay, is literally, "the owner of the earth," a divinity who owns in particular all the animals on which the Tonkawa depended for food. . . . hunters always requested Coyote's permission to hunt and always left a portion of the game killed for Coyote. Failure to observe this rule resulted in failure to find and to kill food animals.

The definiteness of this interpretation of Coyote's name here puzzles me, since in the 1949 dictionary the corresponding meaning, "he who owns the land," was followed by a question mark. Certainly the word contains *ha:c* 'earth, land, country, mud'; and the second element can be related to the verb theme *soko-na-* 'to bury (it), put (it) away, keep (it), own (it)' (Hoijer 1949b:66, no. 844) (although the *-na* is not certainly identified). But having other reasons for thinking Tonkawa distantly related to Penutian, the family to which Chinookan and Takelma belong, I am struck by the similarity of the second element to the Wasco word for "coyote," *-sk'ulya* (cf. the stem for "wolf," *-skilu(-)ks*, and Sahaptin *spilya* 'coyote'). (That an analysis of Tonkawa themes, distinguishing frozen initial elements, shows many Chinookan analogies does not belong in this study. Let me just note two striking similarities to Takelma. Tonkawa *we:'is* and Takelma *mi's* both mean "one"; Tonkawa *we:'il* and Takelma *mi:* mean "now.") The similarity of the second element of Coyote's name in Tonkawa to the Chinookan stem, which itself may have cognates in

Penutian, suggests that the interpretation of the name as "the owner of the earth" may be secondary. If the definite statement of 1972 is due to a note from John Rush Buffalo, perhaps it is a folk etymology or a serious pun, prompted by the belief about Coyote as master of the game. Possibly the expression once had the sense of "world coyote" in Tonkawa, specifically for the world-traveling Coyote of the myth time. Multiple names for coyotes are common in the myths of the Pacific Northwest, and Coyote in the specific role of trickster–transformer is often distinguished. Possibly, on the other hand, the name for "wolf" was once not literally "big coyote," but lexically autonomous, and "earth" or "country" plus -*sokonay* served to distinguish the coyote from *sokonay* alone, which may have served for "wolf." The English expression "prairie wolf" would be analogous; it is not a kind of wolf, but a name for the coyote. In any case, I strongly suspect that the complex expression that designates Coyote in the myths was not the only name for Coyote when Tonkawa was a thriving language.

Titles, headings, openings, closings

We do not know if Hoijer obtained English wording for the titles from John Rush Buffalo. The English wording has a convincing closeness to titles known from other groups and to the identifications sometimes given in notes that John Rush Buffalo supplied. Thus, the third myth in the collection does not name the actors besides Coyote, but only refers to them as "a young man" and "a young and very beautiful woman" (1972:100 n. 3.1). Mr. Buffalo separately identified them as Rabbit and Eagle's daughter, as the published title, "Coyote, Rabbit, and Eagle's Daughter," reflects. I rather think that the titles do reflect, if not Tonkawa originals, collaboration between fieldworker and narrator.

The headings in the present analysis of course are supplied as guides to the structure of the myth and have no Tonkawa warrant. I do think that they summarize understandings of the point of the various sections that a Tonkawa audience would have shared.

The myth has no formal opening, except that the initial expression "Coyote was going along" recurs as an initial line in other texts, such as numbers 2 and 3 (pp. 12, 13). It is not, however, the invariable beginning of a myth involving Coyote. In the other two texts just mentioned, the expression is translated "Coyote was going along," as has been done in this text as well.

Tonkawa myths appear to have formal closings that draw on a few expressions that may occur together or independently. The most common expression by far in the published texts is that which closes this myth, *we:tic* 'So it is'. It occurs by itself in seven texts (nos. 2, 4, 5, 9, 12, 15, 17) (followed by an explanation in 17) and preceded by other material in seven (1, 6, 16; 7, 11, 14; 13). Two myths have material of the sort elsewhere followed by *we:tic*, but without it (3, 8); and three myths have no formal closing (10, 18, 19).

Conclusion

I have tried to honor two traditions, that of the Tonkawa and that of linguistic anthropology, and a representative of each, John Rush Buffalo and Harry Hoijer, through whose collaboration what we can know of the Tonkawa tradition was made possible. I hope this essay serves to show the nature and contemporary interest of the myth of Coyote and Eagle's daughter, and serves as a prolegomena to what will one day stand as Tonkawa poetics – one configuration and crystallization among many of the inherent human ability to shape words and stories in lines and groups of lines, but one whose historical autonomy may make it count for much in generalizations about that human ability, though its witnesses be few.

Notes

This essay first appeared in the volume *On Linguistic Anthropology: Essays in Honor of Harry Hoijer 1979*, by Joseph Greenberg, myself, and Paul Friedrich, edited by Jacques Maquet. The volume was published for the UCLA Department of Anthropology by Undena Publications, Malibu, in 1980, as part of the series Other Realities, of which it was number two. The volume resulted from the 1978–9 Harry Hoijer Lectures, mine being given March 1, 1979. My lecture drew on three languages and traditions with which Hoijer was associated: Takelma, the language of the dissertation of his mentor, Edward Sapir; Tonkawa, the language of Hoijer's dissertation, for which he took Sapir's Takelma grammar as a model; and Kathlamet Chinook, the language of the dissertation I wrote while a student with Hoijer at UCLA in 1954–5. The three full-scale studies constitute a manuscript, "Myth as Verse" (1979), containing also the Takelma "Coyote and Frog" (originally entitled "Coyote Goes Courting," by Sapir), and the Kathlamet "Sun's Myth." Only this Tonkawa essay has been published.

I want to thank Jacques Maquet for inviting me to participate in the first series of lectures in honor of Hoijer, and Mrs. Dorothy Hoijer for aid in making my participation possible. The earlier publication has been revised here with regard to the grouping of verses in the act (scenes *ii*, *iii*, *iv*), a few corrections made, and the references updated. The assignment of numbers to lines has been changed in keeping with reanalysis, which brought to light one or two inconsistencies: A line is added at 50–1 (cf. 117–18).

1   A Takelma (southwestern Oregon) Coyote myth, which I have also analyzed in this way (see Hymes Ms.), "Coyote Goes Courting" (Sapir 1909), can be compared as to both organization and content. Whereas the Takelma text might have been organized in two large parts, but seems to show organization into four, the Tonkawa text might be organized into four but seems primarily organized into two. A broad similarity can be glimpsed in the structural development of these two myths, so distant in aboriginal space from each other. In the first two acts Coyote hears something and puts himself in a position to do something about it. In the third and fourth acts he is in the midst of the event in which he had decided to participate, and cuts a certain figure in public – less heroic than might be desired in both cases (half-right singing, hiding when the monster arrives). As the fifth and sixth acts begin, Coyote has a woman, but the situation is disrupted. In the last two acts,

the seventh and eighth, Coyote is left alone without a woman. There are great differences between the stories, and the parallelism must be phrased loosely to hold; nonetheless the parallelism seems genuine. Perhaps we have here a plot schema of considerable antiquity in Native American tradition, an ancient schema implemented in very diverse particulars of action and language in Tonkawa and Takelma.

2   Let me explain here differences between this analysis and that published in 1980 in regard to the last scenes (VIII *iii* and *iv*). In 1980 I had grouped lines 171–86 as scene *iii*, with four stanzas, each with a pair of verses (173–5, 176; 177–8, 179–80; 181–2, 183–4; 185–6, 187–8). The grouping is regular, and it followed on regular grouping of stanzas and verses from the beginning of the preceding scene, *ii*. In *ii* there were two stanzas, each with two verses: 162–5, 166–7; 168–9, 170–2; and of course the further preceding stanza, *i*, patently has four stanzas, each with two verses.

The difficulty that came to light after the first publication of the analysis was that the sequence of verses in which Coyote laughs in response to the woman saying "Come in" came to seem a unity. As a unity, it would contain the three instances of "Come in" and laughing in response of the 1980 scene *iii*, and a fourth instance that in 1980 was made part of scene *iv* (189–90, 191–4). The change makes the fourth instance outcome of the series, as it should be.

The consequence of establishing lines 176–94 as an integral scene, of course, is to require a reexamination of what has preceded and follows. I came to the conclusion that the wife's first instructions at the outset of scene *ii* stand apart (162–5). There follows a change of place ("going to him"), which often indicates a new unit, and an exchange between the messenger and Coyote. Then the messenger speaks again, and Coyote responds, without verbalization, by going with him. Then the two arrive where the messenger speaks again, and Coyote, responds, without verbalization, by peering in. In short, there is a parallelism, through three pairs, of messenger and Coyote.

Moreover, this analysis places the key point, "come" and the location of the wife, in parallel initial place in each of the four units: "Come!"; "Your wife is summoning you"; "Now come!" (parallel to "Come!" so that the first and third are aligned); and, perhaps significantly, "she is staying here." There follows the fourfold repetition of "Come in" and Coyote's response by laughing.

On this analysis, "peering" occurs once in each of the last three scenes (*ii, iii, iv*). That may be pertinent. On first arrival, that is what Coyote does (instead of going in). The implication may be that the initial command to come implied of course to come to the village, the tipi, and me. Coyote comes to the village and the tipi, but not to her.

This frames scene *iii* in which Coyote is explicitly told to come in, and to which he responds by laughing. Probably he peers in each time (*iii* ABC as well as, explicitly, D). This would fit the mention again of peering in *iv* A. We are to visualize Coyote peering in, being told "Come in!," laughing, and withdrawing (four actions).

The consequence of this reanalysis for what follows scene *iii* of course is to deprive it of what was before its initial stanza (189–94). But the closing formula, which had seemed previously to stand outside the verse patterning, can be included.

And reconsideration of the very end of the myth makes it seem that the next to last line, "She was an Eagle, they say," is not really an integral part of the line that precedes it, in which the wife and her parents fly away. As an explanation of the woman's nature, in character, it seems to pair well with "So it is." Thus the present analysis, in which lines 207 and 208 constitute VIII *iv* D ab.

The ending verses of each of the four scenes now have a consistent theme: (i) he's gambling here; (ii) she's staying here; (iii) she flew away; (iv) she was an Eagle (explaining her nature and her having just flown away with her parents).

References

Bahr, Donald M. 1975. *Pima and Papago ritual oratory: a study of three texts*. San Francisco: Indian Historical Press.

Berman, Judith. 1986. *The seals' sleeping cave: method and theory in the interpretation of Boas' Kwakw'ala texts*. Unpublished ms., Dept. of Anthropology, University of Pennsylvania.

Booth, Stephen. 1969. *An essay on Shakespeare's sonnets*. New Haven: Yale University Press.

Bright, William. 1984. *American Indian linguistics and literature*. The Hague: Mouton.

Brooks, Cleanth and Warren, Robert Penn. 1949. *Modern rhetoric*. New York: Harcourt Brace.

Bulow, Nannette and Bulow, Ernest. 1975. Native American literature and the Whorf hypothesis. In Gina Cantoni Harvey and M. F. Heiser, eds., *Southwest languages and linguistics in educational perspective*. San Diego: Institute for Cultural Pluralism, School of Education, San Diego State University, pp. 49–62.

Dunn, John A. 1984. Some ethnopoetic features of Dorothy Brown's Soaban. In David Rood, ed., *Mid-America Linguistics Conference papers*. Denver: University of Colorado.

Hoijer, Harry. 1933. Tonkawa, an Indian language of Texas. In Franz Boas, ed., *Handbook of American Indian languages*, part 3. New York: Augustin, pp. 1–148.

1946. Tonkawa. In Hoijer, ed., *Linguistic structures of Native America*. Viking Fund Publications in Anthropology 6. New York: Wenner-Gren Foundation for Anthropological Research, pp. 289–311.

1949a. Tonkawa syntactic suffixes and anaphoric particles. *Southwestern Journal of Anthropology* 5:37–55.

1949b. *An analytical dictionary of the Tonkawa language*. University of California Publications in Linguistics 5. Berkeley and Los Angeles: University of California Press.

1972. *Tonkawa texts*. University of California Publications in Linguistics 73. Berkeley and Los Angeles: University of California Press.

Hymes, Dell. 1967. Interpretation of a Tonkawa paradigm. In Hymes, ed., *Studies in Southwestern ethnolinguistics*. The Hague: Mouton, pp. 264–278.

1975. Folklore's nature and the Sun's myth. *Journal of American Folklore* 88: 345–369.

1976. Louis Simpson's "The deserted boy." *Poetics* 5:119–155.

1977. Discovering oral performance and measured verse in American Indian narrative. *New Literary History* 7(3):431–457.

1979. Review of Barry Holstun Lopez, *Giving birth to thunder, sleeping with his daughter: Coyote builds North America. Western Humanities Review* 33:91–94.

1980a. Verse analysis of a Wasco text. *International Journal of American Linguistics* 46:65–77. Revised as chap. 5 of 1981a.

1980b. Particle, pause, and pattern in American Indian narrative verse. *American Indian Culture and Research Journal* 4(4):7–51.

1981a. *"In vain I tried to tell you": essays in Native American ethnopoetics.* Philadelphia: University of Pennsylvania Press.

1981b. Comment on Karl Kroeber, "Scarface vs. Scar-face: the problem of versions." *Journal of the Folklore Institute* 18(2–3):144–150.

1982. Narrative form as a "grammar" of experience: Native American and a glimpse of English. *Journal of Education* 164(2):121–142.

1983a. Victoria Howard's "Gitskux and his older brother": a Clackamas Chinook myth. In Brian Swann, ed., *Smoothing the ground: essays on Native American oral literature.* Berkeley and Los Angeles: University of California Press, pp. 129–170.

1983b. Agnes Edgar's Sun Child: verse analysis of a Bella Coola text. In William Seaburg, ed., *Working papers for the 18th International Conference on Salish and neighboring languages.* Seattle: Dept. of Anthropology, University of Washington, pp. 239–312.

1985a. Language, memory and selective performance: Charles Cultee's Salmon's myth as twice-told to Boas. *Journal of American Folklore* 98:391–434.

1985b. Some subtleties of measured verse. In June Hesch, ed., *Proceedings, Niagara Linguistics Society, 15th Spring Conference 1985.* Buffalo, N.Y., pp. 13–57.

In press. Anthologies and narrators. In Arnold Krupat and Brian Swann, eds., *Recovering the word: essays on Native American literature.* Berkeley and Los Angeles: University of California Press.

Ms. Myth as verse in three Native American languages: Takelma, Tonkawa, Kathlamet. Philadelphia: University of Pennsylvania, Department of Folklore archives.

Hymes, Dell and Zenk, Henry. In press. Narrative structure in Chinook Jargon. In Glenn Gilbert, ed., *Pidgin and creole languages: essays in memory of John E. Reinecke.* Ann Arbor: Karoma Publishers.

Jacobs, Melville. 1945. *Kalapuya texts.* University of Washington Publications in Anthropology 11. Seattle: University of Washington Press.

Kincaid, James R. 1977. *The novels of Anthony Trollope.* Oxford: Oxford University Press (Clarendon Press).

Kinkade, M. Dale. 1983. Daughters of fire: verse analysis of an Upper Chehalis narrative. *University of Oklahoma Papers in Anthropology* 24(2): 267–278.

1984. Bear and Bee: verse analysis of an Upper Chehalis narrative. In David Rood, ed., *Mid-American Linguistics Conference papers.* Denver: University of Colorado, 246–261.

1985. The line in Upper Chehalis narrative: Wren and Elk. Paper presented at the annual meeting of the American Anthropological Association, Washington, D.C.

In press. Bluejay and his sister. In Arnold Krupat and Brian Swann, eds., *Recovering the word: essays on Native American literature*. Berkeley and Los Angeles: University of California Press.

McLendon, Sally. 1982. Meaning, rhetorical structure, and discourse organization in myth. In Deborah Tannen, ed., *Analyzing discourse: text and talk*. Georgetown University Round Table on Languages and Linguistics 1981. Washington, D.C.: Georgetown University Press, pp. 284–305.

Miner, Kenneth L. 1982. A short modern Winnebago text with song. *Kansas Working Papers in Linguistics* 7:91–103.

Sapir, Edward. 1909. *Takelma texts*. University of Pennsylvania Anthropological Publications of the University Museum 22(1). Philadelphia.

Tedlock, Dennis. 1972. *Finding the center: narrative poetry of the Zuni Indians*. New York: Dial. [Reprinted 1978, Lincoln: University of Nebraska Press.]

1983. *The spoken word and the work of interpretation*. Philadelphia: University of Pennsylvania Press.

Toelken, Barre and Scott, Techeeni. 1981. Poetic retranslation and the pretty languages of Yellow Man. In Karl Kroeber, ed., *Tradition in American Indian literature: texts and interpretations*. Lincoln: University of Nebraska Press, pp. 65–116.

Tracy, Robert. 1978. *Trollope's later novels*. Berkeley and Los Angeles: University of California Press.

Woodbury, Anthony C. 1985. The functions of rhetorical structure: a study of Central Alaskan Yupik Eskimo discourse. *Language in Society* 14(2):153–190.

Zenk, Henry and Moore, Robert. 1983. "How we went up to steal a mattress": a comedy in three acts by Clara Riggs. In William Seaburg, ed., *Working papers for the 18th International Conference on Salish and neighboring languages*. Seattle: University of Washington, Department of Anthropology, pp. 353–398.

3

WARM SPRINGS SAHAPTIN NARRATIVE ANALYSIS

Virginia Hymes

Introduction

This study has its origin in the conjunction of my work over the last decade on the Warm Springs dialect of the Sahaptin language and my increasing interest in the work of Dell Hymes and others on the verse analysis of American Indian narratives. It is based most particularly on the discovery by Hymes that Chinookan and at least some other American Indian narratives can be seen, upon close analysis of form and content, to be organized as groups of lines in verses, verses in stanzas and, in extended narratives, stanzas in scenes and acts. This poetic organization is achieved primarily through the narrators' use of parallelism and repetition at all levels of language. Hymes has found further that through all these groupings the pattern number of the particular culture plays an organizing role. In the Chinookan and some other cases that pattern number is five, though for other American Indian groups four is probably most common. For Chinookan he finds, further, that there is an underlying rhetorical organization expressed by the structure of lines, verses, stanzas, scenes, and acts that may be characterized as Onset–Ongoing– Outcome. Sequences of three units at any level are found to have this relationship to each other. Sequences of five rather than three units tend to have the middle unit be, pivotally, outcome of the first two and onset of the last two. This is a rhetorical organization that he finds at all levels of the narrative from lines through acts (D. Hymes 1975, 1977, 1980, 1981a, 1981b).

Hymes's work on the verse analysis of American Indian narratives has been done almost entirely by working with published prose transcriptions of those narratives. It has, therefore, had available as evidence only those levels of language that are accessible in such transcriptions: syntactic, morphological, lexical, and segmental phonological. By working closely with both linguistic form and content, Hymes achieves what he sees as a freeing of the narrative performances from their published prose prisons. This method of verse analysis makes possible, he feels, the discovery of individual voices and a deeper understanding of the meanings of particular narratives as performed by those voices.

62

In recent years a number of other linguists and anthropologists have begun applying Hymes's methods of analysis to narratives in other American Indian languages. Judith Berman has presented analyses of several of the Kwakiutl (Kwakw'ala) narratives collected and published by Franz Boas early in the century. An organization based on the pattern number four emerges clearly from her work, as does the use of initial particles and parallelism and repetition in achieving the rhetorical patterning (Berman 1982). On the basis of further analyses, she has also been able to isolate three distinct styles in the Kwakiutl narratives published by Boas (ibid.). Dale Kinkade has presented analyses of narratives in Chehalis and other Salish languages, working both from previously published prose transcriptions and from his own tape recordings of modern performances. In some Salish languages he has found clear use of four as a pattern number organizing the narratives (Kinkade in press). Sally McLendon, working with her own recordings of Eastern Pomo narratives, has found groupings of clauses into larger units defined by a characteristic intonation contour as well as by the kind of parallelism and repetition and use of particles found by Hymes and others (McLendon 1982). The intonation pattern she describes is one of beginning a verse-sized unit (called a sentence by McLendon) with a high pitch that is not exceeded at all before the final fall of intonation at the end of the unit. In reviewing my own narratives after hearing her presentation at the University of Texas conference on Native American discourse out of which this volume has arisen, I found that an analogous contour, with the addition of thin voice quality and low volume to the initial high pitch, was characteristic of the narratives of several of the Warm Springs narrators. McLendon's work and that of Anthony Woodbury on Central Alaskan Yupik (this volume) illustrate the good fortune of those of us working with languages in which we can still record performances of narratives on tape and so have available the additional level of suprasegmental features, voice dynamics, and voice quality that may work in harmony with or in creative tension with the patterning at the other levels of language with which Dell Hymes's work has dealt.

This study explores the extent to which the kinds of organization of narratives found by Hymes in Chinookan and other narratives are used by narrators in Warm Springs Sahaptin. Further, it attempts to define a set of linguistic features used by Sahaptin narrators to achieve their organization of narrative content. The transcription of one myth narration with its translation is presented on the written page so as to make salient the organization of its lines in verses and larger units. The details of the analysis upon which this presentation is based are also given. Finally, some questions are raised as to how widespread verse structure in oral narratives may be. Readers may wish to turn to the myth itself before continuing with the next section of the chapter.

Background

Warm Springs Sahaptin is a form of the Sahaptin language that has developed at the Warm Springs reservation in central Oregon over the last 130 years. Sahaptin and Nez Perce, a language spoken in eastern Washington and Idaho, compose the Sahaptian family of languages. Sahaptin was spoken by American Indian bands living on both sides of the Columbia River upriver from The Dalles in present-day Oregon. As a result of a treaty in 1855 some of the Oregon Sahaptins and their Chinookan neighbors, the Wascos, were moved to the Warm Springs reservation some ninety miles south of the river. There, under the acculturative influence of churches, work in the white economy and, most important, compulsory schooling, Sahaptin has, like so many other American Indian languages, become a language of limited use by its speakers, most of whom are over forty and all of whom speak English.

The storytelling gatherings on winter nights at which children had to stay awake and listen exist now only in the memories of old people. If stories are told in the language now, it is for the tape recorders of linguist or anthropologist or of the Tribal Cultural Heritage Committee. Most of the narratives I have recorded, including the one presented here, have been told without native-speaking audience. The question naturally arises of whether narratives told under such circumstances will be in any sense performances. Through work with a group of elders who were involved in the Sahaptin language-teaching program in the local school I was fortunate to be able to tape record a number of narratives that were told with that group as audience. There has therefore been opportunity to compare narratives told to the obvious enjoyment of Sahaptin-speaking listeners with the much larger group of stories for which I and my tape recorder were the only ears.

The seven-hour cycle of Coyote stories told by Linton Winishut and the dozen narratives of several genres told by my friend and teacher Hazel Suppah prove on comparison with the others to show little difference in performance features or in overall poetic structure. Direct discourse, taking on the voices of characters, rhetorical vowel lengthening, humor, and sound effects occur in all the tellings. Mr. Winishut, sitting alone with me and the tape recorder at dusk over many evenings, gave performances complete with gestures that cried out for videotaping. Mrs. Suppah, in her performance of the story presented here, gave Raven's cry as she left her children in unabashed full cry, and Basket Woman's song to her children was sung in its full gruesomeness.

Method of analysis and presentation

When I read Dell Hymes's first verse analyses of Chinookan myths, I must confess that I did not wholly believe in their reality: He was a poet and had made verse of prose. William Bright hinted at some of the same feeling in a talk at the Georgetown University Round Table in Language and Linguistics in March of 1981, though he like Hymes is a practicing poet. I am not a poet, but now, after a number of years of work on Sahaptin narratives using the methods Hymes uses, but incorporating attention to intonation, pause, and voice quality, I am convinced that the poets in question are the Native American narrators and that, in writing what they have spoken as prose, we have been hiding their verbal artistry. I now agree with Hymes that in the prose collections of American Indian narratives there is a vast world of poetry waiting to be released by those of us with some knowledge of the languages.

In exploring the applicability in Sahaptin of Hymes's approach to American Indian narratives, I have used a variety of materials. In addition to my own tape recordings and transcriptions of Warm Springs Sahaptin narratives I have made use of the narratives presented as prose in Melville Jacobs's (1929, 1934) two volumes of Northern Sahaptin myths. In using my own materials I have worked in two different ways. My earliest analyses were done from my prose transcriptions without access to the tapes. The whole Coyote cycle was done in this way during a summer when I did not have those tapes at hand. The narrative discussed in this chapter was first done in the same way. All narratives done without access to tapes were then reviewed by listening for features not represented in my earlier transcriptions. Some details of this kind of relistening are mentioned later on in the chapter. What can be said in general, however, is that the difference it makes to have access to tapes is not crucial to the discovery of the major structural organization of the narrative in most cases. It turns out – and this is true also of the narratives in English that I have worked on in the last few years – that most narrators use more than one linguistic device to signal a new unit (verse, stanza, scene) of the narrative and to give cohesion to the lines in a verse, the verses in a stanza, and so on. These features work together, so that a stanza beginning that had been suggested by particle, time word, change of scene or character, will also often turn out to be marked by a sharp change in pitch or in voice quality. Verses that on other evidence seem to cohere as a stanza will often turn out to have parallel patterning of voice quality or intonation or other suprasegmental features. For example, the kind of intonation contour defining verses that McLendon found in Eastern Pomo seems also to be a characteristic device of several of the Sahaptin women narrators whose stories I have analyzed, though it is seldom the only feature marking the joining of lines in the verse. In fact one most often sees the unity of the verse through the parallel patterning and repetition in its lines, and the intonation contour is another cohesive device acting along with that patterning. Recognition of a typical intonation contour for verses has been enormously helpful, however, in isolating verses in some Sahaptin narratives.

Relistening to tapes for which one has already made a verse analysis based on the prose transcription alone can occasionally reveal previously overlooked segmental material, material that is of unsuspected importance. Checking my verse analysis based on the prose transcription of Linton Winishut's Coyote cycle against the tapes served in the most surprising way to confirm a hypothesis I had developed about one of his devices for marking the beginnings of stanzas.

It had appeared that in a large number of cases the first line of a new stanza was marked by a line-final occurrence of the particle *áuku* 'now then', with stress shifted from the first to the last syllable, i.e. *aukú*. This particle is, as line-initial, often a mark of new stanzas and verses. It is usually translated as "so then." It was not the case, in my verse analysis, that all stanzas in which one would, on the basis of the overall pattern, have expected to find final *aukú* did in fact have it. In relistening to the tapes with my verse analysis before me, I found two things. There were a number of cases where missing punctuation or capitalization in my handwritten transcription had made the placement of *aukú* ambiguous – whether at the end of one line or the beginning of the next. I had consistently put it at the beginning of the next line, rather than at the end of the line, where relistening to the tapes showed it to belong. More surprisingly, in other cases I was able to hear *áuku*s and *aukú*s that Hazel Suppah had omitted in her bit-by-bit repetition of the recorded narrative for my transcription. Listening to the tapes of our transcription sessions confirmed that she had indeed omitted them. The point is that the correct placement of the misplaced and the missing particles served to confirm or strengthen the hypothesis that Linton Winishut used line-final *aukú* to mark the first lines of many stanzas.

Hazel Suppah's omission of some of the particles in the narration, even ones that were crucial to the verse structure, points up an important fact about the devices that narrators use. They are largely unconscious. The narrator of the first text I recorded in Sahaptin was appalled when she saw in my transcription of it (in prose of course) that she had used so many *áu*s and *áuku*s. She thought of them as hesitation pauses, and had been unaware that she ever used them much. At the time, I was myself unaware of their function, but have now looked back at the text, an ethnographic one, to find that they were in fact playing a role similar to their role in narratives.

This unconsciousness of devices one uses in oral performance is, of course, not peculiar to Native Americans. How many lecturers in English are aware of how they use such words as "Okay" and "All right" and "Now" to mark the start of new sections? Similarly, how many storytellers in American English are aware of their patterned use of the technique first pointed out by Wolfson (1978, 1982) by which narrators in conversational narratives segment their stories by switching into and out of the historical present tense? In fact, most middle-class speakers of American English feel certain they never use the historical present tense at all, much less use it as an important stylistic device.

With some of my most recently recorded narratives in Sahaptin I have worked directly from tapes and made my first transcription directly in lines.

The lines are usually quite easy to hear. But from that point on, given a transcription in lines, the further work of analysis is quite similar in both cases. Working from tapes has indeed made it possible to explore the contributions of all levels of language to the narrator's shaping of the content in a particular performance. It should be kept in mind, however, that, in working from printed prose transcriptions made by earlier linguists and anthropologists, one is also studying particular performances and not some idealized text. The prose volumes are records in writing of particular tellings, by particular individuals. In those tellings, just as in the ones for which we have tape recordings, the narrator has selected content and used linguistic means at all levels of language to shape that content. There is no question that no written records can capture the contribution made by all linguistic levels, though punctuation often reflects pause and certain intonational phenomena, and many linguists and anthropologists did by various means indicate rhetorical vowel length, extremes of volume, unusual voice quality, and other features of the sort Dennis Tedlock (1978, 1983) has given attention to in his work on Zuni and Mayan narratives. In any case, all published transcriptions do at least present the evidence for the narrators' selection and arrangement of narrative content and do give the data at the level of segmental phonology, morphology, syntax, and lexicon from which one can discover the parallel patterning and repetition at those levels. All my own work up to this point indicates that, important as intonation, voice quality, speed, volume, and other features Tedlock's typographic conventions so admirably capture may be, they work *sometimes in unison and sometimes in creative tension with* devices and patterns at the other levels of language, the levels represented in an ordinary prose transcription.

"Represented" – but not made salient; it is to *making salient* the narrator's use of devices at the levels of phonology, syntax, and lexicon that Hymes's method of analysis is admirably directed. Making those devices apparent on the page has a twofold value. It is a heuristic device for the analyst's insight into the structure and meaning of the narrative in that particular performance. It is also a way of making those insights and the artistry of the narrator most available to readers. A poet, a writer of stories or novels, has control over how his or her art is seen by the reader. The oral narrator is of course best appreciated aurally (if one understands the language and the rhetorical patterns of his or her narrative tradition and individual style). But if the words are to be written down by us we owe it to the narrator to do it in a way that brings out to the fullest extent possible how he or she has used language to artfully shape the content chosen for performance.

What is clear from all the work I have done, and what cannot be stressed too much, is that Hymes's method is not to be thought of as a cookie cutter that you impress on the narrative, or as a pasta machine into which you push a prose transcription to have a verse analysis come out the other end. There is no quick fix; you cannot, having read one article in which particles are seen to organize a narrative, just look for initial particles and finding them assume they have done your work, or not finding them assume there is no poetic organization to the narrative. Rather, what is involved is a patient working back and forth between content and form, between organization at the level of the whole narrative and at the level of details of lines within a single verse or even words within a line, until gradually you arrive at an analysis that seems best *at that stage of your knowledge of the narrative tradition and the particular narrator.* I emphasize the last point because it is only through work with many narratives by many different narrators that the analyst builds up a knowledge of the range of narrative devices used in the language and the variety of uses to which they may be put. The recognition of a rhetorical organization at all levels of narrative that Hymes has found and named Onset–Ongoing–Outcome in the Chinookan narrative tradition was not something quickly or easily achieved, and discoveries of comparable rhetorical principles in other traditions will not come quickly or easily. Co-operative work by many linguists in many narrative traditions will be necessary in order to arrive at knowledge of the range of overarching principles of organization used by Native American narrators.

Getting started

The first step in making a verse analysis of a performed narrative is to work out a tentative division into lines. As mentioned above, when one has a tape recording one can often just hear the lines fall out. This is, however, probably most often the case after one has become familiar with the narrator's style or with other narrators in the same tradition. If one works from a prose transcription the best procedure seems to be to assign one line to each predication. This has been Hymes's practice and that of his students and mine who have worked on other American Indian narratives. (Berman's work on Kwakiutl narratives mentioned above was begun in courses with us.) When narratives written in lines using this procedure are then checked against tapes, two kinds of differences may emerge.

One often finds that a narrator has treated as a line, marked by pause and other features of juncture, a segment that includes no verb. The *łii . . . kw'i* of the first verse of stanza B of the narrative presented here is such a case. In Sahaptin, time words and phrases and stanza-initial particles are particularly apt to be delivered as separate lines, as are lists of nouns. The kinds of nonpredicate material that may be treated as separate lines probably differ for different languages, though in intensive work over the past two years on Appalachian and other English oral narratives it has been found that time words and initial particles are likely there too to be treated as separate lines (see note 2 below for references).

Second, in listening to the tape of a narrative one has already laid out in lines from a prose transcription, one will find cases where two hypothesized lines are not marked off as separate lines by any pause or other suprasegmental feature. When I presented this paper orally several years ago I believed that this was always a case of the narrator "running two lines together" as a poet may do in reading his own work (where he after all has chosen what to write as lines). Although I still feel that many cases are of this sort, I now recognize that narrators may sometimes unite two predications as a unit to be treated as equivalent, in the patterning of a verse, to other lines containing only a single predication. For example, a narrator operating with a pattern of verses with three lines to a verse can make four predications in a verse by uniting two of them in one line, but by maintaining clearly the pattern in threes with other devices. It is not possible to distinguish between a case of this sort and the running together of lines without having reached a stage in the analysis where you have a good sense of the narrator's and the narrative tradition's most typical patterns. This is one reason for never quite feeling a particular analysis is the final one; further work in the narratives of that tradition or that narrator may give new insight and prompt a reanalysis. Even work in a different language may suggest new possibilities. The work is of a spiral nature. Ultimately, I believe, it must be a cooperative endeavor between scholars working on oral narratives in a variety of languages.

Finding verses and stanzas

Having arrived at a segmentation of the text into lines, one does the same for the English translation one is working from and lines the two up opposite each other on facing pages. This arrangement makes for ease in working back and forth between form and content in the next stage: discovering the narrator's grouping of lines in verses and verses in stanzas, and ultimately stanzas in scenes and acts. In some narrative traditions or with some stories of some narrators this job can seem almost done for you, so consistent is the use of particles or other features such as evidentials to mark off verses and stanzas or even larger segments. Hymes found this to be the case with the Wishram narrator Louis Simpson; and his reporting of that fact has unfortunately led some to infer that he is saying that particles are what mark verses and stanzas in all American Indian narratives. Braun (1982) found that in a Teton Sioux narrative an evidential particle translated as "they say" ended every stanza except one in a particular myth. (How nice it would have been to have a tape recording to check whether that one particle had been missed in transcription!) In a Seneca myth evidentials seemed to mark verses rather consistently (Servaes 1982). And in a Cree narrative there were clearly two major sections, each beginning with a particle translated as "Indeed" that occurred nowhere else in the narrative (Blincoe 1982).

Organizing devices such as these are so prominent and consistent that they come to the attention of the analyst rather easily. In most cases of analyzing a text as verse, however, the process is slower and involves a constant interaction between one's understanding of the content and one's increasing awareness of the linguistic devices that are used in that narrative tradition to organize texts. One looks always for parallel patterning and repetition at the morphological, syntactic, and lexical levels as well as at the level of intonation and voice quality in arriving at one's first tentative analysis of the verse and stanza organization of the narrative. It is necessary too to continually step back (or up) and look down from above at the organization of content of the whole narrative as it relates to these small units. The successive stages of the analysis are achieved by a moving back and forth between working from the bottom up (from line to verse to stanza, etc.) and then working down from whole to part. One is never satisfied with an analysis that does not make sense in terms of narrative content. No matter whether a narrator has consistently been using five or three lines in a verse; if one verse seems to make sense as a unit of content only if it has four lines, then so be it. A narrator may occasionally use as a connective in the middle of a verse a particle that he or she otherwise almost always uses as verse- or stanza-initial. There will usually be other evidence that that is indeed what has been done, and it must never be overridden in pursuit of some kind of mechanical consistency. At the same time the analyst must be aware that the organization of content may be quite different from what might be expected from his or her own narrative traditions. The process of analysis gives insight into both ways of organizing of content and linguistic means for doing so. Slowness and patience are necessary and ultimately rewarding.

Warm Springs Sahaptin narrative organization

Role of pattern numbers

The use of the pattern number five is an organizing device in Sahaptin as it is in Chinookan. This is a fact quickly discovered and of which narrators are quite aware. Hazel Suppah even comments metanarratively in one mythtelling that "everything has to happen five times." One is perhaps not surprised then to find that not only do events occur five times but that there are often five lines in a verse, five verses in a stanza, and so on. But one must also not be surprised to find that, as Hymes found in Chinookan, three is also a pattern number for this narrative tradition. It is a pattern number in the sense that one repeatedly finds sets of three verbs, each a line or each a verse, depending on other factors. Sometimes they show the relationship to each other which Hymes has called Onset–Ongoing–Outcome, and which he has found to be a dominant rhetorical structure of Chinookan narratives. As in Chinookan, sets of three quite complex segments – verses, stanzas, even scenes or acts – may also be seen to bear this semantic relationship to each other. In

Sahaptin, however, other sets of three may not be thus related. In Sahaptin storytelling there just seems to be a tendency to fill out a pattern of three verbs in parallel construction, even if one of the three is merely a repetition. An example is in a personal-experience narrative of Hazel Suppah's:

Kútaš kwná wínana,	And we went there,
kútaš wínana áu,	and we went then,
kútaš áu panaitíya.	and we then climbed.

The frequent grouping of five or three units at one level in a unit at the next higher level is probably not at the conscious level in either Chinookan or Sahaptin and in this respect differs from the overt counting of the named five times that events occur or the frequency of the overt mention of five brothers, five nights or days, five implements used, etc. In Sahaptin narratives, the myth genre is distinguished from other narrative genres by the fact that it is only in myths that "things must happen five times." Yet all the narratives I have analyzed, of whatever genre, show the other sort of use of three and five as pattern numbers. For Sahaptin narratives, most often when one has arrived at the analysis that seems most satisfactory in terms of having sections each of which is a plot unit easily described by a title in a table of contents, and in terms of one's being able to give a consistent set of linguistic reasons for each division of the narrative, one finds that the text has been divided into threes and fives.

The text presented here, for instance, had earlier been divided into two acts, one with one scene and the other with four. Stanza A stood apart as Introduction. Certain things about the analysis seemed not quite right. When the thought occurred that the break between acts might in fact be a bit further on, the whole train of consequences of looking at this possibility led to the version presented here with two acts of three scenes each. In the process of reanalysis I found places where I had been inconsistent in weighing the linguistic evidence for divisions of verses and stanzas. By making changes that involved more consistency, an analysis was achieved that reflected the pattern numbers more fully and that had tighter coherence of each unit as a bit of plot.

An experience like this can ease the worry that one may have as a beginning analyst that one is somehow fiddling with the text to make it come out in threes or fives, or for other traditions twos and fours. In my case, earlier experiences of quickly dividing an unfamiliar text from Jacobs's collections into lines for a class, making verse or stanza breaks only at places that were either strongly marked by particles or by obvious breaks in content, and then stepping back from the board to discover three or five lines between each pair of breaks, had given me a rather strong sense that these numerical patterns were really there. The experience with this text and with others has strongly reinforced that assurance.

The role that the overt pattern "five times" plays in organizing the narrative may be fairly complex. It is rarely the case that a narrator spells out in detail each of the five occurrences of an event that is said to have happened five times. Comments from Hazel Suppah indicate that to do so might be considered rather dull. What happens in these myths instead is that there will typically be a set of actions that compose the event. They may be spelled out in full in one "time," usually the first time. Stanza B of the narrative presented here is a good example of this. The event then may be spelled out a second time, usually but not necessarily signaled by *ánč'a* or *ánčaxi* 'again'. This second occurrence may be less fully described and perhaps just mentioned by number. By the third time the narrator is likely to mention that it is the third time, and almost always does so for the fourth time. The fifth time is always mentioned by number and perhaps only by number, but almost always has a different outcome from the other four. That outcome is often related in a new section of the narrative.

For the analyst of these narratives it is useful to begin by looking at all five occurrences in order to determine what the components of the repeated event are. (They are not necessarily all included in any one "time.") One then looks to see which of the components of the event are recounted in each occurrence and whether the narrator has treated them each as a line, a verse, or even a stanza. In the narrative presented here, there is an interesting interweaving of the five components of the fivefold event in Act I, scene 1. These components are: the mother's going to dig for the day, her return home, her request for water, the children's failure to respond, and her response to that failure. It was only the later occurrences of the event, where her response is a threat to leave the children, that made me realize that her getting her own water in stanza B is filling the response slot. It is her first response to their failure to honor her request.

In some narratives, one occurrence of a fivefold event may be a whole scene and have each component of the event a separate stanza. In Linton Winishut's Coyote cycle this sometimes seems to be the case. In other instances, each occurrence of the event may constitute just one verse. And, as happens in the final scene of the narrative presented here, it may be that only the first "time" is related and that a simple "five times and then . . . " may stand for all the rest. The extent to which the different occurrences of fivefold events and the ways in which the component parts of the events are distributed in relation to the verse structure of the narrative constitute one of the important ways in which different tellings of the same story may be compared and insight gained into the narrator's point of view in a particular telling.

Linguistic means in Sahaptin for parallel patterning and marking of narrative segments

Let me now discuss in some detail the linguistic bases in Sahaptin of patterns that group lines and distinguish sets of them. There are six: person marking in the clause; morphological complexity in the verb; shifts in aspect, tense, and direction; use of particles; rhetorical lengthening of vowels; and intonation and voice quality.

Person marking. Like the other dialects of Sahaptin, Warm Springs Sahaptin marks the person and number of the subject and object of the finite verb in each clause through the interaction of a set of clitics attached to the first lexeme in the clause with a small set of verb prefixes. The clitics indicate that either the subject or object is first or second person, singular or plural. They are: *-naš, -aš, -š* in phonemically determined alternation for first person singular; *-nam* for second person singular; *-nataš, -ataš, -taš* in alternation for first person plural exclusive; *-na* for first person plural inclusive; *-pam* for second person plural. With all these clitics the case role (subject or object) indicated depends on the prefix on the verb. If there is no verb person-marking prefix, then the clause is an intransitive construction and the clitic references the subject. If there is a verb prefix marking third person subject (*i-* for singular, *pa-* for plural), then the clitic indicates person and number of the object. For example:

> *Áu-nam q'inú-ta*   Now-you see-will   'Now you will see'.
> *Áu-nam i-q'inú-ta*   Now-you he-see-will   'Now he will see you'.

If the first clause were to have an object that was third person it would be:

> *Áu-nam á-q'inú-ta*   'Now you will see him, her, them'.

With the second person clitics *-nam* and *-pam*, there is one other possibility. The verb may have a prefix *pá-*. In that case the subject is second person and the object is first person. For example:

> *Míš-nam pá-q'inú-na?*   Interrog.-you me-see-past   'Did you see me?'

Two of the clitics reference person of both subject and object unambiguously. They occur of course without a person-marking verb prefix. They are *-maš* and *-mataš*.

> *Q'inú-ta-maš*   See-will-I/you   'I will see you'.
> *Áxwai-mataš q'inú-ta*   Later-I/you see-will   'I'll see you folks later'
> or 'We'll see you or you folks later'.

The clitics are also used in possessive constructions. For first person the regular clitic is used, but for second person possessors *-maš* and *mataš* are used. For example:

> *K'úsi-maš wá*   Horse-2nd.sg. be   'The horse is mine'.

Third person possessors are indicated by the prefix *á-* on the verb.

This system of person marking, coupled with the fact that noun subjects and objects usually follow the verb, makes parallel construction of lines possible in a number of ways. In the discussion above of pattern numbers, I gave an example of the attachment of the person-marking clitic to a particle, *kú*, to create a series of lines beginning with *kutaš*. Since these clitics are always placed at the end of the first word in the clause, except in dependent clauses, when they are proclitic to the first word, one has only to keep the first word constant to create parallel patterning at the beginning of the line. Particles are the most frequently used first words for this effect. Similarly, the third person prefixes can be used to make a series of lines that begin alike, with or without initial particles (cf., e.g. verses 4, 30, and 57). Both these resources for parallel patterning at the beginnings of lines are widely used in all the narratives I have recorded, as well as in those published by Jacobs (1929, 1934).

Morphological complexity in the verb. Sahaptin, like many other American Indian languages, has a tendency to pack a lot of information into the verb word. The possibilities of extending parallel morphological patterning at the front of the verb go beyond the person-marking prefixes. Prefixes in second position like *wi*- distributive and *šapá*- causative, as well as a large number of roots that come in positions at the beginning of the verb stem complex, make possible verb constructions that are alike for quite a stretch at the front of the word. Sahaptin has a very large number of these anterior verb roots. Some have quite concrete meanings like "with the hand, head, feet, pointed object, etc.," "onto the hand, head, etc.," "while eating, sleeping, going along, talking, etc.," "on foot, on horseback, on the belly, etc." While they are often part of fully lexicalized stems, they are also used productively to specify the verb action more finely. The fact that some of them have quite abstract meanings, e.g. *ná*- to specify an action taking place after another has been completed, allows the narrator to create parallel pattern in a series of verbs without as much semantic constraint as the more concrete roots would involve. Linton Winishut's Coyote cycle makes rich use of not only the more concrete roots but also these rarer and more abstract ones. One explanation of his using these abstract roots on a series of verbs was "Linton really likes to make his words long." He is well known as a skilled user of language, and people were said to be glad that in telling his Coyote cycle he was "bringing out" so many of the old words. Yet it is clear that his use of these anterior roots often serves to create parallel patterning within verses or stanzas. The example given below of Hazel Suppah's use of the anterior root *xásu*- 'on horseback' shows use of an anterior root with quite concrete meaning to the same end. There is a word that means "to ride," *wáša*-. But *xásu-naiti*- (*naiti*- 'general locomotion') is also a common more explicit lexicalized stem for the same meaning. Once a narrator has established that a person is on horseback, further uses of *xásu-* in subsequent verbs are clearly a matter of stylistic choice. In what follows Hazel Suppah exercises that choice to good effect. Note also the parallel patterning created by the third person subject prefix *i-*.

Naxš áyat iwínana míi˙ ˙ ˙mi.	1
Ixásunaitima nišákni íčn	2
waníči tiičám Šítaikt.	3
Kwníin áuku ixásutuxa anáštk'a.	4
Áu táa˙ ˙ ˙'aš	5
iwiyálaikika Míllipa,	6
ixásuničanwikika,	7
ixásuwaičnkika,	8
iwínakika.	9

These lines may be translated as follows:

A certain woman went lo-o-ong ago.	1
She rode (horseback) from her house to here	2
the place called Shitike.	3
From there then she rode home, towards evening.	4
Now, getting da-a-ark,	5
she got right along the Warm Springs River,	6
she rode down,	7
she rode across,	8
she went on.	9

The verb words of each line are segmented and given morpheme-by-morpheme translation below. This may help to bring out the full extent of the parallel patterning.

Line 1: *i-wina-na*   3rd.sg.subj.-go-past.
Line 2: *i-xásu-naiti-m-a*   3rd.sg.subj.-on horseback-go-cislocative-past.
Line 3: No verb.
Line 4: *i-xásu-tux-a*   3rd.sg.subj.-on horseback-go homeward-past.
Line 5: No verb.
Line 6: *i-wiyá-lai-kik-a*   3rd.sg.subj.-while going-go right alongside-translocative-past.
Line 7: *i-xásu-ničanwi-kik-a*   3rd.sg.subj.-on horseback-go down to-translocative-past.
Line 8: *i-xásu-waič-n-kik-a*   3rd.sg.subj.-on horseback-cross-stem increment-translocative-past.
Line 9: *i-wína-kik-a*   3rd. sg.subj.-go-translocative-past.

Shifts in aspect, tense, and direction. The Sahaptin system of marking tense aspect and two directions plays two important roles in narratives: grouping lines by parallel patterning at the end of the verb, and segmenting the narrative by shifts in one or all of these grammatical categories. The excerpt from Indianhead Canyon exemplifies both.

Briefly, the linguistic basis for the first role is as follows: Sahaptin has three aspects and three tenses, plus two directionals, cislocative and translocative. The marked aspects are: habitual or usitative, marked by suffix -*xa*, and progressive or continuative, marked by suffix -*ša*. The unmarked aspect usually seems to be perfective, clearly so in past and future. With the present, also unmarked except after the directionals, where it is marked by suffix -*š*, the unmarked aspect refers to actions that have just happened or are just about to. This combination of tense and aspect may also function as a historical present, as may the habitual and progressive presents (cf. e.g. stanzas R and S). The habitual aspect, though in some contexts quite clearly contrasting with perfective or progressive, is used in narratives for actions that are clearly not habitual, and in fact seems to function like a simple past or present. What is important in narratives is that narrators seem to use shifts from one aspect to another, from one tense to another, and from one direction to another, as well as all possible combinations of the three categories, at the boundaries of units of the verse structure of the narrative. A good example of this kind of shift is at the break in Act II between scene 1 and scene 2. Scene 1 has been almost entirely in past, unmarked aspect. Scene 2 shifts into present progressive -*ša*, and continues it through stanzas Q and R. This narrative, like others, is replete with such shifts at boundaries of verses and stanzas, which are sufficiently defined in most cases by other criteria of form or content. Thus Sahaptin narrators seem to be doing with shifts in three verbal categories, tense, aspect, and direction, what Wolfson (1982) found English-speaking conversational narrators doing with the shift between past and historical present. It was my familiarity with her work that led me to look for similar phenomena in Sahaptin.

Morpheme alternations. Two features of morpheme alternation in the tense system give narrators the means to create parallel patterning and end rhyme in a series of lines. The first is the alternation between a zero form and -*š* for the present tense. The -*š*, as mentioned earlier, occurs only after -*m* or -*(k)ik*, the cis- and translocative suffixes. Using a directional then invokes the marked form of the present-tense suffix and creates forms ending in -*mš* or -*ikš*. Usually this is done in one of the marked aspects, creating forms that end in -*šamš*, -*šaikš*, -*xamš*, or -*xaikš*. Often the first use in a series of one of the directionals will seem semantically motivated, direction toward or away from the focus of the narrative at that point. The continued marking for direction of a series of verbs usually seems clearly stylistic – to create parallel pattern and in some cases end rhyme in a series of lines.

The second morpheme alternation, phonemically determined by the last phoneme of the preceding morpheme, involves the past-tense suffix. After *i* it is *-ya*; after *a* and *u, -na*; elsewhere, *-a*. If then a narrator is using past tense with unmarked aspect and no directional suffix, the final phoneme of the verb stem will determine which alternant of the past-tense suffix is to be used, giving as in stanzas E and F of the narrative presented here no particular parallel patterning at the ends of the verb words. By use of *-xa* or *-ša* aspect the narrator can achieve more parallel patterning, as the past-tense suffix is *-na* in both cases. An example of this kind of patterning with *-xana* is stanzas B, C, and D. An interesting case of use of *-ša* that achieves parallel patterning occurs in stanza S and involves the directional suffix *-ik* rather than past tense. The first verb in the stanza itself ends in *ša* (*waaša-*), to which Hazel Suppah adds the translocative and past tense. Below that, verse 64 twice echoes the *-šaik-* part of that first verb by her use on them of the progressive suffix. In the case of those two verses the use of the translocative seems semantically motivated: She is going off from there. Its use on the first verb, where she made her children dance, is not clear semantically and is probably a shift of direction as one mark of the new stanza. In any case, what is striking is that here parallel phonological patterning is achieved by using unmarked aspect in one verse and progressive aspect in the succeeding ones.

Rhetorical vowel lengthening. Another linguistic feature used by Sahaptin narrators to segment their narratives is rhetorical vowel lengthening. I had been aware of this feature as a characteristic of performed narratives but had been unaware until I had begun analyzing narratives as verse that the lengthening occurs chiefly at the beginnings of sections: in the first lines of verses or stanzas. The vowel lengthening is usually in the particle, the person-marking prefix, or in a time word or numeral. Linton Winishut is particularly likely to lengthen the third singular subject prefix *i-* at the beginnings of verses. (See also in the next section his use of *ii* 'yes' as initial particle.)

Particles. Particles play an important role in Sahaptin narratives, both in creating parallel patterning and in signaling new sections of the narrative. The most commonly used particles in these functions are *áu* 'now, then', which I have consistently translated as "now"; *kú* 'and, but, so'; *áuku* 'now then, so then, and then', which I have translated as "now then"; *ánč'a(xi)* 'again (the same)'; *kúš* 'thus'; *kúšxi* 'in the same way'. Linton Winishut also uses *íi* 'yes, indeed' with rhetorical vowel lengthening at the beginnings of verses. The fact that it is homophonous with the third singular subject prefix, which he also lengthens in that position, can lead to confusion. His use of *ii* in this way is interesting in light of the fact that a response by listeners was traditionally required when myths were told, and it was *ii*ꞏ ꞏ ꞏ. Only one of the myths I have recorded has such a respondent. Preliminary analysis of the position of the responses in relation to verse structure suggests that it is usually either at the end of a verse or at the end of the first line of a new stanza. Its occurrence in the latter position seemed clearly expected by the narrator, who waited several times at the end of the first line of a stanza until the delayed response came. In another case, at the end of a verse, she seems to have added a redundant fourth line and then waited until the *ii* ˙ ˙ ˙ came. Research now in progress on a Coyote cycle with native-speaking audience recorded by Eugene Hunn may be able to throw light on the relation of this stylized audience response to verse structure.

Intonation and voice quality. As mentioned earlier, work on the relation of intonation and voice quality to narrative organization was done after earlier versions of this paper had been completed. What is clear from further work is that verses are characterized by an intonation curve similar to that described by McLendon for Eastern Pomo. Most verses begin with raised pitch beyond which there is no rise within the verse. Most end with a final fall of pitch. Further, there is a tendency, among the women narrators I have recorded, for the first lines of verses that have raised pitch to have also thin voice quality and lowered volume, sometimes so faint as to be almost inaudible. This raised pitch and then voice are so regular with the women narrators that the verses – and there are some – that begin with low pitch, rich voice quality, or loud volume are very marked. Similarly a pitch within the verse that rises above verse-initial pitch is marked and semantically important. One example, which turned out to have been quite conscious on Hazel Suppah's part, was in a verse in which people were climbing a very steep hill. The pitch on the word for steep (which was a line in itself) went way up and then way down as they descended the hill. When I pointed this out to Mrs. Suppah several years after she had told the story she said, "Yes" and smiled with satisfaction.

Though most verses end with a final fall in pitch and a pause, there seems to be a pattern of running together the final verses of a scene or act or narrative. This running together is characterized also by increased tempo, almost like a racing to the finish. I have found it with only one narrator, Susan Moses, and it may be idiosyncratic rather than a characteristic of the Sahaptin narrative tradition.

Summary of linguistic features used for poetic organization of Sahaptin narratives

To summarize, the person-marking system and that of aspect, tense, and directional marking, along with the large number of anterior verb roots available to delimit the meaning of the main verb root, and prefixes like the causative and distributive, make possible extensive parallel patterning at both ends of the verb word. The freedom of placement of particles, and the usual placement of noun and verb subjects after the verb enhance these possibilities of parallel patterning. (For exceptions to this placement of expressed subjects that serve

as a narrative device for focus on new characters or refocus on old ones, see
V. Hymes 1982.) Organization of the narrative in verses and stanzas, apart
from that which is achieved by the cohesion of lines through parallel patterning
and repetition, is accomplished by initial and/or final particles, by rhetorical
vowel lengthening, by shifts of tense, aspect, and/or direction, and by features
of intonation, voice quality, and volume. These techniques for parallel patterning
and for organizing content in lines, verses, and stanzas and in scenes and
acts are used in slightly different ways by each narrator. The techniques
interact with each other, with the rhetorical pattern of fivefold repetition of
certain events, and with such aspects of the narrative as change of scene, of
characters, of speaker to create the particular poetic organization found in
each telling.

Some other characteristics of Warm Springs Sahaptin narratives

Before proceeding to detailed explication of the analysis of the narrative
presented here, I would like to mention some features of Sahaptin narratives
that do not relate directly to their poetic organization.

One feature common to all the Warm Springs Sahaptin narratives I know,
and largely absent in those of their Chinookan neighbors (D. Hymes personal
communication), is the frequent use of direct speech without any framing by
a verb of saying. Knowing who is speaking at any point can be a major
problem for an outsider; even recognizing when one turn at speech ends and
another begins may present problems.

Another Sahaptin narrative feature not found in Chinookan is the use of
special suffixes on the names for animals when they are myth characters. For
example, *xuxux* is the ordinary word for raven, an ordinary raven you might
see flying around. *Xuxuxya* is Raven, the myth character. This feature makes
possible a very subtle narrative device, found in this myth. When Raven flies
off, deserting her disobedient children, she flies as *xuxux*, having dropped
her -*ya* suffix along with her maternal responsibilities. Similarly, at the very
end of Linton Winishut's Coyote cycle one realizes that Spilyai has become
spilya, an ordinary coyote, not the trickster, and that the narrative has moved
into the time of the people whose imminent arrival Spilyai has been predicting
and preparing the world for throughout the cycle.

Some comments on the story of Raven and her children

Special features of this myth that warrant mention include the use of a personal
name for the well-known myth character Basket Woman (T'at'aɬiyayái).
Hazel Suppah uses the name Alítɬ'as for her in Act II, scene 1, and explained
that that is her personal name. Furthermore, she has Basket Woman refer to

her child captives as *ktɬ' íktɬ' ima*, a special Sahaptin word used only by Basket Woman which, following Mrs. Suppah, will here be translated as "kids" (in quotes), but may also have connotations of "young game to eat." In addition, the words used in the song for penis and vulva are, says Mrs. Suppah, Basket Woman's special words as well.

Of interest also, in light of much that is written and said about oral narratives, is that this narrative does not have a single time line of events unfolding as they took place in real time. Instead there is a setting up of parallel activities for Basket Woman and the children once she has set her basket down. The focus, then, is first on the children as they cut their way out and begin their escape, then back to Basket Woman, then back to them, then back to her. In each case the shift in focus involves a stepping back in time.

Hazel Suppah herself made a few comments about this narrative that should be shared. It was a story told to children who were slow to get water for their mothers or grandmothers. A parent, even now, in dealing with such a child might just hint at the story by saying "Čauwiyatnaš wáinaša!" 'I'm almost flying!' As we worked on this story and the others about Basket Woman that she told me that year, Mrs. Suppah commented on how strange it was that this woman always *did* the stupid things, the things detrimental to her, that people suggested to her; how she seemed never to suspect them of wishing her ill. In another of the stories, Basket Woman follows Coyote's instructions to pound her legs with rocks so as to make them sound as beautiful as his magically transformed legs. She is a frightening figure but always easily outwitted by others. This myth, of Raven and her children, is one for which the Yakima Sahaptin artist Larry George has prepared a beautiful set of slides to accompany his telling of the story. In those paintings T'at'aɬiya is indeed a frightening creature.

Finally, some comments about Hazel Suppah as a narrator. The tight and finely wrought organization of this story is typical of both her myth narrations and those in other genres. She will not tell a story until she has had time to think it through and feels really ready. Her style is spare. Every detail counts. This contrasts with the rich profuseness in many of Linton Winishut's stories. The predictions at the ends of her myths are concise in contrast to his, which are often interjected many times as a myth progresses and repeated several times at the end. His emphasis on the predictions made by Coyote is consonant with his stated view of the history of the tribe as the working out of what Coyote had predicted in the Coyote cycle. Hazel Suppah on the other hand treats the myths more as just good stories, which may instruct children and are fun to tell and to hear. She is also inclined, in speaking of others' stories, to comment more on the style than on the content. The stories she tells in conversation, riding in the car, or during visits, even though they are new stories being born as the result of some recent experience, and are in English, have the same spareness and analogous stylistic devices of parallelism, repetition, intonation, and voice quality as her Sahaptin stories, long known and told for recording.

Notes on the analysis of *Basket Woman and Raven's Children*

As mentioned at the beginning of the chapter, the detailed table of contents preceding the verse presentation of the myth indicates the coherence of each verse, stanza, scene, and act as a unit of content. The reader should not mistakenly think that these units and their capsule descriptions were the first part of the analysis arrived at. In fact, they were not written out until I was satisfied that the segmentation had linguistic consistency. Content was continually taken into account along the way, but only in conjunction with close attention to linguistic indications of units.

The division into two acts, and the point at which the division is made, are, indeed, dictated most strongly by content. There was some discussion above of how the present division was set into motion by a suggestion by Dell Hymes that I consider the story as having two parts, in the first of which the children are with their mother and in the second with Basket Woman or fleeing her. In reviewing the text with this in mind, it seemed to me that the period in which the children find themselves alone, wander crying, are heard and found by Basket Woman, and are put in her basket formed a scene that should be part of the same act as their fivefold disobedience, which had led to their abandonment and eventual capture. In future support of this division is the fact that Act II then begins with an event that will be repeated five times, just as scene 1 of Act I had done. That this analysis involved revisions in the direction of more consistency in giving weight to the linguistic features discussed in the previous section of this chapter, and that it resulted in scenes that, except for the Introduction, all have either three or five stanzas, strengthened confidence in the new version.

These notes on the details of the analysis of the myth continue following the text with a consideration of each stanza in turn.

Basket Woman and Raven's Children, narrated by Hazel Suppah[1]

Act I
Raven, returning each day from digging roots, asks her children to bring her water. After they have ignored her request five days, she flies away as a raven. Left alone, the children offer, too late, to get water, are finally abandoned, wander crying, and are captured by Basket Woman.

Act II
As she carries them home for her children, they plan and put into effect an escape. She, after discovering they are gone, pursues them, just missing them as Crane helps them across a river. Her request for help leads to her drowning.

Act I

Introduction
Stanza A. Raven and her children are living there.
Scene 1. Five times she asks for water and is refused.
   Stanza B. Raven goes, climbing, to dig wild onions.
      She returns and brings them to her dwelling.
      She asks her daughter for water in vain.
      She gets her own water.
   Stanza C. Raven goes next day for roots.
      She returns.
      She asks for water and is refused.
   Stanza D. Raven goes for roots, the third time.
      She returns and is refused.
      She threatens to leave her children.
   Stanza E. Raven goes the fourth time.
      She returns.
      She makes a vain threat to leave and is ignored by the playing children.
   Stanza F. Raven goes the fifth time.
      She returns and makes a request and a threat.
      She is refused for the fifth time.
Scene 2. Rebuffed five times, Raven turns into a raven and flies away. The abandoned children wander crying and are found and captured by Basket Woman.
   Stanza G. Raven flies off cawing.
      Children offer to get water.
   Stanza H. She flies off anyway, having become a raven out of thirst.
      The children, alone, don't know what to do.
   Stanza I. With no one to care for them, they wander off crying.
   Stanza J. Basket Woman, wandering nearby, hears them.
   Stanza K. Basket Woman looks for the children.
      She finds them.
      She puts them in her basket and packs them on her back.

Act II

Scene 1. The children try out five times a plan for escape from the basket.
   Stanza L. Basket Woman packs the children uphill.
      They cry on the way.
      Sister tells brother to make the bag heavy by dancing.
   Stanza M. Basket Woman climbs.
      Sister says "Let's try it!" (plan).
      They imitate voice calling that Basket Woman's children are burning.

              Basket Woman stops to listen.
              She hurries on.
Stanza N. Sister tells brother to dance hard.
              He dances.
              They call out again.
              Basket Woman stops to listen.
              She runs faster.
Stanza O. Sister tells brother to dance hard.
              Same way for the third time.
              Basket Woman stops to listen.
Stanza P. Basket Woman finishes climbing.
              It's the fourth time.
              They call out that her children have burned.

Scene 2. Basket Woman abandons basket and children escape from it. She runs home to find children safe, promises them "kids" to eat, goes back and finds they have escaped.

Stanza Q. At the fifth time Basket Woman sets her basket down.
              She runs off crying that her children have burned.
              Sister asks brother for flint he has under his nails.
              They cut their way out of basket.
              They escape from basket and run off.
Stanza R. Basket Woman arrives home to find children safe.
              She makes her children dance and tells them about "kids."
              She chants as they dance, promising "kids" to eat.
Stanza S. Basket Woman says she'll go to get "kids."
              She hurries off.
              She heads back to where she's left basket.
Stanza T. Basket Woman comes to a brook.
              She jumps across and gets a thrill.
              She jumps again, and gets a nice thrill.
              She jumps again.
              Five times she jumps.
Stanza U. She goes on.
              She arrives back at her basket.
              Children have escaped and basket is empty.

Scene 3. The children, escaping, reach a river and are helped across by Crane. Basket Woman arrives just after them and is refused help by Crane, until the fifth time when he gives her instructions that cause her to drown. Crane predicts she'll be a harmless thing to scare her children with.

Stanza V. Children arrive at river.
              Wonder how to go on.
              Crane is there.
              They ask his help.
              He lets them cross on his leg.

Stanza W. Basket Woman comes into sight and sees "kids" have crossed.
    She comes down to river.
    She asks Crane how to cross.
    He ignores her.
    At the fifth time he tells her how she can cross.
Stanza X. Basket Woman, following Crane's instructions, stuffs dress with
    rocks.
    She starts to cross.
    She falls into the water.
    She drowns.
    Crane "predicts" her.
Stanza Y. Ending formula.

Act I, introduction

A (1) Áwača lai,   Once it was,
       panišáišana Kakyáyaima.   they were living, Animals.
   (2) Kwná áwača naxš wáutukaš,   There there was one dwelling,
       kwná pawačá Xuxúxya,   there there was Raven, Ravens.
       Xuxuxyáima.
   (3) Áiyat iwačá,   A woman there was,
       áwača miyánaš nápu.   she had two children.
       Náxš áwača pt'iits mi-   She had one girl child and one
       yánaš kú náxš áswan.   boy.

Act I, scene 1

B (4) Imánaxana áiyat,   The woman would go digging for the
                                                  day,
       ipanáitixana túyau,   she'd climb for something,
       ixníxana túna nunásna,   she'd dig some wild onions,
       ɫíi˙ ˙ ˙ ˙ ˙ ˙kw'i.   a-a-all day.
   (5) Iyánawixana,   She'd arrive back,
       ináčičxana íkwn nišáičtyau,   she'd bring those things to the vil-
                                                  lage,
       anakwná pawáutńa.   where they lived.
   (6) 'Ńxana,   She'd say,
       " 'Ša! Čuuš nɨpaiyatam.   "Daughter! Bring me water.
       'Ša! Čuuš nɨpaiyatam."   Daughter! Bring me water."
       Čau patáiknxana kwii-   They wouldn't listen to her,
       ní miyánašiin.   those two children.
   (7) Kúšxi áswainak'a húi imɨ-   In the same way, in vain she'd order
       taxana,   the boy,
       "Nɨpaitam čuuš.   "Bring me water.

Čúut'ašaaš." | I'm thirsty."
Áu čáutya. | Now, not at all.

(8) Áu pníinkni ičúutaxana, | Now she'd go for her water herself,
áuku ičúuxana. | now then she'd drink.

C (9) Áu ánč'a máisx imánaxana, | Now again next day she'd go digging for the day,
áu łíi˙ ˙ ˙ ˙ ˙ ˙ ˙kw'i. | now a-a-a-all day.

(10) Ánč'a iyánawixana. | Again she'd arrive back.

(11) Ánč'a kúšxi imɨtaxana, | Again in the same way she'd order,
"Ámataš čúuš wńpaitamtk." | "You folks bring me water."
Kú čáu patáiknxana. | And they wouldn't listen to her.

D (12) Ánč'a maisx, | Again next day,
ánč'a imánaxana. | again she'd go digging for the day.

(13) Au čáu, čáutya áu. | Now no, not at all now.
Iyánawixana, | She'd arrive back,
áu čáutya áu patánɨpaitaša čúuš. | now not at all now do they bring water.

(14) "Áu˙ ˙ ˙ ˙ ˙ ˙áumataš áu wilálakwta. | "No-o-ow I'm gonna leave you.
C'a'átpamataš áu wilálakwta. | Soon now I'm gonna leave you.
Áu wínataaš au čáat'atki." | Now I'm gonna go because of thirst."

E (15) Áuku imánana, | Now then she went digging for the day,
píinapamyau, | until the fourth time,
iwínana áu, | she went now,
imánana. | she went digging for the day.

(16) Iwiyánawíya áu, | She arrived back now,
húitya áu 'ńna, | in vain now she said,
"Ámataš áu wilálakwta. | "Now I'm gonna leave you.
Wínataaš áu čúut'atki." | I'm gonna go because of thirst."

(17) Čáutya áu patáikša áu; | Not at all now do they listen to her now;
pałq'íwiša áu miyánašin. | those two children are playing now.

F (18) Áu páaxam, | Now five times,
áu máisx, | now next day,
áu páaxatipa łkw'ípa imánana. | now on the fifth day she went digging for the day.

(19) Áu ánč'a iyanawíya áiyat ánašt. | Now again the woman arrived at sunset.

"Ámataš čúuš kwíyaitamtk.   "You folks do my water for me.
Áunaš čauwíyat wáinaša." I'm almost flying!"
(20) Áu čau ` ` ` ` ` ` ` `,   Now no-o-o-o,
  čau ` ` ` ` ` tya áuku. no-o-ot at all now then.

Act I, scene 2

G (21) Áu húi áu paa ` ` `xam áu, Now in vain then fi-i-ive times now,
  paa ` ` ` ` `xamyau áuku until the fi-ifth time, now then, that
  kukúuk,   time,
  áuku iwáčaiča áuku!   now then she took off, now then!
(22) "Ka ` ` ` ` ` " ka ` ` ` ` ` ` ", "Ka-a-a' ka-a-a' ka-a-a' ka-a-a'."
  ka ` ` ` ` ` ` " ka ` ` ` ` `."
  Áuku iwáinana, xúxux, Now then she flew, a raven,
  áuku itxánana.   now then she became one.
(23) "Á ` ` ` ` ` ` `na íɬa! A-a-ah, mother!
  Ámataš čúuš kwíyaiša." We're doing your water for you."

H (24) Áuku iwáinana,   Now then she flew,
  áuku xúxux itxánana, áuku, now then she became a raven, now
     then,
  čáat'atki.   because of thirst.
(25) Áu kwná, áuku, páčtin, Now there, now then, the brother and
     sister,
  áuku patxánana piiliksá áu. now then they came to be alone
     now.
(26) Áuku,   Now then,
  "Maanxánata áuku!" "I don't know where we'll go!"

I (27) Pawínana áuku.   And they went, now then.
(28) Čáukušin kwná túmiš míyái- No one there to do anything for them
  taš áuku.   at all now then.
(29) Panaxtíya áuku.   They cried now then.

J (30) Áu kwná pńč'axašta mná Now somewhere there it must have
  T'at'aɬiyaiyái   been that Basket Woman
  iwiyanínxana.   would wander around.
(31) Kwníin páwiyaikna. She heard them.
  " 'έ! Anakúštxai túman "Hey! Sounds maybe like some
  ktɬ'íktɬ'ima panáwa mná. 'kids' somewhere.
  Áu ` ` tya panáwa ktɬ'ík- Su-u-re does sound like 'kids'!"
  tɬ'ima!"

K (32) Áu ` ` ` ` páwaq'itna. No-o-ow she looked for them.
(33) Áu páyanawiyana, Now she came upon them,
  t'át'aš šápani.   packing her basket.

(34) Áu kwná áu páwnpa,
  pát'aina áu t'át'ašpa kwná.
  pášapa áuku.

Now there now she grabbed them,
she put them now in her basket there,
she put them on her back now
then.

Act II, scene 1

L (35) Áuku pákwnaitiya áu,
    pákwɫtxa áu.
(36) Áuku pawiyánaxtíya áuku
    páčtin.
(37) Áuku pá'nxana pátin,

"Wáašak!
  Qú txanáta!
  Wáašak!"

Now then she packed them now,
she packed them uphill now.
Now then they cried on the way, now
then, the brother and sister.
Now then the older sister would tell
him,
"Dance!
Be heavy!
Dance!"

M (38) Áuku panaitíya áu.
(39) Áu kwníin, áu
    "Áuna áwinawiša!"
(40) "Lúu˙ ˙ ˙ ˙ ˙ ˙'npam.
    Lúu˙ ˙ ˙ ˙ ˙ ˙ ˙ ˙'n,
    á˙ ˙ ˙ ˙ ˙ ˙ ˙'luun,
    Álitɫ'asmí miyánašma."
(41) " 'έ!"
    Ikamcíixwana.
    "Anakúštxai inái
    pawanítša."
(42) Áu ktúktu áuku itúlawaixti-
    kíka áuku.

Now then she climbed now.
Now to him now (the sister said),
"Let's try it!"
"You're bu-u-r-rning.
Bu-u-r-rn, the-e-ey burned,
Alitɫ'as's children."
"Hey!"
She listened.
"It's as if someone's calling me
by name."
And quickly, now then, she walked
on at a brisk pace now then.

N (43) Áuku 'ńxana pt'íic páčtpa,

"Ámaš wáašak!
  Xtúnk!
    Kwná t'át'ašpa."
(44) Áwaašaxa áuku ńni áswan
    áuku.
(45) Ánč'axi,
    "Luu ˙ ˙ ˙'tmaš miyá-
    našma.
    Áluun alitɫ'asmí miyá-
    našma."
(46) Qátutixana ánč'a T'at'aɫi-
    yaiyái.

Now then the girl would tell her
younger brother,
"You dance!
Try hard!
In the basket."
And that boy, now then, dances now
then.
Again,
"Your children bu-u-r-rn.

Alitɫas's children have burned."

Basket Woman again would stop.

"Áutyaaš inái pawanítša."

(47) Áuku maikktú ánč'axi áwi-
la'wixaika áuku.

O (48) Áu˙ ˙ ˙ ˙ ˙ku áu 'nxáika páčtpa.
"Xtúxi wáašak.
Xtún wáašak,
áuku qú kúnki itxá-
nata."

(49) Áu ánč'a áu mɨtamyau,
áu kúšxi áu.

(50) Áuku iwáqatutixana,
iwamcíixwaxana,
"Áutya panáwa,
'Miyánašmaš lúun.' "

P (51) Áu ipanáitinaq'íya áu.

(52) Áu pínapamyau.

(53) Áu,
"Luu˙ ˙ ˙ ˙ ˙ ˙ ˙ ˙ ˙nmaš
miyánašma."

Act II, scene 2

Q (54) Au˙ ˙ ˙ ˙ ˙ ˙ ˙ ˙páaxam
áuku,
kúuk áuku páwašapitša áu
kwná.

(55) Áuku iwilá'wiša áuku.
"Miyánašmaš lúun."

(56) "Ktúxi!
Mánmaš wá sxáukas?"
(Xáštwai míimi áswan
sxáukas ákwiya sx́pas-
pa.)

(57) Áuku kúnki áuku pašátkukša
áuku ɱni,

áu pašáxntkša kwná t'á-
t'ašna áuku,
pašápxnaitša kwaaní áu-
ku.

"Really they *are* calling me by
name."
Now then harder again she started
running now then.

No-ow then now she'd say to her
younger brother,
"Dance hard.
Dance hard,
and then it will become heavy
from that."
Now again now for the third time,
now in the same way now.
Now then she'd stop awhile,
she'd listen,
"Really they are saying,
'Your children have burned.' "

Now she finished climbing now.
Now for the fourth time.
Now
"Your children have bu-u-r-rned."

No-o-ow five times, now then,

then, now then, she sets them down
there now for a moment.
Now then she runs away, now then.
"My children have burned!"
"Quick!
Where is your flint?"
(Already the boy had put flint
under his nails.)

Now then, with it, now then, they're
cutting a hole, now then, with that
(flint),
now they're cutting that basket, now
then,
they're crawling out of there, now
then.

"Ktú!
Áuna wínaninša!"

(58) Áuku pawínanĭnšá áuku,
payakáitiša áuku.

R (59) Tɫ'ánx áu T'at'aɫiyaiyái
yú ˙ ˙ ˙ k áwinačitša,
čítya áu kwná ša'áat mi-
yánašma áwa.
"Čáu, čáu palúuna."

(60) Áu kwná áu išapáwaašaša áu
miyánašma,
"Náptaš ktɫ'íktɫ'iin kúna
wáuxinmš.
Tɫ'íš náčičta.
Áwaš nípatata."

(61) Áwišapawaašaša,
"Átkwátái˙ ˙ ˙ ˙ ˙ tánám
ímalímal.
Átkwátái˙ ˙ ˙ ˙ ˙ tánám
ímalímal.
Átkwátái˙ ˙ ˙ ˙ ˙ tánám
tɫatɫútɫatɫu.
Átkwátái˙ ˙ ˙ ˙ ˙ tánám
tɫatɫútɫatɫu."

S (62) Áwišapawaašaika miyánaš-
sin.
Mɫ áwača nápu.

(63) "Áunaš!"

(64) Áuku ixtúšaikš,
áuku ixáwapanaitišaikš,

anakwná iwášapiča.

T (65) Áu iwínaša áu,
waipxt.
áu kwnáta.

(66) Áu itɫúpwawaičxaikš.
"Ána! Tɫ'ɫkaš.
'šta ánč'axi."

(67) Ánčaxi itɫúpwawaičnxa.
"Ána! Níixaš
tɫ'ɫkaš."

(68) Ánč'axi itɫúpwawaičnxa.

"Quick!
Let's escape!"
Now then they're escaping, now then.
They're starting to run, now then.

Meanwhile now Basket Woman is arriving fa-ar away,
those children of hers now are safe
there.
"No. They didn't burn."
Now there now she's making her children dance now,
"I've laid those two 'kids' there.

I'll bring them.
I'll go get them."
She's making them dance, (chanting,)
"You will e-e-eat his little penis.

You will e-e-eat his little penis.

You will e-e-eat her little vulva.

You will e-e-eat her little vulva."

She made those two children of hers
dance.
Two is how many she had.
"Now I'll go!"
Now then she hurries off,
now then she starts to walk away
fast,
to where she had put them down.

Now she's going now,
a brook,
now right there.
Now she jumps across.
"Aah! A thrill!
I should do it again."
Again she jumps across.
"Aah! A nice
thrill!"
Again she jumps across.

(69) Hái áu,
          páaxam áu.

Until now,
five times now.

U (70) Áu· · · ·ánč'axi iwínaxa.
    (71) I · · · · ·yánawixa.
    (72) "Čáu· · ·k'aaš áu kwná
          ktł'íktł'ima,
          pawinanínxaš,
          čiš au kwná t'át'ašsim
          iwšá."

No-o-ow again she goes on.
She-e-e-e arrives.
"My 'kids' aren't there at a-a-all,

they must have just escaped,
just my basket lying there."

Act II, scene 3

V (73) Áukutya áuku pawínaninša

          pawínaša áu,
          pawanwíša áu,
          wánaiyau payánawiša,
    (74) "Á· · ·na. Máanata tł'í?"

And just now, now then, they're escaping,
    they're going now,
      they're going down now,
        they're arriving at the river,
"O-o-oh dear! Where we gonna go,
  or do?"

    (75) Qw'ášqw'ašya xwśaat aníša
          k'áuk.
          Íšakni aníšamš.
    (76) "Á· · · ·na, púša,
          kwalalínmataš itwápinxa.
          Míškinam nɨpatamtax-
          na?"
    (77) Áuku pášuwaitšamš wxá,
          kú kwnápa pamáwnpša,
          kú páčawawaitšaikš áu.

Old man Crane is making a boat.

On the other side he's making it.
O-o-oh, grandfather,
  a dangerous one is following us.
    Could you somehow come get
    us?"
Now then he puts his leg across,
  and they grab themselves onto it,
  and he pulls them across now.

W (78) Ča áuku míš T'at'ałíya áwi-
          yalpnxamš,
          áuku míimi áu íšaknik'a
          pawá.
    (79) Áu iwánwixaikš,
          Áu kwná áu pakáwamš
          íšakni.
    (80) "Á· · · ·nam, ánam áu kwná
          awít,
          míškinam wáičnxa?"
    (81) Čáu· · ·mišpá'nxanakwaa-
          ní· · · áu.
          Aníša k'áuk.

Just then, now then, Basket Woman
comes over the hill,
  now then, they're already now on
  the other side.
Now she comes down.
  Now they're there now on the other
  side.
"You-u-u, you my in-law there,

  how do you cross over?"
No-o-ot at all would he tell her no-o-
ow.
He's making a boat.

(82) Áu˙ ˙ ˙ ˙ ˙páa˙ ˙ ˙ ˙ ˙xamtya   No-o-ow just fi-i-ive times now,
   áu,
      áu há'ai áu,   now until now,
      "Íi. Kwná áu čí yawá-   "Okay, just come stand in the
      šulalum.   water there.
      Iwá ái tɬ'u'úup či wána.   It's shallow, this river.
      Kwná áu ái maikkwná   There now, a little further on
      áu ái wiyáwaičm.   now, cross over.
      Púnxtanam tɬ'í pšwá,   Put rocks inside your dress,
         kúnam tɬ'í kúnki čáu   so you won't float away, now
         áu áuku yáwaináta."   then."

X (83) Áu áuku ipšátaša pšwá áuku.   Now, now then, she stuffs herself with
                                        rocks, now then.

(84) Áu áuku iwáitša áu.   Now, now then, she crosses now.

(85) Áu ixátamanuuša áu kwná áu.   Now she falls into the water now,
                                        there now.

(86) Íi. Ɬámai áuku itxánaša   Yes. Now then the Basket Woman
   T'at'aɬíya.   drowns.

(87) "A˙ ˙ ˙ ˙," xwśaatin piiní   "O-o-oh," the old man he tells her,
   pá'nša,
   "A˙ ˙ ˙ ˙náxanamata kúš   "O-o-oh where're you gonna be,
   wáta,
   áwitkwatašata tanánmaman?   eating people?
   Áutyanam áu káu ái wáta ša-   You'll now maybe just be something
   páwiyaičukt miyánašmaman.   to scare kids.
   Kúnam čaumná áwitkwatata   And you'll never eat people this way."
   íkuš tanánmaman."

Y (88) Kw'ái áu kwáal.   That's all.

Act I, scene 1

Stanza A is a typical introduction to a myth in Sahaptin. It tells who was "living there." Use of the past progressive form of the verb "to live" is also typical for Sahaptin myth introductions. The division of stanza A into three verses is not strongly motivated, except that (2) seems nicely set off by the parallelism of its two lines beginning *kwná áwača* and *kwná pawačá*. Note that perfect parallelism is precluded by the differing stress on the second words. Verse 3 then is what is left after (2) has cohered as a verse. It has a kind of unity of content and a bit of parallel patterning in the three verb forms *iwačá*, *áwača*, and *áwača*, but not as much as one would like if this were the only criterion for making it a verse. Notice that no particles are involved in the segmentation of stanza A.

Stanza B is set off from A linguistically and in terms of content and the five-times rhetorical pattern. First, there is a shift at this point into habitual aspect, past tense: *-xána*. This combination of aspect and tense continues through stanza D. Particles play no role in the segmentation of B into its five verses. In terms of content, B is the setting out in full of the set of daily events in the lives of Raven and her children that take place on five successive days in the five stanzas of scene 1. The organization of B in verses is almost entirely in terms of the five parts of this five-times-repeated event. They are: (1) Raven's going digging for the day; (2) her return home; (3) her request for water; (4) the children's ignoring her request; (5) her response to their refusal. In B this response is to get her own water, in D to threaten to leave them, and in E the same threat in place of or as a request. Note that B is the only stanza in which all five parts occur. Note also that (3) and (4) are arranged in verses (6) and (7) so that, rather than one request to both children, followed by one refusal by both, there are a request and refusal with one child, in (6), followed in (7) by a request and refusal with the other child. Other mergings and reorderings of the essential five parts of the event occur, as will be seen, in other stanzas.

Stanza C. Though the original division into stanzas of Act I, scene 1 was in terms of the rhetorical pattern of five, i.e. a stanza for each recurrence of the five-part "event," there are also strong linguistic clues for the division. Stanza C begins strongly marked by particles: *áu ánč'a máisx* 'now, again, next day'. Each of the next two verses of C begin with *ánč'a* 'again', giving a parallel pattern that tiers the three verses together as a unit. Furthermore each of these verses parallels in content one of the verses of B: (9) going to dig, (10) returning home, and (11) requesting and being refused water.

Stanza D also is strongly marked by particles: *ánč'a máisx* 'again next day'. The first verse, going to dig for the day, has *ánč'a* repeated in each of its two lines, forming a unit set off from (13). This second verse of the stanza is a fusion of the return and the refusal. No request is explicitly stated in this stanza. The fact that the refusal, *áu čáutya áu* 'now not at all now', is expressed both before and after the return prevents the return from being considered as a verse on its own. Verse 14, Raven's response to the children's refusal to get her water is in this case, as noted above, a threat to leave them. The rhetorically lengthened vowel seen in the first word of (14) is one of Hazel Suppah's devices for marking new segments. It is accompanied here, as it frequently is in her narratives and those of other women, by high pitch and thin voice quality. Thus we see that treating (14) as a verse has both linguistic and content motivation for the analyst.

Stanza E is doubly marked as a new stanza. There is a shift of aspect, from the habitual *-xa-* of the preceding three stanzas to the unmarked aspect. Thus we find *imánana* instead of *imánaxana*. The particle *áuku* lends support to the segmentation, as does the word *píinapamyau* 'until the fourth time', indicating the fourth occurrence of the fivefold event. Verse 15 is a somewhat expanded version of the going for the day to dig. It is a nice example of filling out a pattern of three verbs, even if one is a repetition. Verse 16 is set off as a verse by the rhetorical pattern; this is the return. It is interesting to note, however, that the break is reinforced by the purely morphophonemic circumstance that the pattern of *-na* verb endings on the three verbs of (15) is broken. The stem-final vowel *i* of *wiyanawi-* calls for the *-ya* alternant of the past-tense suffix rather than the *-na*. In this verse the return home and the request for water are joined by intonation. The refusal of the children in (17) is marked as a new verse by raised volume and pitch as well as by the shift to continuative aspect and present tense. The occurrence of three particles, *áu*, *čáutya*, and *áu*, in its first line also marks it as a separate unit.

Stanza F is heavily marked by the occurrence of *páaxam* 'five times' and *máisx* 'next day', as well as by *áu* 'now'. The use of time words to signal new units of the order of stanza or above is common. The heavy marking with line-initial *áu* both unites the three first lines of the stanza as a verse, (18), and the three verses as a stanza. Each of the second two verses has thin, high voice and lengthening of the vowel on initial *áu*, a further signal that each is a separate verse. The first verse of this stanza is a good example of the narrator's treating as lines segments without verbs. The effect is achieved by the initial particles and by pause at the end of each of the first two lines. Indeed, each of these lines is a tone group. These three lines, with the verb withheld until the last, are in terms of the rhetorical pattern "the going digging for the day." Verse 19 represents the return and the request; (20) reports the children's refusal.

Scene 2 is very heavily marked as a new section. The whole line *Áu húi áu páa ˙ ˙ ˙ xam áu* is spoken with high, thin voice that carries over into the *páa ˙ ˙ ˙ xamyau* of the second line. The piling up of particles in verse 21 is remarkable: three *áu*s in the first line, *áuku* and *kukúuk* in the second, and two *áuku*s in the third. The listener is indeed being signaled that this is a major transition in the narrative. This verse is the denouement of all that has happened in the first scene. It sets up the situation for the children's capture by Basket Woman at the end of the scene and act. In the Chinookan narratives that D. Hymes has analyzed, the outcome of the fifth-time part in the pattern often begins a new section of the story. It was this knowledge that led me to reconsider an earlier analysis of this part of the narrative that had placed the first line of (21) as the final line of (20). *Páa ˙ ˙ ˙ xam* had been treated as a verse in itself, making stanza F an anomalous four-verse stanza. Relistening to the tape revealed that *Áu húi áu paaxam au* had the high, thin voice typical of new verses and no final fall before the *páa ˙ ˙ ˙ xamyau* that followed. Furthermore, *páa ˙ ˙ ˙ xamyau* was clearly part of the line including *áuku kukúuk*. Once having arrived at the analysis presented here, it became clear that the first line of (21) summarized scene 1 and that the remaining two lines constituted the outcome of the fifth time, the outcome that had been threatened and that would set the stage for the children's capture by Basket Woman at the end of the scene and act. Looking ahead to Act II, scene 2, one finds a very similar first verse of a new section; again at the fifth time (*páaxam*) something happens that is the outcome of a fifth attempt and also the basis for what happens in the new section.

Scene 2 of Act I consists of five stanzas, G through K. Of these, G, H, and J end in direct speech. The Basket Woman makes her appearance in J and captures the children in K. Act II consists of their eventual escape from her and her death.

The three verses of *Stanza G* are quite easily and clearly set off from each other. Verse 21 has already been discussed. Verse 22 begins with Raven's cry as a raven *ka* ˙ ˙ ˙ *'k* ˙ ˙ ˙ *a'*, and ends with the two lines that tell of her transformation from Xuxúxya, Raven the myth character, to xüxux, raven without the myth suffix *-ya*. These last two lines are both marked initially by the particle *áuku* but are united as one verse with Raven's cry by the lack of any perceptible pause and by the lack of any rise in pitch or loudness on *áuku iwáinana* . . . . Verse 23 is set off by pitch and loudness. It is the children's final response, too late.

Stanza H repeats the content of the preceding stanza to a certain extent. In verse 24, beginning with *áuku* and with a second line that both begins and ends in that particle, Raven's flight and change into raven are repeated and the cause of her flight, thirst, is made explicit (echoing the final line of verse 16, where she warns she will fly away because of thirst). Verse 25 points out the fact that the brother and sister are now alone. This is the first time these kin terms are applied to them, preshadowing the following act in which they will play separate roles in the escape. Verse 26 begins with *áuku*, which introduces their cry of despair and where they will go.

Stanza I consists of three verses of one line each. All have the final fall of verses and end in *áuku*. There were perceptible pauses accompanying the final falls of each of the three verses. This stanza portrays the children as wandering alone with no one to help them and ends with their crying. It is this crying that causes Basket Woman to find them in the next two stanzas.

Stanza J introduces Basket Woman, wandering around, hearing the crying, and commenting to herself that it sounds like some "kids." Verse 30 has high, thin voice. It consists of two lines united in one intonation contour and without the parallel patterning one often finds. Verse 31 contains Basket Woman's hearing the children and the two utterances she makes, separated by pause and with raised pitch at the beginning of each and final fall at end of each.

Stanza K, the final one of this scene and of the act, is doubly marked as a new stanza: by vowel lengthening and high, thin voice, and by the initial particle *áu*. More important, however, in marking this as the beginning of a

new stanza is the parallel patterning the line initiates and which is carried
through the three verses of the stanza, all beginning with *áu* and all having
verbs in simple past tense. Verse 34, the final one, consists of three lines,
each with a past-tense verb and a final *áuku*. Final *áuku* often, in Mrs.
Suppah's narratives, marks the end of a major unit. Here it marks the end of
the children's being either with their mother or alone. For the rest of the
narrative they will be either captives of Basket Woman or fleeing from her
toward ultimate escape.

Act II, scene 1

The break between Stanzas K and L is certainly adequately marked for a
stanza break. The plot organization cited above provides support, moreover,
for a new act. Scene 1 of Act II is divided into five stanzas, L through P.
The reasons for treating it as a separate scene are similar to those that define
scene 1 of Act I. Stanzas L through P are the carrying out in four unsuccessful
attempts of the plan for escape initiated by the sister in stanza L. The fifth
and successful attempt forms the first stanza of scene 2; its beginning is, as
noted above, marked in a way very similar to that of scene 2 of Act I. The
separate parts of the event that is repeated five times are less obvious in this
scene, however, and working out the separation into stanzas has been more
difficult. The first "attempt" can be considered as spread over stanzas L and
M. The clue to the fact that stanza L ends with verse 37 lies in the analysis
of what the five parts of the repeated event are. They are: Basket Woman's
packing the children uphill, the sister telling the brother to dance, their calling
out as if someone is warning that Basket Woman's children are burning,
Basket Woman's stopping to listen, and finally her hurrying on. The clue to
this for me was that the fourth time is in a stanza (P) which begins *Áu
ipanáitinq' iya áu* 'Then she finished climbing then'. Now, if one looks at the
first lines of L and M, one sees that they are in parallel pattern as to particles
and verb morphology. M's first line does indeed tell of Basket Woman's
climbing; L's tells instead of her packing the children on her back. But the
second line of L combines the *kw-* morpheme for "packing" with a morpheme
-łtx- that means "go up." The repetition of the root for packing, *kw-*, with
two different verb roots in L's two lines is of course additional evidence for
the cohesion of that verse. The repetition of *áuku* in each of verses 35–7
gives cohesion to the verses of stanza L. The repetition in verse 38 of the
climbing mentioned in the first verse of L, and the strict parallel patterning
of the first lines of (35) and (38) give strong support to treating (38) as the
beginning of a new stanza M, which together with L constitutes the first time
in the pattern. Together they show all the five parts of the whole event. If
one looks ahead at the rest of the scene, one sees that only the first (verses
35 and 38) and fourth (verse 51) times in the pattern begin with mention of

climbing; in the fourth it is the finish of the climb. The first and second times (verses 42 and 47) each end with Basket Woman's hurrying on; the second and third (verses 43 and 48) begin with the girl's telling her brother to dance.

Stanza N. Linguistic clues to the stanza breaks for L and M have already been mentioned. In Stanza N we find initial *áuku* accompanying a shift into the past habitual to mark the beginning of the stanza. Its end is best indicated by the parallelism at levels of syntax, morphology, and meaning of verse 47 with the final verse (42) of stanza M. Within the stanza, verses are marked off by particles and other features. Verse 44 is set off by change of participant, and linguistically by the double particle *áuku*, especially by its occurrence as line-final. There is a shift too of tense from past to present habitual. Verse 45 is marked by initial *ánč'axi* 'again', and by the direct speech. Verse 46 shifts back to past habitual from the present of (44) and has a change of participant and the particle *ánč'a* 'again'. Verse 47 is marked by initial and final *áuku* as well as by a shift of direction from unmarked direction to translocative indicated by the suffix *-ik-*. Note that the allomorph of this suffix used in the parallel-patterned final verse of stanza M is *-kik-*.

Stanza O is introduced by the initial particle *áuku* with rhetorical vowel lengthening and by a change of focus on participant. It begins, as does stanza N, with the girl telling her brother to dance hard (verse 48). That this is the third time is indicated in verse 49, a verse consisting of two lines each beginning with *áu*. The final *áu* of the second line patterns with the *áu* as third word in the first line; both lines have *áu-particle-áu*, the only difference being the final word "third time" in the first line. Verse 50 is marked by initial *áuku* and by a shift into past habitual and ends with Basket Woman's direct speech.

Stanza P, the final one of this scene, shifts back to simple past, has a first line beginning and ending with *áu*, and holds together as a unit of three verses all beginning with *áu*, and by virtue of the second verse stating that this is the fourth time.

Act II, scene 2

Stanza Q was discussed earlier as being heavily marked for scene break. Its first verse has rhetorical vowel lengthening, a number indicating that this is the fifth and last time (Basket Woman sets her basket down and takes off), and five particles (*áu, áuku, kúuk, áuku,* and *áu*). There is also a shift into present continuative. Very heavy marking indeed. If one looks at the rest of the stanza one notices very heavy use of *áuku*. Verses 55, 57, and 58 begin with it and 55, 57, and 58 have heavy use of it at the ends of lines. And as noted before, the stanza ends with *áuku*. In a sense this stanza is the high point of the story, for the children at least. Their plan succeeds and they get free at least temporarily – and, as it turns out, permanently. Perhaps this heavy use of *áuku*, unusual for this narrator, gives the stanza special weight.

Stanza R begins with an unusual particle *tł'ánx* 'meanwhile', with refocus on the character Basket Woman by preposing of the subject noun before the verb, by changing of locale emphasized by vowel lengthening in *yu ˙ ˙ ˙ k* 'far away'. The verses of stanza R each end with direct speech by Basket Woman. It is the stanza in which Basket Woman runs home to check on her own children, finds them safe, and promises to bring them "kids" to eat. It should be noted in passing that this whole scene is unusual in that there is not a continuous time line but a separate coverage of the same time span, first for the children and their breaking out of the basket after Basket Woman has set it down, and then for Basket Woman from the time she sets it down until, running back to it after checking on her children, she finds it empty. The third scene then opens with the children reaching the river and finding Crane, and eventually being followed there by Basket Woman. It may eventually prove to be a better analysis if one breaks Act II into smaller scenes. For the present I have settled on this analysis in which the final scene involves interactions between the children and Crane and between Basket Woman and Crane but not between her and the children. Scene 1 involved interactions between her and the children; Scene 2, actions parallel in time but with no interaction.

Stanza S is set off by its use of the translocative in its three main verbs, all of which are in the continuative aspect. The middle verse (63) is one word, Basket Woman's saying to her children *"Áunaš"* 'Now I'll go'. Pause and other paralinguistic features set it off from verses 62 and 64.

Stanza T is a little interlude of Basket Woman's finding a brook and jumping across it just for the thrill of it five times. That it was five times is indicated in the final verse (69). Only three times are actually described, each making a verse (66, 67, and 68). Of course, this brief interlude contributes to the children's being able to cross the river before she gets to it.

Stanza U completes scene 2 of Act II with three verses, each begun with rhetorical vowel lengthening. The first two (70 and 71) simply tell that she goes on again and that she arrives. Verse 72 is her direct speech of three lines when she finds that the children have escaped, leaving just her empty basket.

Act II, scene 3
Stanza V. With stanza V we find multiple linguistic indications of a new scene in addition to the considerations of interactions between characters mentioned above as motivation for an analysis that treats this act as having three scenes. There is the double particle marking at the very beginning, in addition to a switch out of the habitual into the progressive. The progressive is sustained throughout the stanza. Within stanza V the verses are set off by vowel lengthening (verses 74 and 76) and by particle *áuku* in (77). Verses 74 and 76 are both direct speech. Verses 75, 76, and 77 are also set off from

each other by shift from one participant to another. The stanza as a whole is unified by content: The children reach the river, are at a loss; Crane is there; they ask him, by kin term "grandfather," for help in crossing; he responds by pulling them across, thus putting the river between them and the pursuing Basket Woman, whose appearance opens the next stanza.

Stanza W is marked as a new stanza by three particles at the beginning of the first line and by a switch from the progressive aspect of the preceding stanza, as well as by a syntactically marked change of character focus, i.e. the placing of the subject noun phrase before the verb. Within W, (78) is set off from (79) by a shift from cis- to translocative for the same subject of the verbs (Basket Woman). They are also distinguished from each other by the different patterning of the particles in their two lines. Verse 80, introduced by vowel lengthening, stands as a separate verse consisting of direct speech. Verses 81 and 82 are each introduced by vowel lengthening, and (82) is, furthermore, a typical fifth-time verse of agreeing to what one has refused the first four times. The stanza ends with Crane's direct speech agreeing to tell Basket Woman how to cross and giving her deadly advice.

Stanza X is as crucial to Basket Woman as stanza Q was for the children, and, as in Q, each of the four lines that are crucial is heavily marked by particles *áu* and *áuku*, enough to set each of these four lines off as a verse. Verse (87) is marked by vowel lengthening. As the final long verse of a stanza, it plays exactly the same role as Crane's speech in the preceding stanza. It is also a typical last part of a Sahaptin myth: Someone who has been doing bad things is set straight about what her behavior will be when the people who are coming have arrived.

Stanza Y. This is not properly a stanza at all but the most common formula for ending a myth.

Conclusions

On the basis of analysis of Sahaptin narratives collected over fifty years ago by the late Melville Jacobs (1929, 1934) and of narratives told and tape recorded over the past ten years at Warm Springs reservation in Oregon, I am left with no doubt that the kind of verse organization of oral narratives that D. Hymes has found in neighboring Chinookan exists also in Sahaptin. The patterning, based as in Chinookan on fives and threes, is apparent from close analysis of the levels of language preserved in written records. Availability of tape recordings of the Warm Springs narratives, however, has made it possible to begin to understand how features of pause, intonation, voice quality, and voice dynamics contribute to verse organization. To put it quite simply, in telling a story a narrator selects content and organizes it using resources from all levels of the language in which the story is told. It is becoming clear that some uses of pause and intonation are as much conven-tionalized aspects of verse organization in particular narrative traditions as are pattern numbers and use of particles, time word, etc. It would be a mistake to think of the suprasegmental features of language as somehow having to do with "performance" and the other features as more part of "the story." What we always have to deal with are particular performances in which all aspects of language and of content are being selected from and used in both culturally conventional and individually expressive ways. Even the choice of what story to tell in a particular context may be individually expressive. It is surely no accident if women who are strong and cope with the problems of children and grandchildren are the chief characters in the myths told by a grandmother who has had responsibility for raising far too many grandchildren, and who was raised by her own grandmother. The resources of content she uses are culturally conventional; her choices and organization of those resources are individually expressive. This fact became particularly clear to me in comparing versions of the same myths told by women narrators with those told by men. Analysis of verse organization of different tellings always aids in seeing how they differ, and in appreciating the viewpoint taken by the narrator.

How widespread verse organization of oral narratives may be is an urgent question for future research. Work with students on written records of narratives in a wide variety of American Indian languages has shown that for some languages at least there are clear patterns of verse organization. Much more research is needed by specialists in those languages. A certain amount of work my students and I have done over the past five years with materials collected by them and others in the Department of Folklore at the University of Pennsylvania has indicated that traditional narratives in a range of non-Indian communities also have thoroughgoing verse organization based on pattern numbers and using devices at all levels of language to achieve parallel patterning and repetition that are the basis of the verse organization. We have found that narratives recorded in conversation and in oral history interviews, narratives of a personal-experience sort, also show parallel patterning and repetition and a looser kind of verse and stanza organization.[2]

What seems to be basic to all oral performance we have looked at (including sermons, oratory, medicine show, and carnival spiels) is delivery as lines and grouping of at least some of those lines by parallel patterning and repetition. A strong tendency for the number of lines grouped together to be fairly consistent for individual performers is also emerging. What is clear for all the materials we have looked at is that writing oral performances at least as lines, if they are delivered as lines, makes them much more accessible both for readers' appreciation and for researchers' analysis.

Notes

1 This story was narrated for tape recording at Warm Springs, Oregon, in July 1979. It was transcribed and translated by me with the assistance of Hazel Suppah, who gave no title to the story.

2 Most of this work has been done in connection with my course "Ways of Speaking" in the Department of Folklore and Folklife at the University of Pennsylvania. My own work has concentrated on Appalachian women's narratives collected by Charlotte Ross and narratives collected by Kenneth Goldstein in England, Ireland, Scotland, and the United States. A close analysis of one long Appalachian narrative, "Tremble Dove," has been reported on in a talk at the Center for Intercultural Studies, University of Texas at Austin (February 1983), and at the Folklore Colloquium of the University of Washington (May 1984). A number of students from the course participated in a panel, "Discovering rhetorical structure in oral performance," which I organized and chaired for the American Folklore Society annual meetings in Minneapolis, Minnesota, in 1982. The panel included my overview of the method of verse analysis and results of applying it to a variety of traditions: Douglas de Natale's analysis of North Carolina mill workers' narratives; Charlotte Ross's analysis of an Applachian traditional narrative, "Muttsmag" (which is part of her dissertation); Elaine Eff's analysis of a Baltimore screen painter, former carnival pitchman's handwritten autobiography.

In the years since 1982 we have worked on close analysis and comparison of five tellings of one traditional Irish narrative, "How Fin McCool got the thumb of knowledge," told by the late Joe Heaney, a well-known folksinger and storyteller, and recorded by Kenneth Goldstein. I am in the process of completing an article with my own analyses of these tellings and the comparison made possible by verse analysis.

Professor Goldstein also made available to the 1985 class narratives by each of four outstanding storytellers from Ireland (Joe Heaney), England (Ruth Tongue), Scotland (Belle Stewart), and the United States (Sarah Cleveland), and has given me permission to use my analyses of the narratives for publication. The narratives offer particularly interesting evidence of the differences in oral traditions as to length of line and relationships between lines within verses.

Course papers completed by students working on their own materials (all in English unless otherwise noted) have included analyses by Simone Rudoler of two narratives told to children by her Polish great-aunt; Joseph Gibney of his Syrian grandmother's traditional and life history narratives; John Benoit of black Vietnam veterans' war narratives; Ray Allen of narratives told by men who congregate at a working-class Philadelphia bar; Janice Gadaire of her Canadian great-uncle's life history narratives; Susan Vorscheimer of Martin Luther King's "I have a dream" speech; Camile Bacon Smith of an American Indian Philadelphia engineer's narratives about his Winnebago–Menominee background; Lisa Null of four different narrators' tellings of a traditional Newfoundland narrative; William Westerman of sermons and narratives coming out of the Sanctuary movement; Benedicte Johnson of Pashtun narratives collected from women in Afghanistan and Pakistan; Elizabeth Wickett of women's laments recorded in Egypt in Egyptian Arabic. The analyses of Johnson, Wickett, and Benoit are connected with their dissertation work. All are on deposit at the Folklore Department at the University of Pennsylvania. Together, they form the basis for my strong conviction that oral narrative and other forms of oral discourse, such as sermons and carnival pitches, are produced in lines that are grouped in larger units such as verses and stanzas, and that the kind of verse organization demonstrated for an American Indian narrative in this chapter will be found to be widespread.

References

Berman, Judith. 1982. Deictic auxiliaries and discourse marking in Kwakw'ala narrative. In Wayne Suttles et al., eds., *Working Papers for the 17th International Conference on Salish and Neighboring Languages.* Portland, Oreg.: Portland State University, pp. 355–408.

1983. Three discourse elements in Boas' Kwakw'ala texts. In William Seaburg, ed., *Working papers for the 18th International Conference on Salish and Neighboring Languages.* Seattle: University of Washington.

Blincoe, Deborah. 1982. [Analysis of Coming Day, Wisahketchahk preaches to the wolves (Plains Cree).] Ms. Philadelphia: University of Pennsylvania, Dept. of Folklore.

Braun, Barry, 1982. [Analysis of Iktomi takes his mother-in-law on the warpath (Teton Sioux).] Ms. Philadelphia: University of Pennsylvania, Dept. of Folklore.

Hymes, Dell H. 1975. Folklore's nature and Sun's myth. *Journal of American Folklore* 88:345–369.

1977. Discovering oral performance and measured verse in Native American narrative. *New Literary History* 8:431–442.

1980. Particle, pause, and pattern in American Indian narrative verse. *American Indian Culture and Research Journal* 4(4):7–51.

1981a. *"In vain I tried to tell you": essays in Native American ethnopoetics.* Philadelphia: University of Pennsylvania Press.

1981b. Reading Clackamas texts. In Karl Kroeber, ed., *American Indian literatures: texts and interpretations.* Lincoln: University of Nebraska Press, pp. 117–159.

Hymes, Virginia. 1981. Warm Springs Sahaptin verse analysis. In *Working Papers for the 16th International Conference in Salish Languages.* University of Montana Occasional Papers in Linguistics 2. Missoula: University of Montana.

1982. A Sahaptin narrative device: from Sahaptin to English and back again. In Wayne Suttles et al., eds., *Working Papers for the 17th International Conference on Salish and Neighboring Languages.* Portland, Oreg.: Portland State University, pp. 178–200.

Jacobs, Melville. 1929. *Northwest Sahaptin texts, I.* University of Washington Publications in Anthroplogy. Seattle: University of Washington Press, pp. 175–244.

1934. *Northwest Sahaptin texts.* Columbia University Contributions to Anthropology XIX, pts. 1, 2. New York: Columbia University Press.

Kinkade, Dale. In press. Bluejay and his sister. In Arnold Krupat and Brian Swann, eds., *Recovering the word: essays on Native American literature.* Berkeley and Los Angeles: University of California Press.

McLendon, Sally. 1982. Meaning, rhetorical structure, and discourse organization in myth. In Deborah Tannen, ed., *Analyzing discourse: text and talk.* Georgetown University Round Table on Languages and Linguistics 1981. Washington, D.C.: Georgetown University Press, pp. 284–305.

Servaes, Brita. 1982. [Analysis of The bean and the corn (Seneca).] Ms. Philadelphia: University of Pennsylvania, Dept. of Folklore.

Tedlock, Dennis. 1971. On the translation of style in oral narrative. *Journal of American Folklore* 84:114–133.

1978. *Finding the center: narrative poetry of the Zuni Indians.* Lincoln: University of Nebraska Press.

1983. *The spoken word and the work of interpretation.* Philadelphia: University of Pennsylvania Press.

Wolfson, Nessa. 1978. A feature of performed narrative: the conversational historical present. *Language in Society* 7(2):215–238.

1982. *CHP: the conversational historical present in American English narrative.* Dordrecht: Foris.

4

POETIC STRUCTURING OF KUNA DISCOURSE: THE LINE

Joel Sherzer

A basic, central feature of the oral discourse of the Kuna Indians of Panama is the line, a unit independent of and yet related to conventionally recognized grammatical units such as phonemes, morphemes, and sentences. Investigation of the structuring of lines in Kuna discourse requires attention to the intersection and interplay of linguistic, sociolinguistic, and poetic structures, patterns, and processes. This exploration of the nature of the Kuna line reveals the diversity, complexity, and richness of Kuna discourse and, in addition, sheds light on issues that have emerged in the study of Native American discourse and oral discourse more generally.

The Kuna are more than 25,000 agriculturalists who inhabit, mainly, a string of islands along the northeast coast of Panama known as San Blas. Kuna verbal life provides a laboratory for the study of the structuring and performance of oral discourse. The Kuna have a very diverse range of linguistic varieties, styles, and genres, from colloquial and everyday to formal and ritual, in both spoken and chanted form.

One way to approach this diversity is in terms of ritual traditions. There are three, marked by distinct languages, settings, sets of official actors, and speech events: the gathering-house tradition, in which *saklakana* (chiefs) and other political leaders address their villages in chants and speeches; the curing–magical tradition, in which specialists address many different kinds of spirits; and the puberty-rites tradition, in which a specialist addresses a single spirit, that of a long flute. Within this general threefold classification, there is a considerable range of grammatical and discourse styles, as there is as well within colloquial, informal speech.

The three ritual traditions involve a distinction found widely in the world, between a flexible "text," in which a general idea, theme, or set of metaphors is adapted to fit a particular situation; and a fixed or relatively fixed text, which must be memorized. Among the Kuna, the first is characteristic of the gathering house, that is, in human-to-human communication. The second is found in curing, magical, and puberty rites, that is, in human-to-spirit communication. Not the slightest linguistic variation is tolerated in the performance of puberty-rites texts. These texts can be compared to the fixed "compulsive word," characteristic of Navajo and other native North American southwestern curing rituals (Reichard 1944). It is clearly not the case, in spite of the arguments to the contrary by Albert Lord and Jack Goody, that there is no pure memorization of fixed texts in nonliterate, oral societies (see Goody 1977; Lord 1960). The native southwestern "ways" and the Kuna puberty texts demonstrate the contrary (see also Finnegan 1977). The oral discourse of nonliterate societies provides a rich diversity of possibilities with regard to the relative fixity or flexibility of speech, as well as with regard to other dimensions of language and speech. The Kuna also consider curing–magical texts to be fixed. But although curing–magical texts and puberty-rites texts are both memorized directly from a teacher-specialist, there are interesting differences in their actual performance. In curing–magical texts, slight variations of an essentially nonreferential nature are tolerated, involving very superficial aspects of the phonology and morphology of noun and verb suffixation. Thus there exist at least two types of memorization in Kuna.

Before turning to the structuring of lines in the three Kuna ritual verbal traditions as well as in more everyday speech, it seems appropriate to comment on the distinction "oral/written," especially since this distinction has recently been given considerable attention (see for example Goody 1977; Ong 1977; Tannen 1982). Whereas there are literate Kuna, Kuna discourse, and in particular the verbal art that is the focus of this paper, is oral. This does not mean that Kuna discourse is oral rather than written in some simple general or universal sense. There is no single feature that characterizes Kuna discourse as a whole; rather there is a set or complex of such characteristic features. While some of these features may be more characteristic of oral than of written discourse, others are found in written discourse. Empirical research clearly indicates that there is not a simple set of features that uniquely characterize oral discourse, in spite of the recent flurry of pseudoempirical theorizing on this topic. Nor can one sharply dichotomize ordinary and literary Kuna language and speech. Rather it is necessary to recognize poetic structures and processes in a wide range of forms of Kuna discourse, from everyday and informal to ritual and formal. This range includes conversational narration, lullabies, myth performance, and magical chants. And it includes spoken as well as melodic, chanted speech. Different poetic–linguistic devices are used in different verbal genres and in different ways in the different genres. Finally, as distinct from the published literature of literate societies, which is often conceived of as a body of masterpieces that a few educated people are able to read and enjoy, Kuna verbal art is a central, instrumental part of various aspects of Kuna social and cultural life, for example politics, curing and magic, greeting, conversation, and social control (see Sherzer 1983).

I turn now to the poetic organization of Kuna discourse and to a focus on the line. An important aspect of my discussion here is the existence of a very diverse range of Kuna verbal styles and genres, differentiated in a number of ways, including phonology, morphology, syntax, semantics, lexicon, and in particular line structure. I focus on the line because the line is in several ways the basic poetic unit of Kuna discourse. It is the most overtly marked discourse unit linguistically and, in chanting, musically. And it is most useful for a diagnostic comparison and typological classification of Kuna genres of speaking. In fact it is impossible to compare Kuna verbal styles without paying serious attention to line structure, just as a grammatical and discourse analysis of line structure requires a sociolinguistic analysis of the variety of Kuna verbal genres. Basic to my approach is the recording of the range of forms of Kuna discourse in actual, natural settings.

In each of the Kuna verbal styles and genres, it is possible to recognize the existence of lines. These lines are marked by a set of distinct devices. Not all of the devices are operative in every case. In addition, the devices have other functions besides marking lines. As a result there is not always congruence among them. In fact, a most interesting aspect of the various line-marking devices in Kuna is the ways in which speakers play them off against each other, creating contrasts and tensions among them. There are four principal line-marking devices:

(1) Lines are marked grammatically by means of an elaborate set of initial and final words, particles, and affixes. Among the various other functions of these elements is metacommunication; they signify such notions as "say," "see," "hear," and "in truth." They are furthermore simultaneously sociolinguistic markers in that different verbal styles and genres have distinct sets of these elements.

(2) Especially in more formal and ritual styles, lines are marked by extensive syntactic and semantic parallelism. This parallelism is organized in terms of line structure and in turn contributes to this structure.

(3) Lines are marked by intonation patterns; in particular in spoken speech by the structuring of pauses and the rising and falling of pitch, as well as tempo, and in chanting by melodic shapes involving volume, duration, and tempo, along with pauses and, in some genres, the structured use of coughs or coughlike noises.

(4) Lines are marked according to a coparticipant dialogic interactional structure in which an addressee responds with one of a set of ratifiers after each line. This pattern is common in many styles of speaking; it is formalized in certain forms of ritual chanting.[1]

Attention to line structuring in Kuna speech thus reveals an intersection of referential and nonreferential, grammatical, sociolinguistic, social interactional, and musical factors and patterns. In addition, the study of line structure reveals function and pattern in the traditional components of grammar (phonology, morphology, syntax, and lexicon) that are otherwise impossible to discover.

In the presentation of illustrative examples, I will point to ways in which the various line-marking devices interact and intersect, focusing on the types of congruence among them as well as the types of contrast and tension. I will provide examples in two ways – first, a selection of short, illustrative lines or groups of lines from the wide variety of Kuna verbal styles and genres; and second, a more extended presentation of two cases that demonstrate the ways in which the same basic narrative content can be structured into different line organizations by different performers or by the same performer in different verbal styles and genres.

I begin with more formal and ritual styles and genres, which are frequently chanted. It is in these that there is the greatest tendency for there to be a combined, cooperating, congruent, and reinforcing use of all the line-marking devices just listed. The first example is gathering-house chanting, the performance of myths, legends, and personal experiences to a gathered audience every other evening. In this genre, lines are often grouped together into clearly marked verses (see Hymes 1977 for a discussion of line, verse, and other poetic units in Native American discourse). Verses typically consist of two lines. Verses often begin with *sunna* 'truly' or *al inso* 'thus' and end with *soke* 'say; it is said', *oparye* 'utter; it is uttered', or *takleye* 'see'. The first line of a verse often ends with the phrase, sometimes combined into a single word, *taylesokelittole* 'see it is said it is heard'. Lines and especially verses drop in pitch at the end and final vowels are lengthened. There is also a decrease in volume and tempo at the ends of lines and verses.

Gathering-house chanting is performed in the form of a ritual dialogue between two chiefs. The second chief, called the *apinsuet* (responder), chants *teki* 'indeed' after each verse, thus quite clearly marking verse endings. The *apinsuet* begins to chant during the lengthened final vowel of the principal chanting chief, who in turn begins his next line during the lengthened *i* of *teki*. In gathering-house chanting there is thus never silence, since each chanter begins his turn by overlapping the long, held vowel of the previous voice.

Here are two short selections from two different performers, Muristo Pérez of Mulatuppu and Mastaletat of Mulatuppu. The verse of the chanting chief is labeled CC; the line of the responding chief, RC.

Muristo Pérez
CC: sunna sukkun kaluse tayle soke 1 ittole.
　　kirmar patto 1 an apintakkwici ipiti sunna tar kutayleye.
RC: teki.
CC: Truly I arrived at Sukkun it is said it is heard.
　　The brothers were already waiting for me truly see.
RC: Indeed.

Mastaletat
CC: we yalase papa 1 anparmialimarye soke 1 ittole.
　　eka masmu 1 akkwekarye oparye.
RC: teki.

CC: eka l inso tarkwamu l akkwekarye soke l ittolete sunna ipiti oparye.
RC: teki.

CC: To this mountain (world) God sent us it is said it is heard.
To care for banana roots for him it is uttered.
RC: Indeed.
CC: In order to care for taro roots for him it is said it is heard truly it is uttered.
RC: Indeed.

The two performers have different musical styles, which are shown in Figs. 4.1 and 4.2, diagrammed in terms of pitch, tempo, and duration.[2] Mastaletat illustrates a contrastive use of line-marking devices typical of gathering-house chanting – the interplay of one- and two-line verses. The first verse represented here consists of two lines, with *soke l ittole* followed by a distinct pause marking the end of the first line; the second verse consists of one line only, with *soke l ittolete* occurring in the middle of the line.

Next, I present two of the many examples of medicinal-curing–magical chanting, performed by specialists to representatives of the spirit world, in a linguistic variety quite distinct from chiefs' chanting. Lines in this genre are marked primarily by the suffix -*ye*, which has several grammatical functions, including subjunctive-optative, vocative, and quotative. In curing–magical chanting, -*ye* has primarily a line-marking function. Line-final vowels are lengthened. There is a notable pause between lines and for some performers a slight cough or cough-like noise between structured groups of lines, which I call a verse (again utilizing the terminology of Hymes 1977). There is extensive lineal parallelism.

Pisep ikar (the way of the sweet basil plant), used to insure successful hunting, as performed by Pranki Pilos of Mulatuppu, demonstrates remarkable congruence and synchrony among the various line- and verse-marking devices. Here is the opening portion of this performance.

Inapiseptili olouluti tulalemaiye.
olouluti tulallemaiye.

Inapiseptili olouluti sikkirmakkemaiye.
olouluti sikkirmakmamaiye.

Inapiseptili olouluti wawanmakkemaiye.
olouluti wawanmakmainaye.

Inapiseptili olouluti aktutumakkemaiye.
olouluti aktutulemainaye.

Inapiseptili olouluti kollomakkemaiye.
olouluti kollomakmainaye.

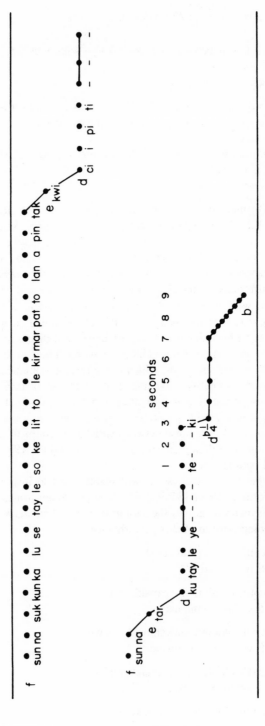

Fig. 4.1. Gathering-house chanting: Muristo Pérez. Dots indicate beats; letters, pitch levels.

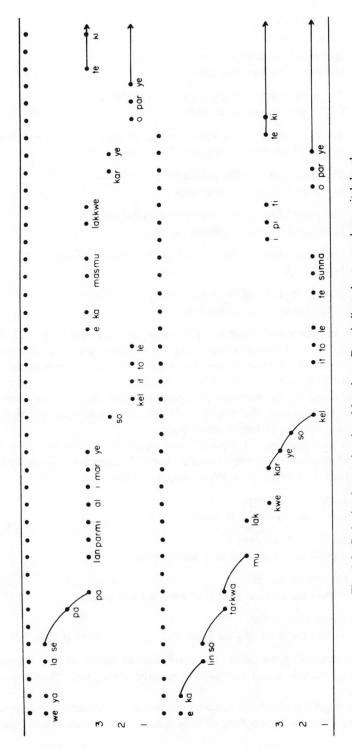

Fig. 4.2. Gathering-house chanting: Mastaletat. Dots indicate beats; numbers, pitch levels.

Inapiseptili olouluti mummurmakkemaiye.
olouluti mummurmakmainaye.

The pisep plant, in the golden box, is moving.
In the golden box, is moving.

The pisep plant, in the golden box, is swinging from side to side.
In the golden box, is swinging from side to side.

The pisep plant, in the golden box, is trembling.
In the golden box, is trembling.

The pisep plant, in the golden box, is palpitating.
In the golden box, is palpitating.

The pisep plant, in the golden box, is making a noise.
In the golden box, is making a noise.

The pisep plant, in the golden box, is shooting out.
In the golden box, is shooting out.

In Pranki Pilos's performance of *pisep ikar*, lines are marked by a clearly audible final pause. Lines are grouped into two, constituting verses, represented here by an extra space between lines. Following every verse there is an audible cough. Every line ends with the suffix *-ye*. And there is a mosaic of overlapping syntactic, semantic, and morphological parallelism, all organized in terms of this same line structure. The resulting effect is a neat isomorphic stacking of line-marking devices on top of one another.

Kurkin ikar (the way of the hat), used to combat headaches, provides another illustration of a curing–magical chant. Here are the first two verses of this chant, as performed by Olowitinappi of Mulatuppu.

kurkin ipekantinaye.
olopillise pupawalakan akkuekwiciye.

kurkin ipekantinaye.
olopillise pe maliwaskakan upoekwiciye.

Owners of the hat.
Within the level of gold your roots are reaching.

Owners of the hat.
Within the level of gold your small roots are being placed.

Lines are marked by the suffix *-ye*, morphological, syntactic, and semantic parallelism, pauses, and a very regular melodic shape, which is shown in Fig. 4.3.

Olowitinappi's performance of *kurkin ikar* manifests considerable congruence among the different line-marking devices, but, as distinct from Pranki Pilos's

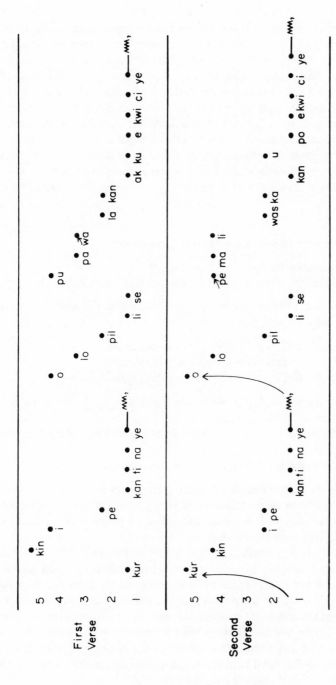

Fig. 4.3. *Kurkin ikar*: Olowitinappi. Dots indicate beats; numbers, pitch levels. *Key*: ⤴ indicates a slight upward glide in pitch; ∿ indicates laryngealized (creaky) voice quality; ↗ indicates an intake of breath.

performance of *pisep ikar*, Olowitinappi introduces certain contrasts and tensions among them. Thus, in the first three verses, there is an isomorphic congruence in the use of grammatical affixes and words, musical and grammatical parallelism, and pauses. Each verse begins with a vocative line and ends in the suffix *-ye*. The second line of each verse begins with *olopillise* and ends with a verb with the following sequence of suffixes: *-kwici* 'standing; vertical position' *-ye*. Final vowels are lengthened. In the fourth verse, while continuing to use the same musical and pausal structure, Olowitinappi introduces a new model, creating a moment of nonparallelistic contrast. In this new model, *kurkin ipekantinaye*, which was in the first position of lines and verses, is now in final position in lines and verses, and *-kwici-ye* now no longer marks the end of lines.

> kurkin ipekantinaye.
> olopillipi apikaekwiciye kurkin ipekantinaye.

> Owners of the hat.
> Within the level of gold you are resisting owners of the hat.

This line is used to create a new system of parallelism in which each verse consists of only a single line.

> olopilli aktikkimakkekwici kurkin ipekantinaye.
> olopilli kwamakkekwici kurkin ipekantinaye.
> olopilli aktitimakkekwakwiciye kurkin ipekantinaye.

> Within the level of gold you are weighing very much owners of the hat.
> Within the level of gold you are being well-placed owners of the hat.
> Within the level of gold you are moving owners of the hat.

This kind of contrastive interplay between grammatical and musical parallelism occurs frequently in the performance of curing–magical chants. In this way, performers are able to demonstrate individual creativity in the performance of texts that they have memorized word for word.

Next, I present puberty-rites chanting, a third distinct ritual genre of chanting. Here lines are marked by syntactic and semantic parallelism, lengthened final vowels, and a particular, unique melodic shape, involving extremely regular lineal repetition. Of the three ritual genres, puberty-rites chanting involves the most regular, congruent, isomorphic stacking of line-marking devices. It is thus interesting that the Kuna consider the puberty-rites tradition to be the most archaic and immutable. Here are three lines of a puberty-rites chant, *iet ikar* (the way of the ritual haircutter), performed by Ernesto Linares of Mulatuppu. The musical shape is shown in Fig. 4.4.

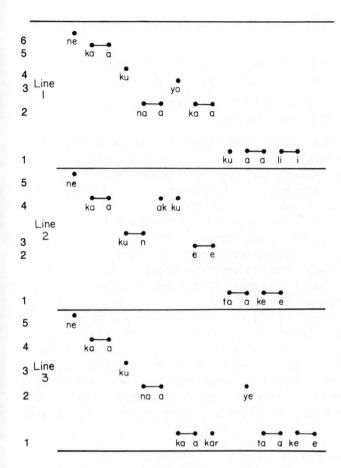

Fig. 4.4. Puberty-rites chanting: Ernesto Linares. Dots indicate beats; numbers, pitch levels.

neka kuna yoka kuali.
neka kun akkuetake.
neka kuna kakaryetake.

It is dusk.
It has become night.
It is getting darker.

So far I have discussed forms of chanting. I turn now to an examination of speaking styles, beginning with the most formal, that of chief's spokesman, who follows a chief's chanting, retells the chant, and interprets it for the gathered audience. Here are two lines of a spoken interpretation by Armando, of Mulatuppu.

> tek inso taylekuti "pillikwense taylekuti nerti aytetee."
> kusun pittosursokeye.

> Well thus indeed "one level down indeed the prophet descended."
> Truly don't you hear it is said.

Tek 'well', *inso* 'thus', and *taylekuti* 'indeed' are common line openers of spokesmen's speeches, often bunched together, as in this example. A very common line-final marker in this style is *pittosursoke* 'don't you hear it is said', often coming at the end of several consecutive lines, a unit that, again, I label a verse, even though it is marked rather differently than in the chants discussed above. Tempo slows dramatically at the ends of lines and verses and there is a falling pitch contour. There are short but clearly audible pauses between lines, longer pauses between verses. The types of contrasts and tensions that performers introduce among these various line- and verse-marking devices will be discussed below after a fuller presentation of the speech event from which I have extracted these lines.

Kwentomala 'stories' are told in a less formal style than the speeches of chiefs' spokesmen. Typical line openers are *te(k)* 'well', *takkarku* 'so; in truth', and *emite* 'now'; line-final markers, *soke* 'say; it is said', *napir soke* 'in truth it is said', *soysunto* 'it is said in truth'. There is even less congruence, that is, there is even more contrast, among the various line markers than in spokesmen's speeches. There is not a clear demarcation of verses. Here are the first two lines of one story, the hot-pepper story, performed by Mastayans of Mulatuppu.

> "te takkarkute, mu warkwen mai" soysunto.
> muu.

> "Well in fact there was a grandmother" it is said in truth.
> A grandmother.

This example nicely illustrates the way in which pause structure and a large set of grammatical elements and words are jointly used as resources in the marking of lines in the spoken performance of stories. This performer marked his first line with both a set of words and grammatical elements and falling pitch and a pause, and his second line with a pause alone, thus providing a striking contrast between these two lines of basically identical referential content, as well as a contrapuntal rhythm to his delivery.

As an example of everyday, more informal speech, I have chosen a conversation between two individuals. The narrative told within this conversation has a line structure, marked, in this very small portion of it, by the line-final quotative *soke* 'say', in the second line followed by the suffix *-sunto* 'in truth', as well as by regular ratification by the addressee–listener, involving the utterance after each line of *a*, *mm*, or a key word in the line, a pattern which is an everyday, informal version of the ritual chiefly dialogue described above. In the two lines of the narrative presented here, the narrator is T; the addressee–listener–responder is O.

> T: "mottorkin kwenti" anka soket.
> "They had a motor" he said to me.
> O: a.
> T: "purwa noar" soysunto.
> "The wind came up" he said in truth.
> O: mm.

Contrasts between lines involve mainly the presence or absence of initial and final words and phrases as line-framing elements.

The examples I have provided here by no means exhaust the full set of Kuna forms of discourse. They do illustrate, however, the range of line-marking devices and the ways in which these line-marking devices are combined in actual performance. Two more extended examples will provide a fuller sense of the poetic structuring of Kuna discourse and especially the quite varied possibilities available to speakers. First I will examine two versions or tellings of the same Kuna myth, performed as constituent parts of a single speech event. Every other evening, in the central gathering house of the village, Kuna chiefs perform myths, legends, or personal experiences, in the form of a ritual dialogue with another chief in the presence of a gathered audience (see above). I present here two portions of the myth of *nele sipu* (the White Prophet) as performed by Chief Olowitinappi on April 9, 1970. The chant is in an esoteric language, phonologically, morphologically, syntactically, and semantically different from ordinary Kuna. The chanted version of the myth was followed by a spoken version by a chief's spokesman, Armando (see above). Armando, in his performance of the myth, serves as reteller, translator, interpreter, and editor. This speech-event structure was normal; chiefs' chants are always followed by spoken interpretations by their spokesmen. It is precisely the structure of the event that permits me to compare the two performances or versions of the same myth.

I find it useful to distinguish two aspects of the poetic structure of the performance of *nele sipu*; first the macrostructure, the overall general organization; and second the microstructure, especially the structuring of lines and verses. With regard to macrostructure, the two performances of *nele sipu* are practically identical. The chanted version opens with a statement of the health of the performing chief, a ritual greeting with which chiefs always open their chants. Then both chanted and spoken versions have the same general structure. First there is a reflexive description of the event itself (the spokesman's spoken version opens with this) – the arrival of the members of the village at the gathering house, organized according to named roles in the community. After this reflexive description, the story proper begins with a story preface, announcing the myth of *nele sipu*. Then comes the body of the story, the visit of *nele sipu* to four levels of the afterworld. Each level determines an episode in the structuring of the story: (1) the level of reborn dirt; (2) the level of reborn birds; (3) the level of reborn *paypa* birds; and (4) the longest episode, a description of the human afterworld. I find the term episode appropriate for these segments or units within the text; they share features with both act and scene of Hymes's (1977) terminology. The performance ends with a coda – a list of renowned Kuna chiefs of the past who also chanted about *nele sipu*. A comparison at a more micro level reveals both similarities and differences.

Here then is the opening and the first episode of the myth of *nele sipu*, as chanted by Olowitinappi and as spoken by Armando. In this representation, verses, as performed by the chanting chief and the spokesman, are numbered consecutively (inside parentheses) within each portion. As above, the lines of the responding chief are labeled RC.

Opening: Chief Olowitinappi chant

     (1) al emite tule tummakanakwaleee.
        sunna nase nonimaryeee.
RC: tekiii.
     (2) tule saylakanakwal arkarmalakwaleee.
        na nase nonimaryeee.
RC: tekiii.
     (3) tule polisiakanakwaleteee.
        nase nonimaryeee.
RC: tekiii.
     (4) papa olokansupilli mesisa kwatse nasiknonimaryeee.
RC: tekiii.
     (5) al inso sunna sia tulekan kapur sikkwimala panse nonimaryeee.
RC: tekiii.
     (6) tule inatulekanakwar tule kanturkanakwar nase nonimaryeee.
RC: tekiii.
     (7) al inso tule purwa ikar wisimalatti noniteee sokeee.
RC: tekiii.
     (8) papa oloittokunnekaki olokansuseka 1 upononimarteee.
RC: tekiii.
     (9) sikwa 1 ammalakwar siamalakwale panse 1 upononiteee.
RC: tekiii.

(10) tule sikkwikaemala nase noni kacisopemalateee.
RC: tekiii.
(11) tule mornattulekan noni wini onimalat noniteee.
RC: tekiii.
(12) amma iete panse nonimarteee.
iemalakwar nase nonimaryeee.
RC: tekiii.
(13) pela olokansuse pani anpakkunonimarteee.
olokarta nikkapukkwamaryeee.
RC: tekiii.
(14) papati oloniptolapa tule tummakan otenonimarteee.
RC: tekiii.
(15) tule ankermala aktenoni.
paliwicurmar aktenoni.
anpalittokekakumarteee.
RC: tekiii.
(16) papati 1 ittoket neka upepeparteee.
olokalalatupa opaksa nasikteee.
RC: tekiii.
(17) papa oloittokuna upepeparteee.
na olotupa otenoniyeee.
RC: tekiii.

Opening: chief chants (translation)

(1) Now all the important persons.
Truly arrived.
RC: Indeed.
(2) All the chiefs all the spokesmen.
Really arrived.
RC: Indeed.
(3) All the policemen.
Really arrived.
RC: Indeed.
(4) God left golden seats and we come to sit in them.
RC: Indeed.
(5) Thus truly cocoa men (specialists) and hot-pepper birds (specialists) you arrived to me.
RC: Indeed.
(6) All the medicinal specialists and all the *kanturkana* (puberty specialists) really arrived.
RC: Indeed.

(7) Thus the knowers of the way of the wind came I say.

RC: Indeed.

(8) They came to enter their golden seats in God's golden listening house.

RC: Indeed.

(9) All the female relatives all the nieces (women) you came to enter with me.

RC: Indeed.

(10) All the bird grabbers (midwives) really arrived and the hammock makers.

RC: Indeed.

(11) Those who make molas arrived those who string beads arrived.

RC: Indeed.

(12) Ritual hair cutters you arrived to me.
All the hair cutters really arrived.

RC: Indeed.

(13) All of you have arrived to sit in your golden benches.
There is the golden list (of people present).

RC: Indeed.

(14) God left the golden prophets.

RC: Indeed.

(15) Angels descended.
Those who have no feeling (angels) descended.
In order to hear us.

RC: Indeed.

(16) God in the corners of the listening house.
Hung a golden recording wire.

RC: Indeed.

(17) God in the corners of the listening place.
Left the golden wire.

RC: Indeed.

Opening: spokesman Armando speaks

(1) "tule nuy. nikka nikka taylekutina.
we neyse upononi" takken soke.

(2) "tule saylakanakwar tayle nase nonimala, tule arkarkanakwar takkenye," sayla anmar owiso takken.

(3) "tule taylekuti polisiakanakwar" takken soke.

(4) "tule kapur tule kanakwar tayle nase upononimala.
we neyse kup" ittosursoke soy takken.

(5) inso taylekutina.
"inaturkanakwar tayle nase nonimar" takken soke.
"pap ittoet neyse" pittosursoke takken.

(6) "papti taylekuti anka ittoet nek mette natmala.
(7) e nuy piekar" pittosurso pittosursokene.
(8) " 'ipakwenpa tayleku panse wis korpukkwa taylekuti nanamaloe.'
    papti kotte nat" takken soke.
(9) "nan tummatti kotte nat" pittosursoke soy takken.
(10) "papti taylekuti we nekki taylekutina.
    anka kan nuekan taylekuti urpis natmala.
    aa kanse an anpa kunonimarye," anmarka soy pittosursokene.
(11) "inso taylekuti punmar upononikki.
    nuy nikka nikka tayleku panse upononimarye."
    sayla anmar owiso pittosursokene.
(12) inso taylekutina.
    "kwena kwena panse pe upononima taylelekuti.
    tule kaci wisimalat noni" takken soke.
(13) "tule moray tulekan tayleku nonikki.
    we neyse" pittosursoy takken.
(14) inso taylekutin win onimalat noni takken soke.
(15) "iemalat nonikki, timimmimalat noniye," sayla anmal oisomar
    takken.
(16) "pela taylekuti nuy nikkatpi" pittosursoke soy takkenye.

Opening: spokesman speaks (translation)

(1) "The people with names with names (important people) indeed.
    Came to enter this house" see it is said.
(2) "All the chiefs indeed really arrived, all the spokesmen see,"
    the chief informs us see.
(3) "All those indeed who are policemen" see it is said.
(4) "All those who are hot-pepper men (specialists) indeed really
    have come to enter.
    Into this house" don't you hear it is said it is said see.
(5) Thus indeed.
    "All the medicinal specialists indeed really have arrived" see
    say.
    "To God's listening house" don't you hear it is said see.
(6) "God indeed left us this listening house.
(7) So that we may speak his name" don't you hear it is said don't
    you hear it is said.
(8) " 'One day indeed you will call a bit indeed to me.'
    God called" see it is said.
(9) "The great mother called" don't you hear it is said it is said
    see.

(10) "God indeed in this house indeed.
Left us indeed good benches.
To these benches we still come," he says to us don't you hear
it is said.

(11) "Thus indeed the women have entered.
You who have names indeed have entered here with me."
The chief informs us don't you hear it is said.

(12) Thus indeed.
"One by one you entered with me indeed.
Those who know how to make hammocks have arrived" see it
is said.

(13) "Those who know how to make molas indeed have arrived.
To this house" don't you hear it is said see.

(14) Thus indeed "those who string beads have arrived" see it is
said.

(15) "The ritual haircutters have arrived, the ritual water carriers
have arrived," the chief informs us see.

(16) "All those indeed with names" don't you hear it is said it is
said see.

The White Prophet, first episode: chief chants

(1) al inso sunna "teki pillikwense aytetteee" takku 1 ipitikuyen
oparye.
RC: tekiii.
(2) al inso " 'weti oloturwakkapilliteee.'
tule 1 anka sokeeen" oparye.
RC: tekiii.
(3) "papati weki turwa nana mesisteee.
papa weki turwa papa mesisyeee.
RC: tekiii.
(4) oloturwakkapilliseteee" soke.
"turwatulekana turkupukkwayeeen" oparye.
RC: tekiii.
(5) "oloturwakkaki papa olopanter pukkipnekateee papa.
olokappan pukkipnekkuyeee.
RC: tekiii.
(6) oloturwakka olonekinpa tarmakkemaite 1 olopikuyen" oparyeee.
RC: tekiii.
(7) "ammamarye nuelanpalittokoteee" takku.
nele sipu namakketeeen oparye.
RC: tekiii.

(8) "ammamarye nue neka turwioeye" soketeee.
 "melle pani sioteee.
 turwapilli mioteee."
RC: tekiii.
(9) al insoti "kakka yalapar" soke "nue pani turwapilli urpoteee"
 sokeee.
RC: tekiii.
(10) al inso "wese turwatulekana turkupukkwateee."
 nele sipu namakketeee.
RC: tekiii.
(11) al inso teki "neka taktetee takku.
 pillikwense palakte noniparteee" oparye.
RC: tekiii.

The White Prophet, first episode: chief chants (translation)

(1) Thus truly "well one level down (I) descended" see I utter.
RC: Indeed.
(2) Thus " 'This is the level of the golden dirt.'
 The man (guide) said to me" I utter.
RC: Indeed.
(3) "God placed the dirt's mother here.
 God placed the dirt's father here.
RC: Indeed.
(4) At the level of the golden dirt" it is said.
 "The dirt people come to life" I utter.
RC: Indeed.
(5) "In the place of the golden dirt God left many golden flags
 God.
 Left many golden bells.
RC: Indeed.
(6) The golden streets of the place of the golden dirt shine brilliantly
 like gold" I utter.
RC: Indeed.
(7) "Women listen to me well."
 The white prophet chanted I utter.
RC: Indeed.
(8) "Women clean the house well" it is said.
 "Don't leave (dirt) around for me.
 You must throw away the dirt."
RC: Indeed.
(9) Thus "along the mouth of the river" it is said "you must place
 the dirt for me" I say.

RC: Indeed.
(10) Thus "there the dirt people come to life."
The white prophet chanted.
RC: Indeed.
(11) Thus well "he saw this place.
He descended again one level" I utter.
RC: Indeed.

The White Prophet, first episode: spokesman speaks

(1) tek inso taylekuti "pillikwense taylekuti nerti aytetee."
kusun pittosursokeye.
(2) "ney pillikwense aytes taylekutina.
oloturwana pillise aytetapye," anmar oiso takken.
(3) inso taylekutina " 'we nap nekki pani neyturwitimala.
aakwat pillikwense pattemaye,' " anmar oiso pittosursokeye.
(4) " 'aaki taylekuti turwakan taylekuti mai' " takken soke.
(5) emit taylekutina.
" 'aase turkupuyye,' " soy pe ittosursokeye.
(6) inso taylekutina " 'pe neyturwioet nue mio' takken soke.
(7) 'mer tipa miar saoye' nerti nek owisos" pittosursokeye.
(8) " 'aaki taylekutina.
papti taylekutin nek urpitappi.
nek nuet, taylekuti papti kal urpis' " takken soke.
(9) " 'olo ikar nuet tayle kar mesisa.
neyti kuye' " soy pittosur sokken.
(10) inso taylekuti.
" 'olo panter pukkipney takkenye,' anmar oiso" pittosursokene.
(11) inso taylekuti.
" 'papti pel immar akkaloma sokku, ney nutaymait mai' " takken
soke.
(12) " 'immal icomasurye,' anmarka soy" takken.
(13) en taylekutin " 'a tule puymarye,' soy" pittosursokeye.
(14) inso taylekuti "nerti tey ney taysa.
pal aytes" takken soke "pillikwense.
natsun" pittosursokeye.

The White Prophet, first episode: spokesman speaks (translation)

(1) Well thus indeed "one level down indeed the prophet descended."
In truth don't you hear it is said.
(2) "To the first level of the earth he descended indeed.
To the level of the golden dirt he descended there" he (the
chief) informs us see.

(3) Now indeed " 'what you sweep for me on this earth.
It falls to the first level' " he informs us don't you hear it is said.

(4) " 'There indeed is indeed the dirt' " see it is said.

(5) Now indeed.
" 'There it comes to life,' " it is said don't you hear it is said.

(6) Now indeed " 'you must throw away the dirt well' see it is said.

(7) 'Don't throw it in the sea' the prophet informed" don't you hear it is said.

(8) " 'There indeed.
God indeed left a home.
A good home, indeed God left for them' " see it is said.

(9) " 'He placed a good golden road indeed for them.
And houses' " it is said don't you hear it is said.

(10) Thus indeed.
" 'There are many golden flags see,' he informs us" don't you hear it is said.

(11) Thus indeed.
" 'Since God is changing all things, is arranging things' " see it is said.

(12) " 'He does not do bad things,' he says to us" see.

(13) Now indeed " 'there are many of these men (of dirt),' he says" don't you hear it is said.

(14) Thus indeed "the prophet then saw this place.
He descended again" see it is said "one level.
He went" don't you hear it is said.

Differences between the two performances of *nele sipu* have mainly to do with the very different styles used in these performances, with the very different resources the performers have at their disposal in order to structure lines and verses. Let us examine first the chanted version. In Olowitinappi's chanting, lines and verses are quite clearly marked by a reinforcing combination of melodic shape, pause pattern, and ratification by the second chief. It is these devices that I have used to determine lines and verses in my representation and translation. Grammatical and lexical line-framing devices tend to coincide with musical, intonational, and social-interactional markers of lines and verses. Verses often begin with *al inso* 'thus' or *al inso sunna* 'thus truly' and end with *oparye* 'utter' or *soke* 'say' and/or with the suffixes -*ye* or -*te*. The first line of a verse often ends with the suffix -*te*. Some first lines end with the word *takku*, derived from *takke* 'see'. Others end with *soke* 'say'. There are certain contrasts and tensions created among the various line- and verse-marking devices, however. Notice for example the interplay of one-, two-, and three-line verses in my representation. While the usual pattern is a two-line verse, verses 4–11 and 14 in the opening and verses 1, 6, and 9 in the first episode break this pattern by having only one line. Three-line verses are rare but also occur, as in verse 15 in the opening and verse 8 in the first episode. Verse 1 of the first episode is particularly striking in that it includes in the middle of a line the long verb-final vowel *-eee* and the word *takku*, both of which are practically always line-final markers. Another usual line-final marker, *soke*, appears in the middle of verse 9 of this episode. While predications usually occur as lines, in verse 5 of the first episode *papa*, which is the first word of the second sentence of this verse, occurs as the last word of the first line, producing a contrast between sentence structure and line structure. Similarly, quotations often occur within single lines, but they can also cut across lines (as in verse 2 of the first episode) or even across verses (as in verses 3 and 4 of the first episode).

Turning now to my representation and translation of Armando's spoken version of *nele sipu*, I have used the slowing of tempo, coupled with falling pitch and short and long pauses, to determine lines and verses. Although there is a fair degree of congruence among the various line- and verse-marking devices, there tends to be less than in the chanted version. Poetic contrasts and tensions are created in various ways: the interplay of one-, two-, and three-line verses; the insertion of the line-initial marker *taylekuti* (as a line-initial marker it is used conjointly with *tek*, *inso*, or *emi*) in the middle of lines; and the use of line-framing words all by themselves to constitute a line without referential content (as in verses 5, 10, and 11 of the first episode).

Another most interesting type of contrast in the performance(s) of *nele sipu* involves line-by-line and verse-by-verse correspondences between the chanted and spoken versions. The chanted version of the opening is structured into seventeen verses; the spoken version, sixteen. The chanted version of the first episode is structured into eleven verses; the spoken version, fourteen. The basic content is the same, but each version includes referential details not found in the other. Thus in the opening the chief and spokesman provide slightly different lists of individuals who arrive in the gathering house. And they mention God at different moments in their listing. On the other hand, certain verses correspond exactly or almost exactly with regard to referential content while differing strikingly in poetic structuring. Here are some examples.

(1) The first verses, chanted and spoken, of the opening. Differences include the verse-initial *al emite*, the line-initial *sunna*, and the lengthened line-final vowels of the chief, in contrast with the line-final *taylekutina* and the verse-final *takken soke* of the spokesman; the chief's use of *tummakana* (literally "big ones") and the spokesman's use of *tule nuy nikka* 'people with names' to express the meaning "important people"; and the chief's use of the verb *noni* 'arrived; came' as a verb stem and the spokesman's use of the verb stem *upo* 'enter' with *noni* as a suffix to it.

(2) The second verses, chanted and spoken of the opening. Here the major differences are the lengthened line-final vowels of the chief; the use of the words *tayle* 'indeed' and *takkenye* 'see' by the spokesman, words that are sometimes but not in this case line-final markers; and the spokesman's concluding metacommunicative phrase.

(3) Verse 11 of the chanted version of the first episode and verse 14 of the spoken version. Here lexical correspondences are quite close. Differences involve the chief's verse-initial *al inso teki* and verse-final *oparye* and the spokesman's verse-initial *inso taylekuti* and verse-final *pittosursoke*. The spokesman also inserts *takken soke*, usually a verse-final marker, in the middle of line 2.

The spokesman's role is as repeater, translator, interpreter, and editor of the chief's performance. His version moves the original along several dimensions and continua: from esoteric to everyday, from unintelligible to intelligible, from chanted to spoken, and from stricter to freer. Further comparison of these two performances would reveal other linguistic reflections of these dimensions.

For my second extended illustration, I return to the performance of *kwento-mala* (stories). In addition to spoken performances, such as the spoken performance of the hot-pepper story I used for illustration above, stories can also be chanted by chiefs, in their ritual language, to a gathering-house audience. It is thus possible to compare the poetic structure of two performances of the same story, one chanted and one spoken, one in a ritual language and style, one in a more colloquial language and style. My example consists of two performances, by the same individual, Chief Muristo Pérez of Mulatuppu, of the same humorous story, *us kwento* (the Agouti story), the first spoken and the second chanted. The first performance took place in the most usual context for the performance of humorous stories, an informal gathering of men within the village gathering house. It occurred on a morning in the spring of 1970, on a day on which a group of men were present in the gathering house, resting, relaxing, and joking among themselves. Muristo performed *us kwento* for their pleasure and amusement as well as to demonstrate his own verbal virtuosity. This spoken version of *us kwento* is in the linguistic style of storytelling, in some ways like, but less formal than, the gathering-house speech-making style. While the audience for the story is the gathered group of men, the immediate addressee is Armando, a Mulatuppu spokesman. Such dialogic performances are quite common among the Kuna and are related to the ritual dialogic chanting of chiefs. (See Sherzer 1983: 196–200.)

The second performance of *us kwento* is related to the fact that humorous stories can also be performed as chants by chiefs, in the gathering house, to an audience of men and women, in which case a moral is developed and a spoken interpretation is also performed by a chief's spokesman. Muristo's second performance, in 1976, of *us kwento*, is in this chanted form. However, it was not chanted in the gathering house, but in Muristo's own house, a setting in which chiefs sometimes practice their chants and perform them for an intimate group such as family and close friends. This performance of *us kwento* is in the style characteristic of gathering-house chanting.

A comparison of these two performances, at a six-year interval, is most interesting. Against the backdrop of their striking linguistic–stylistic differences, there is a remarkable similarity in narrative content, right down to minute detail. With regard to the most general level of organization, the macro, the 1970 spoken version consists of seven episodes, all involving Agouti tricking Jaguar, in the following order – (1) opening the *ikwa* fruit, (2) holding a big rock in place, (3) looking for bread under the water, (4) eating an avocado, (5) burning a field for planting, (6) Jaguar being frightened by Agouti on a tin roof, and (7) Jaguar being frightened by touching Agouti within a tree trunk – in addition to an interlude, between episodes 5 and 6, in which Jaguar visits his wife at home. The 1976 chanted version consists of seven episodes in the following order – (1) opening the *ikwa* fruit, (2) looking for bread under the water, (3) holding a big rock in place, (4) eating an avocado, (5) burning a field for planting, (6) Jaguar being frightened by the possibility of a tree falling, and (7) Jaguar being frightened by Agouti on a tin roof, plus an interlude, between episodes 5 and 6, in which Jaguar visits his wife at home, and a coda describing Agouti robbing Jaguar's clothes and including a moral explaining how animals used to be robbers and tricksters.

Here I present two episodes for comparison, the opening of the *ikwa* fruit and holding a big rock in place. In the spoken version, which I present first, lines are numbered consecutively within each episode. They are determined by pauses together with falling pitch. Spaces indicate long pauses without falling pitch; commas, short pauses. I do not find a salient verse organization as, for example, in the spokesman's performance of *nele sipu* which I presented above or in the chanted performance of *us kwento*. Dashes between syllables indicate speech that is slowed down and stretched out. Capitalization indicates words that are pronounced extra loud. Repeated vowels (e.g. heeeld) indicate expressive vowel lengthening. Other explanations are found in parentheses after lines. In the chanted version, verses are numbered consecutively (in parentheses) within each episode. They are determined by a reinforcing combination of melodic shape and pause pattern. Lines end in periods and in the English translation begin with a capital letter.

Us kwento, performed by Chief Muristo Pérez: first episode (1970; spoken)

1   tek itto Armando.
2   takkarku anmar kwento wis ittoerkepe a.
3   kwento.

4   us kwento masunto.
5   takkarkua   usteka   acu epokwa   penkusokkarsunto.
6   acute   us epokwa usu   us yartakke a.
7   acu soetit.
8   taytapsunto a.
9   takkarku us kan−na−re−ke−siit.
10 kir takkarsunto acu.
11 palimaytesunto.
12 palimatku   wepa soysunna, napir soke.
13 takkarku usu maskunsi.
14 takkal "ikwa kunsi" soke.
15 ipepirki   sisunto.
16 ipepirki sii, maskunsiit, wepa kirka   us soysunna   kirka.
17 "emite   kunmoko soke" soke. (Quoted portion is slightly faster
        in pace and slightly higher in pitch)
18 "palimaynatappit a, kunno" sokket "e nono kunnoye." (Slightly faster
        and slightly higher in pitch)
        (Armando interjects: *napir e nono kalekoku an epinsa.*)
19 sursoke, "ipu pe kunsiye napir soke kunnosoke weye." (Quoted portion
        is slightly faster, slightly higher in pitch)
20 napir soke.
21 "pe iki maris?" soysunto a. (Slightly higher in pitch)
22 "iki pe marisye?" (Slightly higher in pitch)
23 sursoke "an aluki maris takken soke." (Quoted portion is slightly
        higher in pitch)
24 "aluki an maris" takken ittos. (Slightly higher in pitch)
25 "pe takko soke" a. (Quoted portion is slightly higher in pitch)
26 akkwa amicunto akkwa akkwa   amis.
27 us alu ekaaarsunto alu ekaa ipepir apin mesicunto. (Last three words
        uttered very rapidly)
28 TAK ikwa TAC AK
        (Armando interjects: *manna pureke.*)
29 pe takken soke a.
30 napir soke.
31 a acu key takke a.
32 "wey pe samoko" kar soysunto. (Quoted portion faster, slightly higher
        in pitch)
33 tekka akkwa kal amismosunna.
34 ikwa eti alu pirki nue sicunnat a.
35 ittosa.
36 usti yamu yartaysat.
37 eti akkwa akkwa apin eti sarsosatwa aluki imaculit.
38 acuti aluki nue sioet.

39   kep immmaysat   TAK.
40   takkarku matunki sarsocunto.
      (Audience laughs uproariously)
      (Armando interjects something unintelligible)
41   napir soke.
      (Armando interjects something unintelligible)
42   teki   takkarku   immma aluper sokku.
43   us macitar oesto o–i–co–may–ti–sunto. (Last word is stretched
      out, higher in pitch)
44   a.
45   acu tule wiles.
46   nekoette   oete. (Last word is higher in pitch)
47   us sateparto aparmatparto.
48   apparmaysi apparmaysi apparmaysi appar (uttered rapidly, in repetitive
      fashion) o–al–le–na–tap–pi ikarpal a.

The Agouti story: first episode (translation)

1   Well listen Armando.
2   So let's listen to a bit of a story now.
3   A story.
4   It's the Agouti story.
5   So   and Agouti   Jaguar the two of them   they were about
      to compete with each other.
6   And Jaguar   Agouti the two of them Agouti   Agouti is a trickster
      ah.
7   Jaguar is a hunter.
8   He got there and saw him ah.
9   So Agouti is sitting–up–straight
10   Uncle saw him Jaguar did.
11   He started chasing him.
12   When he started chasing him   over there say, it's true it is said.
13   So Agouti is sitting eating.
14   So "I'm sitting eating *ikwa* fruit" he says.
15   On top of a hill   seated.
16   Sitting on top of a hill, sitting eating, there to Uncle   Agouti says
      to Uncle.
17   "Now   you are going to eat too say" he says. (Quoted portion is
      slightly faster in pace and slighter higher in pitch)
18   "He is going along chasing him ah, he is going to eat" he says "he
      is going to eat his head." (Slightly faster and slightly higher in
      pitch)
      (Armando interjects: It's true his head is going to be caught I think.)

19   Nope, "what are you sitting eating it's true I am going to eat some
      too" he says. (Quoted portion is slightly faster, slightly higher in
      pitch)
20   It's true it is said.
21   "How did you split it open ah?" he said. (Slightly higher in pitch)
22   "How were you able to split it open?" (Slightly higher in pitch)
23   No "I split it open with my balls" see it is said. (Quoted portion is
      slightly higher in pitch)
24   "With my balls I split it open" see hear. (Slightly higher in pitch)
25   "You watch" he says ah. (Quoted portion is slightly higher in pitch)
26   He got a rock a rock a rock   he got.
27   Agouti ooopened up his balls his balls he op he set them against the
      side of the hill. (Last three words uttered very rapidly)
28   TAK the *ikwa* fruit TAK AK.
      (Armando interjects: Wow what pain!)
29   You see it is said ah.
30   It's true it is said.
31   Ah Jaguar is astounded ah.
32   "Here you're going to do it like that too" he said to him.
      (Quoted portion faster, slightly higher in pitch)
33   Well he got a rock for him too.
34   But the other one placed the *ikwa* fruit right on top of his balls ah.
35   Did you hear?
36   This Agouti he tricked him for the hell of it.
37   This one he smashed against the stone the stone he didn't do it on
      his balls.
38   But Jaguar is going to place it right on his balls.
39   Then he diiid it   TAK.
40   So he smashed him in the banana. (Reference to a humorous event
      that had occurred in the village)
      (Audience laughs uproariously)
      (Armando interjects something unintelligible)
41   It's true it is said.
      (Armando interjects something unintelligible)
42   Well   so   he diiid it he finished off his balls it is said.
43   That boy Agouti almost fainted   he−was−jump−ing−a−round.
      (Last word higher in pitch)
44   Ah.
45   Poor Jaguar.
46   He passed out   he fainted. (Last words higher in pitch)
47   And Agouti took off again   started running again.
48   Running running running run (uttered rapidly, in repetitive fashion)
      laugh−ing along down the path ah.

Us kwento, **performed by Chief Muristo Pérez: first episode (1976; chanted)**

(1) insoki.
sunna tar kuye.
sunna al emiti.
sunna tayle l aikwa tar mai tayle.
kilu tar mai kue soke.

(2) kiluka sokku napir sokittole "na pe takke" tayleye.
kilu ipikwa l imasi tar kuye.

(3) sunna tayle we ekwatpa maciti tar nate tayleye soke.
ai l usukwa kannarre sii taytappi kueye.

(4) sunna tayle masikwa l ittosi tayle soke ittole.
kilukwa taytappiye soke.

(5) wepa sokku napir sokittole "pete l ipi kunsi?" sokittole.
"ante we l ikwa kunsi" sokittole.
"napir kulleye yer kulleye" oparye.

(6) "kiluye pe kunmoko?" soke sokittole.
"anti kunmoko" soke tayleye.
"ittomokarkepeye."

(7) ai usu sokku "napir wete l ante aluki marrisa" tayle soke.
"aluki pe marremokarkepoye."

(8) sunna teki tayle sunna l akkwa al amisa tayle sokittole.
akkwapa mesa alukwa tar ikwa par sisa tar kuye.

(9) teki sunna tayle l okwicitappi alukwakwakinpi okwicisa soke.

(10) sunna kilu tar nek oete tayleye soke.
usu l aparmakkemo l oallema kiluka kuwe.

The Agouti story: first episode (translation)

(1) Thus.
Truly it is.
Truly now.
Truly see friend (Agouti) is there see.
Uncle (Jaguar) is there it is said.

(2) He (Agouti) said to Uncle it is true it is said it is heard "I have come to see you" see.
Uncle is sitting doing something he is.

(3) Truly see that one (Jaguar) that boy he left see it is said.
He saw Friend Agouti sitting up straight there he did.

(4) Truly see he is sitting eating see it is said it is heard.
And Uncle saw him there it is said.

(5) He (Jaguar) said it is true it is said it is heard "you there what are you sitting eating?" it is said it is heard.

"I am sitting eating this *ikwa* fruit" it is said it is heard.

"And it tastes good it tastes delicious" it is uttered.

(6) "Uncle will you eat some too?" he says it is said it is heard.

"I will eat some too" it is said see.

"To try some too then."

(7) Friend Agouti said "it is true I split it open with my balls" see it is said.

"You will split one open with your balls too then."

(8) Truly well see truly he took a stone see it is said it is heard.

He placed the balls against the stone and set the *ikwa* fruit down he did.

(9) Well truly see he (Jaguar) smashed with all his might against his balls he smashed it is said.

(10) Truly Uncle lost consciousness see it is said.

And Agouti runs away laughing at Uncle he does.

Us kwento: **second episode (1970; spoken)**

1 kir neywiskuarsunto acu.

2 acu neywiskuarparku napir soke.

3 "pia tule nate?

4 anki toto" soke kep palimayteparsunna, ka–te–pa–li–par.

5 partaytapku parkaletapparsunto.

6 takka ipe kwicis ipepir weki a.

7 ar–kwan–ta–ni–kwi–ci–sun–to.

8 napir soke.

9 wepase warmakkarku kar soysunna "ai iki pe kukwisye?" ka sok "pentaytae kirye," soke. (Second quoted portion is higher in pitch)

10 "emi tayleku, purwatar tummat tani takkenye akkwa anki arkwantamalo teysokku apinka an pentayye" kar soysunto a. (In last word of quoted portion pitch is higher and larynx is tightened)

  (Laughter from gathered audience)

11 acu kinmoka kep apin katapsunto weki a.

12 "apin pe weki kao" kar soysunto "anti peka siynakweloye ittosa.

13 suarki anmal apinmakkoette" soysunto "tek an purkwemaloye."

14 acu al–laa–ma usti pinna pinna iptatmosunto aparmaytemosunto.

  (Last word uttered rapidly)

15 suli suar kwen arkusku sii sunna arkwantakoe?

  (Laughter from gathered audience)

16 "tule pinsa pe yartaysat."

17   mm us sateparto.
18   ittosunto us o–al–le–na–tap–pi ittokwicunto "a al an yarta" iptakkarsunto pinna pinna (last two words said rapidly) arsuntakoe? arkusku siit.
      (Laughter from gathered audience)

The Agouti story: second episode (translation)

1   Uncle came to Jaguar did.
2   When Jaguar came to again   it's true it is said.
3   "Where did that guy go?
4   He's making fun of me" he says then he started chasing him again, catch–ing–him–a–gain.
5   When he got there he saw him again   he got there and reached him again.
6   So he was standing on a hill here on a hill ah.
7   It–was–fall–ing–straight–down.
8   It's true it is said.
9   Whe he got there he says to him "friend how can you be standing there like that?" he (Jaguar) says to him "come help Uncle," he (Agouti) says. (Second quoted portion higher in pitch)
10   "Now indeed, a big wind is coming see the rock is going to fall on us therefore help me   against it" he said to him ah. (In last word of quoted portion pitch is higher and larynx is tightened)
      (Laughter from gathered audience)
11   Jaguar is ready   then he went there and held against it ah.
12   "Against it here   you hold" he said to him "and I'll go and cut a stick for you did you hear.
13   With the stick we'll hold it tight" he said "well if not we would die."
14   Jaguar heeeld–on and Agouti slowly slowly left he ran on again.
      (Last word uttered rapidly)
15   But the stick was well in place   truly how was it going to fall?
      (Laughter from gathered audience)
16   "This guy tricked you for the fun of it."
17   Mm and Agouti took off again.
18   He heard Agouti go–ing–a–long–laugh–ing he stood listening "he tricked me"   he left slowly slowly (last two words said rapidly)   how could it fall? it was in place.
      (Laughter from gathered audience)

Us kwento: **third episode (1976; chanted)**

(1)   kilu tar purkweti l ukkakase nononiparye soke.
       kilu pinsama tayleye.

"nika l anki toto" sokeye.

(2)   sunna l "emiskin sunno sokittole anse nonokwa kullesunno" soke.
kilu tar palimayteparye.

(3)   inso wiluppa pal aparmaysapar soke ittole.
usukwa tar sii taytappi ipepilli ulupa kuye.

(4)   ipepilliki alamakkesi soke l ittole.
kiluse tar kolekwiciye "an pentakkeye" soke "ipepilli piciali" soke.

(5)   "wete l anki maluarmala ani tayle purkwemaloye" sokittole.
"teysokku pe anka kamokweloye apinkaeka peka suar siynakweloye."

(6)   kiluti l ipepilliki l alamakkekwici tayleye soke.
usu l aparmayte tayleye soke.

(7)   nue pe yartaysa tayleye.
oallenatappi l usu tar kuye.

(8)   pinapinakwa kilu l ipepillikwa l iptayte sokittole.
kwen ayaliculi tayle sokittole.
"nue nika l an yartaysa" tayleye.

The Agouti story: third episode (translation)

(1)   From the edge of death Uncle came out again it is said.
Uncle is thinking see.
"Nephew is making fun of me" he says.

(2)   Truly "now truly it is said it is heard his head will be eaten by me"
he says.
Uncle began pursuing him again.

(3)   Thus having run again a while again it is said it is heard.
He discovered Agouti sitting under a big rock he did.

(4)   He is sitting holding up the big rock it is said it is heard.
He stands up and calls out to Uncle "help me" he says "the big rock
is going to break" he says.

(5)   "And it is going to fall on us and we see will die" he says it is heard.
"Therefore you must also hold on for me I will go get you a stick
to push against it."

(6)   Uncle is standing holding up the big rock see it is said.
Agouti ran away see it is said.

(7)   He tricked you well see.
He went laughing along Agouti did.

(8)   Little by little Uncle let go of the big rock it is said it is heard.
But nothing came undone see it is said it is heard.
"Nephew tricked me well" see.

Muristo's two performances of the Agouti story are remarkably similar in referential content, especially given the six-year interval between them. Differences reflect the stylistic differences between the ritual chanting of chiefs and the spoken telling of stories.

Let us look first at the 1970, spoken, version. While I have used the slowing of tempo, coupled with falling pitch, to determine lines, these features intersect with others, notably the line-initial words *tek*, *takkarku*, *emite*, and *kep* and the line-final suffixes *-sunto* and *-to*, the line-final particle *a*, and the line-final words and phrases *soke*, *napir soke*, and *takken soke*. Poetic contrasts and tensions are created by the interplay of short and long pauses with and without falling pitch and the interplay of pause patterning with the line-framing words, phrases, and suffixes.

In Muristo's 1976 chanted version of the Agouti story, grammatical and lexical line-framing and verse-framing markers tend to coincide with musical and intonational patterning. Verses often begin with *sunna*, *sunna tayle*, or *inso* and end with *soke*, *sokittole*, *kuye*, *oparye*, or *tayleye*. *Soke*, *sokittole*, *kuye*, and *tayleye* are also used to terminate lines that are not verse-final. The suffix *-ye* is a very common line-final marker. As in the spoken version, the poetry of performance involves the interplay of the various line-marking and line-framing devices, including their presence or absence and their somewhat variable placement.

The spoken version of the first episode of the Agouti story is structured into forty-eight lines; the chanted version into ten verses with twenty-four lines. The spoken version of the second episode of this story is structured into eighteen lines; the corresponding chanted version, into eight verses with eighteen lines. Interesting line-by-line comparisons and correspondences include the following.

(1) Line 13 of the spoken version of the first episode and verse (4), line 1, of the chanted version. The spoken version begins with the quite common storytelling line-initial *takkarku*, while in the chanted version the line-framing markers *sunna tayle* and *tayle soke ittole*, characteristic of chiefs' chanting, are employed. In the spoken version, the short, syncopated form *mas* of *masi* 'food' is prefixed to the verb *kunne* 'eat'; in the chanted version the longer form *masi* is used and it is an independent word rather than a prefix. Instead of *kunne* 'eat', Muristo uses *ittoe* 'hear; feel; taste', a more metaphorical expression, in the chanted version.

(2) In the "holding a big rock in place" episode, line 12 of the spoken version and verse (5) of the chanted version. The spoken version consists of two very colloquial quotations and the metacommunicative *kar soysunto* 'he said to him' between them in the middle of the line. *Soysunto* usually, but not always, occurs at the ends of lines. None of the set of line-initial and line-final grammatical and lexical markers are employed. In the chanted version the first line of the verse ends with *sokittole*, a common line-final marker in chiefs' chanting. The verse ends with the suffix *-ye*. In spite of the fact that it is chanted, this verse seems relatively bare and even colloquial, in part because of the quoted speech and in part because of the absence of the usual line-initial and line-final framing markers. The form of the verb, *siynakweloye* 'I'll go and cut' (lit. "cut-go-first-future-optative"), is identical in the two

versions, as is *purkwemaloye* 'we would die', which appears in line 13 of the spoken version and verse (5) of the chanted version. Further investigation of these two performances would reveal other similarities and differences between Kuna ritual chanting and colloquial spoken versions of myth and story narration.

In general, Muristo's chanted version of the Agouti story differs from his spoken version along the same dimensions that the chanted and spoken performances of the White Prophet differ – the chanted version is more ritual, more grammatically esoteric, and less intelligible to ordinary Kuna individuals than the spoken version. They are, however, remarkably similar in content, including potential for humor. This potential seems to be exploited more in the spoken version, both because of its immediate intelligibility for the audience and because of the direct interactions with this audience.

The different versions of the White Prophet and the Agouti story provide us with a glimpse of the Kuna view of the translational relationship between chiefly ritual chanting and colloquial spoken retellings. Translations and re-formulations in different styles of chanting and speaking are a centerpiece of the Kuna ethnography of speaking. (See Sherzer 1983: 201–7.) In addition, the existence of these translations, as performances within actual naturally occuring speech events, makes possible controlled comparisons, contrasting different poetic and discourse organizations and structures, in spoken and chanted speech, in different styles: ritual, formal, informal, and colloquial.

Claude Lévi-Strauss (1964, 1966, 1968, 1971) studies variations of the same myth, in different South American Indian societies, in order to create his own abstracted version of the basic structure of myth. My approach here, on the other hand, has been to record, transcribe, and analyze different versions, actually performances, of the same myths and stories, within a single community, in different contexts and verbal styles, in order to more fully comprehend Kuna theories and practices of the poetics of performance, the creation and artistic structuring of meaning through discourse.

This focus on translation also provides us with insights into the nature and actual practice of memory among the Kuna. Memory is clearly related to oral performance. The performance of ritual chanting involves a structural edifice that seems to include mnemonic devices (see Yates 1966) that are used by chiefs in order to remember their chants and by chiefs' spokesmen to translate and reformulate them on the spot. Armando's performance/interpretation of the myth of the White Prophet is remarkable in that the chanter, Olowitinappi, was a visiting chief from a distant region and the chant was not one particularly familiar to Armando. Muristo's performances of the Agouti story are remarkable for their similarities, given the six-year interval between them.

The texts I have examined here clearly involve an interplay of shared tradition and individual creativity. With regard to both the myth of the White Prophet and the Agouti story, there is clearly a general structure shared by all knowers and performers, both in content and in canons of performance appropriate to particular genres. This enables memorization and replication of similarities in performance. At the same time and against this background of shared tradition, the diversity of linguistic–poetic devices – grammatical, semantic, lexical, intonation, musical, and social-interactional – provides a set of resources that are drawn on in different ways by performers who are thus able to produce line and verse patterns, meanings, and metaphors which, while steeped in the traditions of Kuna verbal art, are also their own unique and personal creation.

The aim of this paper has been to show the significance of the line as a central, basic unit in Kuna discourse, from ritual chanting to colloquial and conversational speech. Elements of traditional grammatical analysis – phonology, morphology, syntax, and lexicon – contribute to the structuring of lines. In addition, attention to lines reveals structure in phonology, morphology, syntax, and lexicon that does not appear elsewhere or otherwise. Furthermore, intonation, musical pattern, and the social organization of speech function along with grammar in the creation of line structure. Lines are not named units in Kuna. Nonetheless there is strong evidence for the Kunas' perception of them. In addition to the textual evidence presented here, the teaching of the most esoteric ritual chants, magical–curing and puberty-rites texts, by specialist-teachers to students, is line by line.

I have used the term poetic for the kind of discourse organization focused on here. In this respect I follow Hymes (1977) and others in arguing that discourse organized in terms of lines is poetry. This usage demystifies the term poetry and makes it available, as I believe is appropriate, for the verbal artistry of nonliterate as well as literate societies, colloquial and conversational speech as well as formal and ritual language.

Recent research in American Indian discourse has pointed to lines and verses as significant structured units in a large areal perspective. Two basic approaches have emerged. Dennis Tedlock has stressed the importance of expressive features of performance in the structure of Zuni and Quiché narrative; in particular, he uses pause patterns to identify line structure. Dell Hymes has shown that in Chinookan and other languages of western North America, various grammatical devices are used to mark narrative lines and verses (groups of lines) and that larger units are structured in terms of rhetorical–cultural organization. William Bright, Sally McLendon, and Anthony Woodbury, investigating Karok, Eastern Pomo, and Central Alaskan Yupik Eskimo, have discovered a fair degree of convergence between lines and verses determined by pauses and intonation and lines and verses determined by grammatical and lexical features. (See Bright 1979; Hymes 1981, this volume; McLendon 1981; D. Tedlock 1978, this volume; Woodbury 1985, this volume.) My investigation of Kuna discourse has revealed that each of the line-marking devices – grammatical, intonational, musical, and social-interactional – is highly elaborated and developed in and of itself, and enters into different types of relationships with the others, sometimes congruent, synchronic, and isomorphic, sometimes creating contrasts, tensions, and counterpoint. It is worth noting that it is in the most ritual verbal genres, which from the Kuna point of view are the most archaic and traditional (see Sherzer 1975 for a phonological reflection of this), that there is the most isomorphic, congruent stacking of line-marking devices.

The existence of poetic contrasts and tensions among the different line-marking devices should not be an unfamiliar phenomenon for students of written poetry. In fact we might appropriately speak of two aesthetic principles in Kuna verbal life, one that involves harmonious synchrony and symmetry and one that involves dynamic contrast and tension. Both have been noted among Native Americans. (For dynamic lack of symmetry and synchrony as an aesthetic principle in North America, see Philips 1974 on the structure of Warm Springs communicative events and B. Tedlock 1982 on Zuni pottery and other visual expressive forms.) Kuna speakers and chanters draw on both of these aesthetic principles in their individual structuring of verbal forms. I use the term structuring rather than structure in order to stress the dynamic process involved. Against the backdrop of linguistic and cultural traditions, speakers and chanters develop individual creative styles. The fact that different verbal genres or different speakers can utilize distinct poetic organizations is very much in keeping with Kuna social, cultural, and verbal life, which is characterized by a remarkable organization of diversity (see Sherzer 1970 and Howe and Sherzer 1975).

Kuna discourse, because of its ongoing diversity and vitality, provides a virtual laboratory for the study of Native American discourse in particular and for an exploration of the complex nature of oral discourse more generally. Central to my approach here has been a controlled comparison of different verbal genres with the goal of describing the various structuring principles and processes involved in the actual performance of oral discourse. These structuring principles and processes constitute what I have called the poetics of performance.

I have argued here that the line is a useful, indeed necessary, unit in Kuna discourse. It must be viewed as separate from while nonetheless relatable to other units, such as the sentence, the speech act, and the turn at talk. Research I have referred to here demonstrates that the line is also relevant to the study of the discourse of other groups in the Americas. I suggest that it should be investigated as a potential universal unit of oral discourse. My primary focus has been the line, but I believe that my perspective on oral discourse and the methods I have used have implications that go beyond lines and beyond the Kuna.

Notes

This paper is a revision and expansion of a paper of the same title that appeared in *Language in Society* 11:371–390 (1982). I am indebted to Dell Hymes for extensive comments on an earlier draft. Hymes (1977, 1980) provided the impetus to investigate the interaction of the various line-marking devices in Kuna. I am also grateful for conversations about an earlier draft of this paper with Richard Bauman, William Bright, Sally McLendon, Dina Sherzer, Dennis Tedlock, Sammie Wicks, and Anthony Woodbury. Research for this paper was supported by the John Simon Guggenheim Memorial Foundation, NIMH, and the University of Texas at Austin.

1   Such ritualized dialogues seem to be fairly common in tropical-forest South America. Fock (1963) suggests an areal distribution. Burns (1980) describes a somewhat different pattern among the Yucatec Mayan. See also Sherzer 1983:196–200.
2   The drawings of the various musical shapes in this paper were made by Sammie Wicks, adapting a system used by James Reid.

References

Bright, W. 1979. A Karok myth in "measured verse": the translation of a performance. *Journal of California and Great Basin Anthropology* 1:117–23.
Burns, A. F. 1980. Interactive features in Yucatec Mayan narratives. *Language in Society* 9:307–319.
Finnegan, R. 1977. *Oral poetry*. Cambridge: Cambridge University Press.
Fock, N. 1963. *Waiwai: religion and society of an Amazonian tribe*. Copenhagen: National Museum.
Goody, J. 1977. *The domestication of the savage mind*. Cambridge: Cambridge University Press.
Howe, J. and Sherzer, J. 1975. Take and tell: a practical classification from the San Blas Cuna. *American Ethnologist* 2:435–460.
Hymes, D. 1977. Discovering oral performance and measured verse in American Indian narrative. *New Literary History* 8(3):431–457.
    1980. Particle, pause, and pattern in American Indian narrative verse. *American Indian Culture and Research Journal* 4(4):7–51.
    1981. *"In vain I tried to tell you": essays in Native American ethnopoetics.* Philadelphia: University of Pennsylvania Press.
Lévi-Strauss, Claude. 1964, 1966, 1968, 1971. *Mythologiques*. Paris: Plon.
Lord, A. B. 1960. *The singer of tales*. Cambridge: Harvard University Press.
McLendon, S. 1981. Meaning, rhetorical structure, and discourse organization in myth. In D. Tannen, ed., *Analyzing discourse: text and talk*. Georgetown University Round Table on Language and Linguistics 1981. Washington, D.C.: Georgetown University Press, pp. 284–305.
Ong, W. J., S.J. 1977. *Interfaces of the word*. Ithaca: Cornell University Press.
Philips, S. U. 1974. Warm Springs "Indian time": how the regulation of participation affects the progression of events. In R. Bauman and J. Sherzer, eds., *Explorations in the ethnography of speaking*. Cambridge: Cambridge University Press, pp. 92–109.
Reichard, G. G. 1944. *Prayer: the compulsive word*. New York: Augustin.
Sherzer, J. 1970. Talking backwards in Cuna: the sociological reality of phonological descriptions. *Southwestern Journal of Anthropology* 26:343–353.

1975. A problem in Cuna phonology. *Journal of the Linguistic Association of the Southwest* 1(2):45–53.

1983. *Kuna ways of speaking: an ethnographic perspective.* Austin: University of Texas Press.

Tannen, D. 1982. Oral and literate strategies in spoken and written narratives. *Language* 58:1–21.

Tedlock, B. 1982. Aesthetics as interaction: creativity and criticism at Zuni. MS. prepared for the conference "Native American Interaction Patterns," University of Alberta, Edmonton, Alberta.

Tedlock, D. 1978. *Finding the center: narrative poetry of the Zuni Indians.* Lincoln: University of Nebraska Press.

Woodbury, A. C. 1985. Functions of rhetorical structure: a study of Central Alaskan Yupik Eskimo discourse. *Language in Society* 14(2):150–193.

Yates, Frances. 1966. *The art of memory.* Chicago: University of Chicago Press.

5

HEARING A VOICE IN AN ANCIENT TEXT: QUICHÉ MAYA POETICS IN PERFORMANCE

Dennis Tedlock

Seven generations before Guatemala fell under the dominion of the Hapsburgs of Spain, the highland Maya kingdom ruled by the Caweks of Quiché entered upon its greatest days. The Keeper of the Mat, the head of state, took the name of a mythic god-king, Plumed Serpent, and he founded a new citadel with three major temples atop pyramids, twenty-three palaces, a ball court for a game whose movements symbolized those of heavenly bodies, and, cut into the rock beneath all this, an artificial cave corresponding to the underworld. Three generations before the reign of Plumed Serpent, representatives of the leading Quiché lineages had gone on a pilgrimage to the lowlands of Tabasco (or perhaps Yucatán) to obtain the regalia that gave rulers "fiery splendor," including canopies, thrones, musical instruments, cosmetics, jewelry, gourds of tobacco, and the paws, hooves, and feathers of various creatures of the forest (D. Tedlock 1985:204, 212). Along with all these things they brought back a hieroglyphic book, the Popol Vuh or "Council Book." For their descendants, including Plumed Serpent, this book served as an *ilbal* or "seeing instrument" (1r, 50r),[1] making it possible for Quiché lords to recover the limitless vision of the first four humans who ever existed. If it was like the surviving Maya hieroglyphic books, it set forth a coordinated account of astronomical events and earthly conditions, and of the past actions of gods and humans, that served as a complex navigation system for those who wished to see and move beyond the present.

In 1524 the citadel founded by Plumed Serpent was destroyed by Pedro de Alvarado; shortly thereafter it was replaced by a new town named Santa Cruz Quiché, built a short distance away. It was in Santa Cruz, between 1554 and 1558, that members of the Cawek lineage created a new version of the Popol Vuh, writing in the Quiché language but using an alphabetic orthography that had been worked out by the missionary Francisco de la Parra in 1545. If these writers had chosen to transpose the ancient Popol Vuh on a glyph-by-glyph basis, they might have produced a terse, schematic, and highly mathematized text that would have made little sense to anyone but a diviner. What they did instead was to transcribe what the reader of the ancient book would *say* when he transformed the glyphs into what they call his "long

140

performance and account" of "the emergence of all the sky-earth" (D. Tedlock 1985:71–2). Marking their act of quotation with such phrases as "This is the account here," they begin before the first dawn, when the world contained only an empty sky and a calm sea, and continue all the way down to the time of their own writing, when the legitimate heir to the title of Keeper of the Mat bore the adopted name Juan de Rojas.

Another source for Quiché discourse of past centuries lies in manuscripts that contain the dialogue for various dramas that were performed during the colonial period and (in many cases) continue today. Most of the material in these scripts goes back no further than the sixteenth and seventeenth centuries, when missionaries made repeated efforts to transform traditional dramas into something more in conformity with Christian teachings (Mace 1970:31–47). With the aid of their converts they wrote new parts for the characters, partly in Spanish and partly in the native languages, and recast some of the plots along the lines of stories of the saints. Whether the scripts written during this period displaced ancient ones or supplanted what was previously a purely oral tradition, the surviving examples do include some passages of a clearly pre-Columbian character. In the case of the drama called Xajoj Tun 'Dance of the Trumpet', or Rabinal Achi 'Man of Rabinal', the dialogue is entirely in Achí (a dialect of Quiché) and bears no obvious marks of the Christian presence.[2]

To have the alphabetically written text of an ancient performance is one thing, and to hear a full voice in that text is another. The difficulty of hearing the Popol Vuh is something like the problem faced by Junajpu and Xbalanque, the twin heroes of many of its mythic episodes, when they attempt a conversation with the skull of their dead uncle. "He had wanted his face to become just as it was," we are told, "but when he was asked to name everything, and once he had found the name of the mouth, nose, the eyes of his face, there was very little else to be said" (D. Tedlock 1985:159). In other words, his speech was as spare as his facial features. Given the condition of his vocal organs, his problems must have begun all the way down at the phonetic level, and that is where the problems begin in the Popol Vuh.

The writers of the Popol Vuh use an orthography that provides for all Quiché phonemes that have no equivalent in Spanish, with the exception of a tense-lax vocalic distinction that plays only a small role in the differentiation of otherwise identical words. But they are inconsistent in their spelling of certain Quiché consonants, creating numerous lexical ambiguities. In the case of the Quiché alveopalatal stops, for example, they always use *ch* for the voiceless version, which is correct, but they sometimes use it for the glottalized version as well, which should have been written *4h*. A greater problem stems from the fact that Quiché has four different *k* sounds: a velar stop, like *k* in English; a uvular stop, pronounced farther back in the mouth; and glottalized counterparts of both of these. When the writers of the Popol Vuh used *c* (before *a*, *o*, and *u*) or *qu* (before *e* and *i*), they should have done so only to indicate the plain velar stop, but they frequently used these same spellings for the plain uvular stop (properly *k*), for the glottalized velar stop (properly *4*), and for the glottalized uvular stop (a backwards *3*). When they did use *k*, *4*, and *ɛ*, it was usually to indicate *k* sounds other than the plain velar one, but they were unstable in their choices. The net result is that one word in the Popol Vuh text may have many different readings, all equally allowable if the reader's sole purpose were to establish a phonologically and syntactically correct text, without regard to meaning.

The problem of multiple readings may be illustrated by a sentence that begins a Popol Vuh narrative episode, given in the manuscript as follows: *Are chic uchacatahic, ucamic zipacna* (9v). There is no problem with *chic*, despite the fact that it has both a *ch* and a *c*, because it is part of an easily recognized phrase that begins many Quiché sentences, *are chic*, meaning something like "now this is"; moreover, the phrase is correctly spelled. As for the word *zipacna*, an earlier passage identifies it as the name (*bii*) of a character; the fact that this character hangs around riverbanks and eats fish and crabs helps alert us to the fact that his name is derived from the Nahua name Cipactli (with a nonglottalized velar stop after the *a*), referring to a god with crocodilian attributes. The word given in the text as *uchacatahic* poses much greater problems. Given that it has one *ch* and two occurrences of *c*, purely phonological considerations would permit a total of thirty-two possible readings (2 × 4 × 4), but since *-tahic* is readily identified as a correct rendition of a passive and resultative verb suffix, we can immediately cut that number down to eight. Eliminating what the Quiché lexicon disallows, we are still left with five possibilities. If we choose *uchacatahic*, just as the text has it, the meaning is "his getting stood up on four or more legs." The other possibilities are *uchakatahic* 'his getting disillusioned', *uchaɛatahic* 'his getting cooked', *u4hacatahic* 'his getting defeated', and *u4hakatahic* 'his getting hung up to dry'. The situation with the next word, *ucamic*, is much simpler: It could be correct as it is, meaning "his dying," or it could be *u4amic* 'his arriving'.

At this point, then, we know that we are about to hear a story in which a crocodilian character will come to be stood up on all fours, disillusioned, cooked, defeated, or hung up to dry, in some combination with arriving or dying. As it happens, the question of Sipacna's fate can be solved through an appeal to context, in the older, narrower sense of intratextual context. If we work our way through the story of Sipacna, slipping past further lexical ambiguities, we will be able to decipher the fact that his destiny was to be crushed under the weight of an entire mountain, at which point he "breathed a last sigh and was calm" (D. Tedlock 1985:98). This terrible death was brought about by the trickery of Junajpu and Xbalanque. They did not stand Sipacna up on all fours (far from it), nor did they cook him or hang him up to dry. As for disillusionment, he hardly had any chance to feel that, having had no idea he had been tricked until the moment the mountain crushed him. So our victory in the struggle with *uchacatahic* must lie in the only other possibility, which is defeat. An idiomatic English translation of the sentence that opens the story of Sipacna might run as follows: "Now this is the defeat and death of Sipacna."

Not all of the phonological and lexical mysteries presented to the reader of the Popol Vuh text admit of intratextual solutions. The search through the motley crowd of colonial and contemporary Quiché word lists, lesson books, and dictionaries, including those pertaining to closely related languages, together with the search for parallel passages elsewhere in the Popol Vuh or in other Quiché writings of the same period, combined in turn with a widening of context to include the published ethnographic sources, may still fail to yield a convincing answer to a particular problem. The only way a paleographer can get beyond such limits is to become an ethnopaleographer, taking the Popol Vuh text back to those who continue to speak the language in which it was written. Here is one respect in which the translator of an ancient Quiché text has an advantage over Old World classicists, even with their magnificent dictionaries of ancient Greek and Latin. Not only do contemporary Quichés speak a language that is no more distant from that of the Popol Vuh than modern English is from Elizabethan, but they have yet to make the kind of peace with Christian ideology that was made so long ago in Greece and Rome.

Reading through the Popol Vuh text with a speaker of the Quiché language is far more than a mere linguistic task, and finding that speaker involves much more than simply locating an adult who grew up speaking Quiché. When the task is not only to overcome the confused spelling and punctuation of an old text but to interpret the meaning of that text, it requires a speaker who has access to knowledge that lies beyond ordinary linguistic competence. This might be a knowledge of passages in contemporary formal oratory that resemble passages in the Popol Vuh, for example. It might even be knowledge that goes beyond language as such, as when a Popol Vuh passage recalls an aspect of contemporary culture such as a ritual devoted to the planting of maize, or an aspect of the natural environment such as the way the dawn sky looks at a certain season in a certain region. A reading arrived at on the basis of such knowledge must then be further weighed in the context of existing scholarly knowledge about the state of the Quiché language, discourse, culture, and environment at the time and place of the writing of the text, or the time and place described by the text. Considered in its entirety, the work of the ethnopaleographer will have more resemblance to research in oral history, folklore, sociolinguistics, and cultural anthropology than to plain linguistics.

The most extreme case of a narrowly phonetic approach to the reading of the Popol Vuh may be found in the unpublished manuscripts of J. P. Harrington. In 1922 he worked through a printed version of the text with Cipriano Alvarado, a Quiché who had been brought to Charlottesville, Virginia, by William E.

Gates.³ As Gates explained it, Alvarado read aloud and Harrington, "knowing nothing of the meanings," strove for an accurate phonetic rendition of what Alvarado said. The result is a text that makes considerable sense at the phonetic and even at the grammatical level, but is full of absurdities when it comes to the question of meaning. Where the published text had the divine name *tzakol*, Alvarado spoke the word *tzacol*, meaning "one who cooks," rather than hitting on *tz'akol* 'maker', which is the reading indicated by the weight of the evidence that dates from the colonial period. Where the text had *gucumatz*, Alvarado decided on *cucumatz*, which might be translated as "burning serpent," rather than *k'ucumatz* 'quetzal-feather serpent', the Quiché name for the divine Plumed Serpent once known over the whole of Mesoamerica but no longer named in Quiché prayers. Harrington's transcription displays problems of this sort on every page, producing an effect that verges on Dadaism.

Contextual problems like those in the work of Harrington and Alvarado are also abundant in the more recent work of Adrián I. Chávez, a Quiché-speaking urbanite from Quezaltenango. He reads the *4ucumatz* of the Popol Vuh manuscript not as *k'ucumatz* but as *k'u'cumatz* 'concealer of the serpent', as if to put the Plumed Serpent in the position of denying himself (Chávez 1979:1–1a). In the case of *uucub caquix*, a divine name interpretable as *wukub cakix* 'Seven Macaw' on the basis of colonial dictionaries, he reads *wukub kac'ix* 'Our Seven Disgraces' (ibid.:12–12a), giving the story of the defeat of Seven Macaw the tone of a medieval Christian morality play. A Christian bias also shows up in the work of Dora M. de Burgess, a missionary at the Insituto Bíblico Quiché near Quezaltenango, and Patricio Xec, a Quiché Protestant convert (Burgess and Xec 1955). As Barbara Tedlock has pointed out (1983:347–8), they properly read the *zaqui coxol* of the manuscript as *saki c'oxol*, which can be translated as "White Sparkstriker," but instead of acknowledging that this is the name of a deity who is alive and well to this day, even to the extent of being impersonated in masked dramas, they somehow interpret it as referring to the coral snake, thus transforming an anthropomorphic and primarily beneficent Quiché deity into a poisonous reptile and a Christian symbol of evil.

Each of the past encounters between the Popol Vuh text and a speaker of modern Quiché has fallen short of a dull dialogue between the knowledge that scholars have accumulated and the knowledge of Quichés who occupy positions of authority of the kind that have existed since before the time when the alphabetic Popol Vuh was written. Qualified *ajk'ij* 'daykeepers', men and women who know how to interpret illnesses, omens, dreams, internal bodily sensations, and the workings of the Maya calendar, are quite numerous in a number of Quiché towns. Some male daykeepers hold the title of *chuchkajaw* 'mother–father', which properly belongs only to those who serve as the heads of patrilineages and look after the shrines that every proper patrilineage has on its lands. In at least one town there is a hierarchy of mother–fathers in which the highest level is occupied by two men who look after shrines that belong to the town as a whole. This is the town of Chuwa Tz'ak 'Before the Building', better known today as Momostenango, a Nahua name meaning "Citadel of Shrines." It is without rival among contemporary highland Maya towns in the degree to which its ceremonial life is timed according to the Maya calendar and mapped according to the relative elevations and directional positions of outdoor shrines (see B. Tedlock 1982). It was here, during the summer of 1975 and the whole of 1976, that I conducted an experiment in ethnopaleography.

From the beginning it was my desire to do more than merely use the Popol Vuh as a means of devising questions for interviews. I wanted to find a Quiché who could read the text itself, though Munro S. Edmonson had categorically stated that "with the exception of students of the Instituto Bíblico Quiché, the modern Indians cannot read the Popol Vuh in Quiché" (1971:xv). Success came when I met Andrés Xiloj, who is not only a daykeeper but a mother–father, the head of his patrilineage. His prior experience with alphabetic literacy was limited to Spanish, but when he was given his first chance to look at the Popol Vuh text, he produced a pair of spectacles and began reading aloud, word by word. He needed very little help with the orthography; on the syntactic front it was necessary to point out, for example, that *xch-* (a composite prefix no longer used in Quiché) is something like the future tense in Spanish. I offered glosses of archaic words when it was apparent he was not going to come up with anything from his own vocabulary; in time, of course, he readily recognized the more frequent archaic forms.

At the lexical level, Xiloj's contributions to the reading of the Popol Vuh may be exemplified by some problems occurring in a passage that deals with a divination done by Xpiyacoc and Xmucane (3v–4r), the husband-and-wife team who are the daykeepers in the ancient Quiché pantheon. Like contemporary daykeepers, they use the red seeds of the palo pito, called *tz'ite* in Quiché. What is done with these seeds is described in the Popol Vuh as *xmalic*, which gives us a choice between two homonymous readings, one meaning that the seeds were annoyed by someone and the other that they were lightly rubbed by someone's hand. Edmonson, apparently thinking of divination as a "casting of lots," decided that the seeds were being "cast" (1971:22). Xiloj, a practicing diviner, had no trouble in seeing that a hand was being passed over the seeds, since that is exactly what a Quiché diviner would do with his or her hand, mixing the seeds up and spreading them out flat on a table before grabbing a random handful.

The divination in the Popol Vuh is further described as involving something called *cajic* (*cahic* in the orthography of the manuscript), for which the Quiché lexicon allows four possibilities. There is no *cajic* as such, exactly as given in the text, but there are two homonyms that take the form *kajic*, one meaning "descending" or "dropping" and the other meaning "borrowing." The other two possibilities are *c'ajic* 'crumbling' and *k'ajic* 'breaking'. Edmonson, in keeping with his notion of divination as a casting of lots, amended the text to read *kajic* (*qahic* in his orthography) and gave "throwing" as his translation (1971:22). Xiloj also chose *kajic*, without a moment's hesitation, but his translation (to render it in English) was "borrowing." He explained that when a daykeeper prays at the beginning of a divination, he or she asks to "borrow" the sheet lightning, cool breezes, and clouds and mists of the world, which are message-bearing media, from the lords of the days of the calendar, who are the ultimate sources of the information necessary to answer the question asked by the client. At the end of a divination these media, which have not been given but lent to the daykeeper, are returned to their owners.

On a larger scale than the problem of correctly hearing the phonemes and words of the Popol Vuh text is that of hearing how whole phrases, sentences, and longer segments of discourse might have been intoned and paced. The surviving manuscript, a copy made by the missionary Francisco Ximénez around 1701, has only scattered punctuation marks and lacks capitalization almost entirely, which gives it a strong resemblance to the work of modern descriptive linguists. A knowledge of Quiché syntax may permit the identification of clauses and sentences, but does not tell us to what degree such units were grouped or separated through the use of pauses and intonational contours.

Ximénez wrote out the text of the Popol Vuh in solid gray columns of prose. The only real break in this format comes near the end, where lists are used to present lordly titles and the names of those who succeeded to them, but there are many other passages that conceal a highly formal verse structure within their undifferentiated masses. The development of this structure is guided more by recurrent figures of meaning than by recurrent figures of sound. In other words, Quiché verse is characteristically parallelistic rather than metrical; in this it is like the verse found in other Mesoamerican texts and oral performances, in the texts of the ancient Middle East (which are far older than the Homeric and Vedic texts), and in all living oral traditions that stand free of the influence of metrical systems from written traditions.[4] Mesoamerican parallelism, regardless of language, is dominated by a twofold or coupleted pattern, but there are frequent variations, most often in the form of a triplet (D. Tedlock 1983:chap. 8).

The pioneering work on Mesoamerican verse was done by Angel María Garibay K., who called attention to parallel couplets in colonial texts of Nahuatl songs (1953). It was Miguel León-Portilla, a student of Garibay's, who first called attention to the presence of verse in the Popol Vuh, publishing rearrangements of several passages from the translation of Adrián Recinos in 1964 (see León-Portilla 1969).[5] At the same time he left one passage in prose format, recognizing, correctly, that the tendency toward formal verse in the Popol Vuh is stronger in some places than in others. But then there came the work of Edmonson (1971), who let the search for parallel couplets dominate his entire reading of the text; he obscured all variations with a uniform typographical scheme and even supplied "missing" lines.

At a level of organization above that of phrases, sentences, and lists, the Popol Vuh text offers even less help to the eye than at the lower levels; it often runs on for whole pages without a paragraph break. A closer look at the text reveals that it has a system of paragraphing all its own, apart from the format in which the manuscript was written. These hidden divisions are signaled by the recurrence of phrases consisting of what Dell Hymes calls "initial particles" (1980). Among the most frequent such phrases are *are c'ut* 'and here' or 'and this is', *c'ate c'ut* 'and next' or 'after that', and *queje c'ut* 'and so'. These occur at the beginnings of sentences, most frequently when there is a change of topic or a shift in the time or place of narrative action. But Quiché narrative does not display "measured verse" of the kind Hymes describes for some North American languages (1981:chap. 9). A given particle or set of particles may be used just once, or two or three or (once in a great while) four times in succession before a different choice is made; in other words, such particles do not resolve a text into stanzas according to sustained numerical patterns.

For all that we may divide the Popol Vuh into paragraphs and rearrange some passages as verse, this process still will not tell us, in and of itself, how a performer might have emphasized or elided the boundaries of such segments of discourse through the use of intonational contours, or how he might have varied his timing through the placement of pauses. As in the case of phonological and lexical problems, the solution to this one calls for ethnopaleography. But here it is not only the ancient text and a pen and notebook that must be taken into the field, but a tape recorder. For these purposes it will not do to have the contemporary speaker of the language reading aloud from a difficult text rather than performing what is familiar. The fieldworker will be seeking after contemporary speeches, prayers, songs, and narratives, looking for patterns in the wording that have analogs in the ancient text and noting the ways in which such patterns are actualized in performance.

In the case of the present ethnopaleographic project, Andrés Xiloj was sometimes reminded of contemporary stories in the very course of reading and interpreting the Popol Vuh; true to Quiché conversational style, he told these stories on the spot rather than saving them for some special occasion (D. Tedlock 1983:14–15 and chap. 15). Another source of narrative was Vicente de León, himself a daykeeper and mother–father, who introduced a long narrative into our very first conversation. The search for more formal discourse than that of Quiché narrative led to Paulino Ixchop, who coaches the performers in a drama called Xajoj C'oy, or "Monkey Dance," and to Esteban Ajxub, a specialized daykeeper who works full time as an *ajbix*, or "singer." For a fee, a singer will augment the prayers of a less eloquent daykeeper with chants or songs, together with further prayers. In addition to making tapes of prayers and dramatic speeches, I was able to record public announcements by the current *ajk'ojom* 'player of the slit drum', the town crier for Momostenango.

The prayers recited by the contemporary singer, like some passages in the Popol Vuh, display sustained parallel verse based on both syntax and meaning, most often in the form of couplets and triplets. At the smallest scale, a couplet may consist of a pair of unmodified and uninflected nouns totaling only two to four syllables. An example occurring both in contemporary prayers and in the Popol Vuh consists of *caj* 'sky', and *ulew* 'earth'. The knowledge that these two items occur independently as separate nouns might lead a careless transcriber of sound recordings to overlook the fact that when they follow one another they are pronounced as a single word, *cajulew*, with a single stress on the final syllable. Combined in this way, sky and earth become complementary metonyms whose referent approximates the abstraction we call "world" in English, but they accomplish this level of inclusiveness without any final reduction of the difference between sky and earth. Other examples of compound nouns are *juyubtak'aj*, composed of *juyub* 'mountain' and *tak'aj* 'plain', producing the sense of "earth," and *chopalo*, composed of *cho* 'lake' and *palo* (or *plo* in modern Quiché) 'sea', producing a term for all the pooled water of the world.

I have assumed that these and some other paired nouns would have been pronounced as single words by the reader of the hieroglyphic Popol Vuh, just as they are by contemporary speakers of Quiché. Wherever the examples given above occur in the text of the alphabetic Popol Vuh they are written as two separate words, but the two words are never separated by a comma, though they may be preceded or followed by one. In my translation I have chosen to join the two halves of these pairs with hyphens, as with "sky-earth," in order to bring them closer together while at the same time keeping them readable, but ideally they should be written as "skyearth," "mountainplain," and "lakesea."

At a level above the pairing of plain nouns is a couplet in which two nouns carry parallel modifiers or parallel affixes, or participate in parallel prepositional phrases. Sustained runs of such couplets are well represented in prayers and other oratorical passages in the Popol Vuh. The following example comes from a speech in which the gods who are the makers and modelers of humankind call upon older gods who are diviners and artisans to help them (4r). Like many other such passages, this one is introduced by a phrase that stands outside the parallel scansion:[6]

Chic'utun ibi':	Fulfill your names:
Junajpu Wuch',	Hunahpu Possum,
Junajpu Utiw,	Hunahpu Coyote,

camul alom,	bearer twice over,
camul c'ajolom,	begetter twice over,
nim ak,	great peccary,
nima tz'i's,	great tapir,
ajc'ual,	lapidary,
ajyamanic,	jeweler,
ajch'ut,	sawyer,
ajtz'alam,	carpenter,
ajraxa lak,	maker of green plates,
ajraxa sel,	maker of green bowls,
ajk'ol,	incense maker,
ajtoltecat,	master craftsman,
ratit k'ij,	grandmother of day,
ratit zak.	grandmother of light.

Esteban Ajxub creates passages with a similar structure when he prays to the ancestors on behalf of his clients. If we were to make a conventional transcription of such a passage, turning off our tape machine after completing a division of the recorded sounds into phonemes and words, and then going on to determine punctuation by syntactical considerations and distributing the words among stichs according to scansion, we might end up with the following:

Sacha la numac comon nan:	Pardon my sins all moms:
comon wak remaj,	all six generations,
comon wak tic'aj,	all six jarsfull,
comon chuch,	all mothers,
comon kajaw,	all fathers,
comon ajchac,	all workers,
comon ajpatan,	all servers,
comon ajbára,	all mixers,
comon ajpúnto,	all pointers,
comon ajtz'ite,	all counters of seeds,
comon ajvaráje,	all readers of cards,
uc'amic,	who received,
uchoquic,	who entered,
wa chac,	this work,
wa patan,	this service,

```
chiquiwa ri nan,                    before the moms,
chiquiwa ri tat.                    before the dads.
```

Note that *comon nan*, in the opening phrase, occupies an ambiguous position between the singularity of *Sacha la numac* and the parallel stichs that follow; given the pairing of *nan* and *tat* in the last couplet, we are left wondering whether *comon nan* should have been followed with *comon tat*, making for an additional couplet of the kind that repeats the word *comon*. Moving on to the couplets that Ajxub actually produced, we may note that the first five of them, like the couplets quoted from the Popol Vuh, have what might be called a paradigmatic verticality; there are some small syntactic changes in the construction of the nouns, but at the scale of sentence building there is no horizontal syntagmatic movement at all. It is Ajxub's last three couplets that get the sentence moving again; paradigmatic verticality is retained within each couplet, but syntagmatic horizontality enters in the movement from one couplet to the next. Beginning with the last of the opening five couplets, we might represent this combined vertical and horizontal movement as follows:

```
comon ajtz'ite,
comon ajvaráje,  ucamic,
                 uchoquic,  wa chac,
                            wa patan,  chiquiwa ri nan,
                                       chiquiwa ri tat.

all counters of seeds,
all readers of cards,  who received,
                       who entered   this work,
                                     this service,   before the moms,
                                                     before the dads.
```

Here is an example of a similar diagonal movement from the text of the Popol Vuh (1r):

```
ri  tz'akol,
    bitol,    uchuch,
              ukajaw,  c'aslem,
                       winakirem,
                                   abanel,
                                   c'uxlanel,

the  maker,
     modeler,  mother of,
               father of   that which is alive,
                           that which is human,
                                       with breath,
                                       with heartbeat,
```

It should be noted that when the structure of two successive couplets changes in a way that moves the sentence forward, the transition between them is different in degree, but not in kind, from the transition between such singular opening phrases as "Pardon my sins all moms" (in Ajxub's prayer) or "Fulfill your names" (in the Popol Vuh passage) and the couplets that follow them. From the point of view of the kind of commonsense poetics that scans for the presence of verse and leaves prose as a negatively defined category, these opening phrases are "prose" in the sense that they stand outside the "verse" that follows them. But I find it more useful to describe Quiché poetics in terms of a dialectic between paradigm and syntagm, or between the vertical movement of verse and the horizontal movement of prose. In a dialectical poetics the same eye that scans texts that are written in a prose format for the presence of verse must also catch the movement of prose even where verse patterns seem obvious.

Having temporarily turned off our tape recording of Ajxub's prayer in order to work out matters of punctuation and scansion on the basis of phonemes and words alone, we may now return to the question of what he was doing with intonation contours and pauses while he was producing these phonemes and words. Competent speakers of any language, far from surrendering all uses of intonation and pausing to the marking of the boundaries between syntactical units, retain the ability to control them independently. A contour may unify a group of words while at the same time signaling that there are more words to come, or it may end with a steep fall in pitch of the kind that marks the end of a complete utterance, whether that utterance is a sentence or not. I shall call the strings of words marked in these ways *cola* and *periods*, respectively, in order to distinguish them from phrases, clauses, and sentences, with which they may or may not coincide. At one extreme several sentences may be treated as cola and linked to form a single period; at the other a single word (and one that does not make a sentence) may form a period all by itself. Pauses, for their part, may or may not fall in places where they mark cola and periods, or clauses and sentences, or the stichs indicated by scansion. I shall call the strings of words marked by pauses *lines*, in order to contrast them with stichs.

What follows is the same modern prayer passage that was already presented above in scanned form, but this time it is given as Ajxub actually performed it, with cola and periods determined by intonation and lines determined by pauses. A comma marks the end of a segment in which the highest pitch falls on the first stressed syllable, that being the final syllable of the first word or (where the first word is monosyllabic) the final (or only) syllable of the second word, and in which the lowest pitch falls on the final syllable of the last word, though this last pitch remains higher than would mark a complete sentence. In the case of a dash the last syllable of a segment is brought up to the level of the first high syllable rather than lowered; such a rise emphasizes, even more than a moderately low terminal pitch, that there is more to come. A period at the end of a segment would indicate a pitch markedly lower than that indicated by a comma, signaling completeness, but there is no point of completeness in this particular passage. In fact, prayers are often delivered with many cola but only one grand period, no matter how many complete sentences they may contain.

> Sacha la numac comon nan –
> comon wak remaj,
> comon wak tic'aj,
> comon chuch, comon kajaw,
> comon ajchac, comon ajpatan, comon ajbára, comon ajpúnto, comon ajtz'ite, comon ajvaráje,
> uc'amic, uchoquic, wa chac, wa patan, chiquiwa ri nan, chiquiwa ri tat,

> Pardon my sins all moms –
> all six generations,
> all six jarsfull,
> all mothers, all fathers,
> all workers, all servers, all mixers, all pointers, all counters of seeds, all readers of cards,
> who received, who entered, this work, this service, before the moms, before the dads,

Note that while each of the stichs we reckoned earlier is at least marked as a colon, most of the boundaries between cola fall within lines. The original seventeen scannable stichs, ranging from three to eight syllables each, have become six audible lines, ranging from five to thirty syllables. At the beginning the words *comon nan*, which we earlier thought might be the first half of an incomplete couplet, are smoothly joined to *Sacha la numac* in a single colon and line, set firmly apart from all later cola and lines by the uniqueness of its intonation. It is as if the second half of the hypothetical couplet had given way to the singularity of *Sacha la numac*, or had been swallowed up by the emphatically incomplete intonation of the first half.

Following the opening line, only the first of the couplets is neatly divided into two lines by a pause; its internal unity is preserved by the fact that it stands out as the only couplet delivered in this way, and by the fact that its two halves not only share *comon*, which they have in common with the couplets that follow, but *wak* 'six' as well, which belongs to them alone. The internal unity of the second couplet is emphasized by its isolation between two pauses. But the remaining three couplets that begin with *comon* are run on as a single line, with no more marking of the transition between one couplet and the next than between two parts of the same couplet; in other words, it is meaning alone that divides this line into pairs of phrases. The next line, beginning with *uc'amic*, consists entirely of couplets of the kind that allows the forward motion of prose to give each of them a place further along in the sentence, but the transition from one stitch to another within a given couplet is treated no differently from the transition between one couplet and the next.

Turning once again to the text of the Popol Vuh, we may now attempt a reconstruction of the oral delivery of the passages quoted earlier, beginning with the one that started with a singular introductory phrase and followed with eight couplets. We must make three assumptions in order to do this. The first is that the audience for the recitation could have been intimate enough to permit a level of amplitude allowing for lines as long as those in Ajxub's prayer; his audience (in addition to the ancestors) was limited to several nearby people and did not tax his lung capacity. The second is that the performer of the Popol Vuh, in quoting from a speech in which some of the gods summoned up others in a prayerlike manner, would have imitated the way in which actual prayers were delivered by his own human contemporaries. And the third assumption, of course, is that his contemporaries delivered prayers in the same way as present-day Quichés.

Given that larger-scale syntactical shifts than the ones occurring between some of the couplets of this Popol Vuh passage do not necessarily call for line breaks in contemporary prayers, it may be that the fifth line below should have been run on with the fourth, and that the last line should have been run on with the one preceding. In any case, with the exception of the last line, I have tried to follow Ajxub's tendency to accelerate (or increase his line length); he generally slows back down only when a change of sentence is accompanied by a major change of subject matter. Since the present passage does not end the speech in which it occurs, I have ended it with a comma rather than closing off a complete period.

> Chic'utun ibi' –
> Junajpu Wuch',
> Junajpu Utiw,
> camul alom, camul c'ajolom,
> nim ak, nima tzi's,
> ajc'ual, ajyamanic, ajch'ut, ajtz'alam, ajraxa lak, ajraxa sel, ajk'ol,
>   ajtoltecat,
> ratit k'ij, ratit zak,
>
> Fulfill your names –
> Hunahpu Possum,
> Hunahpu Coyote,
> bearer twice over, begetter twice over,
> great peccary, great tapir,

> lapidary, jeweler, sawyer, carpenter, maker of green plates, maker
> of green bowls, incense maker, master craftsman,
> grandmother of day, grandmother of light,

The other Popol Vuh passage quoted earlier, illustrating the combined movements of verse and prose, might have been delivered as follows, once again following Ajxub's pattern:

> ri tz'akol, bitol,
> uchuch, ukajaw, c'aslem, winakirem, abanel, c'uxlanel,
>
> the maker, modeler,
> mother of, father of that which is alive, that which is human, with
> breath, with heartbeat,

In Quiché narrative the balance between prose and verse, or between paradigm and syntagm, swings more toward the prose side than in prayers and oratory. There may be groups of parallel stichs, but these are commonly isolated fragments, each one separated from the next by strings of unparalleled words rather than participating in a sustained run of verse. Here are two sentences from a Popol Vuh narrative (10r):

> C'ate c'ut, ta xquicoj uco'c chuxe pek, chuxe nima juyub, Meawan
> ubi juyub, xch'acataj wi. C'ate c'ut, ta xepe ri c'ajolab, xquic'u ri
> Sipacna chiya'.
>
> After that, when they put the shell beneath an overhang, beneath a
> great mountain, Meawan is the name of the mountain, he was defeated
> there. After that, when those boys came along, they found that
> Sipacna by the water.

The closest thing to a couplet like those discussed earlier is *chuxe pek, chuxe nima juyub* 'beneath an overhang, beneath a great mountain', but it is complicated by the addition of an adjective to the second stich, and it is not followed by another couplet. There is a semantic overlap between "beneath a great mountain" and "Meawan is the name of the mountain," but these two phrases are quite different syntactically. At a larger scale there is the repetition of the initial particles *c'ate c'ut* 'after that', together with certain similarities in the structure of the two sentences that follow these particles (though the first sentence is much longer), but this tentative pattern is not carried through in what follows the quoted passage.

Turning to contemporary narrative, the passage quoted below is from a story by Andrés Xiloj; it is given as performed rather than as scanned. Note the isolation of the initial particle *entónses* (used twice) in lines to itself, where it serves to break the story into paragraphs; note also the isolation of the final phrase, which marks the line before it as a sort of quotation – or better, a citation of common knowledge, in this case a place name. As often happens when an unparalleled proper name is introduced for the first time in a particular narrative, this one is given a line to itself. A lack of punctuation at the end of a line indicates an interrupted intonational contour rather than a rise (dash) or fall (comma or period).

Entónses	So then
ri Yewa'chi, xbe pa tak'aj,	that Yewachi, he went to the coast,
xuc'am ulok jun cacáxta k'an caney,	he brought back one backpack load of yellow guineas,
cupajo como	weighing about
tres quintáles!	three hundred pounds!
Ri jun cacáxta k'an caney,	That one backpack of yellow guineas,
ri vanáno, pwes.	those bananas, then.
Entónses	So then
xpetic, xel ulok chuwi	he came back, he got as far as the pass
Chuwi Saka',	Diligence Pass,
cujch'aroj che.	as we came to call it.

In this passage the force of prose reduces the tendency to construct parallel verse to a mere trace. The two verbs of the second and third lines, *xbe* and *xuc'am*, are parallel in sharing the complete aspect (*x-*) and a third person singular subject (*-∅-* or *-u-*), but the clauses in which they are contained are developed differently; the same goes for the two verbs in the third line from the end, *xpetic* and *xel*. The repetition of *jun cacáxta k'an caney* in the third and sixth lines is a step in the direction of verse, but the two occurrences are separated from one another by words that are unparalleled. The second occurrence, preceded by *ri* 'that', is semantically parallel with the words that follow it, *ri vanáno*, but a full syntactic parallel would have demanded a much longer phrase as a second stich. Finally, there is the repetition of *chuwi* in the second and third lines from the end, which hardly constitutes the basis of a couplet.

Returning to the narrative passage from the Popol Vuh, we might reconstruct its delivery as follows. If we were to treat "beneath an overhang, beneath a great mountain" on the model of most of the couplets in Ajxub's prayers, its two stichs would not be separated by a line break; indeed, Xiloj often runs the stichs of his narrative couplets together, though he is most likely to do so when they match perfectly, unlike the stichs of the present couplet. In the present case I have decided to break the couplet apart on the model of the break between "That one backpack of yellow guineas" and "those bananas." As in the case of Xiloj's performance, initial particles and a newly introduced proper name are given lines to themselves:

C'ate c'ut	After that
ta xquicoj uco'c chuxe pek,	when they put the shell beneath an overhang,
chuxe nima juyub,	beneath a great mountain,
Meawan	Meawan
ubi juyub,	is the name of the mountain,
xch'acataj wi.	he was defeated there.
C'ate cut	After that
ta xepe ri c'ajolab,	when those boys came along,
xquic'u ri Sipacna chiya'.	they found that Sipacna by the water.

In contemporary narrative the phrases that introduce quotations, like the initial particles that introduce paragraphs, are given lines to themselves. When clauses that refer back to quotations consist of a single word such as *xch'a* 'he said', they may be run on in the same line with the end of the quote itself, but otherwise they, too, are given lines to themselves. The following passage is taken from the same narrative by Xiloj that was quoted earlier. He engages in code switching here, in both directions, between Quiché and Spanish. In the translation I have left the Spanish words as they are except where I reckon them as constituting loan words rather than code switching. The initial particle *entónses* or *entónse*, a favorite in contemporary Quiché, poses a problem here; in the translation, I have reckoned it as Quiché when it occurs alone or shares a line with Quiché words and as Spanish when it shares a line with Spanish words.

Entónses	So then
Yewa'chi díjo,	Yewachi dijo,
"Entónse éste éste capitan	"Entonces este este capitán
entónse wa wachi, wa capitan	so this man, this captain
mucuxij ta rib chi nuwach,"	shows no fear before me,"
Yewa'chi díjo,	Yewachi dijo,
xch'a ri Yewa'chi.	said that Yewachi.

The third and fourth lines might be described as a quatrain built from two couplets, except that *entónse* does not fit the internal scansion of either of them. Note that the repetition of *éste* in the third line, although it might appear at first to be a stumble on the part of the speaker, turns out to be a partial realization of a couplet that receives full treatment in the next line, after the switch from Spanish to Quiché and from *éste* to *wa*. The couplet consisting of *wa wachi, wa capitan* illustrates a fairly common feature of contemporary Quiché verse, already illustrated by the fifth couplet in the opening sentence of Ajxub's prayer to the ancestors, which is that one of the stichs in a parallel unit may be constructed by substituting a Spanish loan word or phrase for an older Quiché word or phrase. In the present passage Xiloj follows a Spanish stich with a Quiché one in the last two lines, but in most cases the change moves in the other direction, with Spanish entering in the second stich of a couplet or in the third stich of a triplet or quatrain.[7]

There follows a Popol Vuh narrative passage (4r) that illustrates the framing of a quotation, with its cola, periods, and lines already reconstructed:

Ta xquibij usuc'uliquil,	Then they spoke straight to the point,
"Utz are chuxic ri ipoy, ajamche',	"It is well that there be your mannikins, wood carvings,
chich'awic, chitzijon, bala!	talking, speaking, indeed!
Chuwach ulew.	On the face of the earth.
Ta chuxok,"	Then let it be,"
xech'a c'ut.	so they said.

Given that *bala* 'indeed!' is normally period-final and line-final in contemporary discourse, I have let it be so here, even though it interrupts an ongoing sentence. Interruptions of an exclamative nature also occur in the earlier of the two passages quoted from the narrative by Xiloj, where the line "three hundred pounds!" interposes a period before a sentence is complete, and in a passage to be quoted later from another narrator, where *bay* 'well!' ends both a line and a period.

An interruption of a different sort may occur when a speaker hesitates over a choice of words. This seldom happens in the prayers of a professional singer, unless he has to stop to ask an unfamiliar client for personal information that fits into a particular place in the discourse – for example, in the midst of a prayer devoted to the Mundo, the "World" or Earth deity, he might stop to ask the names of the mountains where the seeds and crystals in the client's divining bundle were obtained. Such an interruption is handled in such a way as to maintain a high degree of formality: the performer does not stutter, or use some equivalent of English "uh", or linger in puzzlement, but rather stops abruptly and cleanly and immediately turns to the client to ask for the needed information, resuming the prayer exactly where he left off. From the perspective of the prayer itself, there is no interruption at all in phrases, stichs, or cola, but only an unusually long pause.

In the more casual context of Quiché narrative, hesitation over a choice of words can be quite a different matter. In the extreme case the pause may not only interrupt a colon but may fall immediately after an article or demonstrative and leave the hearer in doubt as to what the noun will be, as in this two-line, one-colon passage from a narrative by Vicente de León:

Sach chi ri ri ri ri	Lost is the the the the
ri ri ri ajch'amiy,	the the the staff bearer,

If someone were to repeat "the" seven times in English we would take it as the mark of a stutterer; a more normal hesitation would have been something like "the uuuuuh [pause] staff bearer." But Xiloj sometimes produces repetitions of *ri* similar to de León's, as do other Quiché narrators, and in fact there is no Quiché equivalent of "uh." A tentative formulation of the difference would be this: The English-speaker's lengthened "uh" is not so much a hesitation as a false horizontal move produced by the syntagmatic force, whereas the Quiché-speaker's repetition of *ri* is a false vertical move, produced by the paradigmatic force. Here we have an indication of the strength of the vertical movement in Quiché discourse: it even has an effect on the way speakers make mistakes. I say mistakes because whenever speakers of Quiché helped me transcribe tapes, repeating what they heard until I was satisfied with my phonemic notation, they ignored repetitions of *ri* and similar phenomena. As for the text of the Popol Vuh, such repetitions have long since been edited out of existence.

Except for the sevenfold repetition of *ri* and a potential quatrain based on a code switch, our examples of the paradigmatic or verse dimension in Quiché discourse have been limited to couplets. The most common Quiché variation on the couplet, as in Mesoamerican verse in general, is the triplet. Some Quiché triplets have three stichs in perfect syntactic parallel, but just as often the third stich varies from the other two, commonly by means of deletion of affixes or words. Here are two successive triplets from the Popol Vuh (1v), preceded by a singular introductory phrase and followed by a resumption of the forward movement of the sentence. What follows the introductory phrase is to be understood as a direct quotation from the actual performance given by the reader of the hieroglyphic Popol Vuh:

Are utzijoxic wa'e: This is the account here:

    "C'a catz'ininok,   "Now it still ripples,
    c'a cachamamok,   now it still murmurs,
    catz'inonic,   ripples,

    c'a casilanic,   it still sighs,
    c'a calolinic,   it still hums,
    catolona puch   and it is empty

upa caj."   under the sky."

Triplets may also be found in contemporary formal discourse. The following passage, which happens to display two triplets in succession, comes from a prayer that Ajxub addressed to the various aspects of the Earth deity. Note that the last line of the first triplet, *comon mundo*, or "all worlds," is abbreviated by comparison with the pair of stichs that precedes it, and that one triplet is separated from the other by the unparalleled words *petinak wi wa* 'whence come these'. The second triplet is woven together from what could also be reckoned as three couplets. The entire passage was delivered as a single line with nine cola:

múndo chirélabal k'ij, múndo chukájibal k'ij, comon múndo, petinak
wi wa k'áni tz'ite, sáki tz'ite, k'áni piley, sáki piley, k'áni baraj,
sáki baraj,

world where the sun rises, world where the sun sets, all worlds,
whence come these yellow seeds, white seeds, yellow beans, white
beans, yellow mixtures, white mixtures,

In reconstructing the delivery of the triplets quoted from the Popol Vuh,
we must first set aside the single introductory phrase as a single line. As for
the transition between the two triplets themselves, we have even less reason
to interpose a line break than Ajxub did. The Popol Vuh triplets are neither
divided by a singular phrase nor differ from one another as much as his do.
Here is the result:

Are utzijoxic wa'e –
"C'a catz'ininok, c'a cachamamok, catz'inonic, c'a casilanic, c'a
calolinic, catolona puch upa caj."

This is the account here –
"Now it still ripples, now it still murmurs, ripples, it still sighs, it
still hums, and it is empty under the sky."

Triplets often occur at or near the beginning or end of a series of couplets.
When this happens, the scanning eye is sometimes confronted with ambiguity,
as in this passage from the Popol Vuh (1v):

Majabiok   There is not yet

jun winak,   one person,
jun chicop,   one animal,
  tz'iquin,   bird,
  car,   fish,
  tap,   crab,

che',   tree,
abaj,   rock,

jul,   hollow,
siwan,   canyon,

c'im,   meadow,
qu'echelaj.   forest.

There are several possible readings of the stichs shown here as a group of
five. If we scan the first three stichs as a triplet with a shortened third line
(from which *jun* has been deleted), the next two stichs and the rest of the
passage fall out in perfect couplets. On the other hand, we might scan the
first two stichs as a couplet, given that they both include *jun*, and leave the

next three stichs as a triplet, semantically unified by the fact that all three words refer to subcategories of *chicop* 'animal', whereas the following words do not. The first of these solutions undervalues the semantic attraction between "bird" and "fish," which pulls "bird" away from the generic "animal," while the second undervalues the attraction between "animal" and "bird," which pulls "animal" away from "person." A third solution, based on the fact that a list of animals elsewhere in the Popol Vuh includes the couplet *quej, tz'iquin* 'deer, bird' (2v), would be to posit a scribal error and insert "deer" ahead of "bird," leaving nothing but couplets. The trouble with this solution, which is the one chosen by Edmonson (1971:9), is that the alternative list is simply a series of paired animals, without the semantic complexity of the movement from "person" to "animal" to "bird." If there is a "deer" in the present passage, I would suggest that it has been semantically swallowed, so to speak, by "animal," rather than falling victim to a scribal error.

Ambiguities of scansion also occur in contemporary discourse. We have already seen one example, where the opening line of Ajxub's prayer to the ancestors seemed to include half of what could have been a couplet. The following example occurs in the second sentence of the same prayer:

C'o in quimúlta,	Here is their fine,
c'o in quipreséntere,	here is their present,
c'o in quichac,	here is their work,
quipatan,	their service,
quibára.	their mixing.

The third stich is pulled into a triplet with the first two by the fact that it is perfectly parallel with them syntactically; such a reading would leave the last two stichs as a couplet. But *chac* and *patan*, in the third and fourth stichs, frequently form a couplet, as they do in the opening sentence of this same prayer (where they are prefixed with *aj-*); this consideration would pull the third stich into a couplet with the fourth and leave the last stich dangling. Noting that *bára* (in the last stich) is frequently paired with *púnto* (again exemplified in the opening of the present prayer), we might speculate that the performer has left out a potential sixth stich, just as we earlier wondered whether the writers of the Popol Vuh had left out a stich between "animal" and "bird." This would permit us to resolve the whole sentence into three couplets, the first of them consisting of the first two stichs as given above. The second couplet would consist of the next two stichs, though if we wished to remove all irregularities we would still have to decide whether the performer should have left *c'o in* out of the third stich or added it to the fourth stich. The third couplet would require the addition of *quipúnto* 'their pointing' as the last stich.

On the other hand, if we wish to recognize Esteban Ajxub's status as a professional prayermaker, and to consider the fact that he produced the present prayer at my request and as a deliberate demonstration of his art, we must be prepared to see this passage, with all the tension in its third stich, not as the imperfect realization of an abstract set of rules but as sparkling moment of improvisation amid the dullness of convention. Lewis Turco puts the matter of variation in verse patterns as follows, though he happens to be speaking of written meter rather than oral parallelism: "Scansion attempts only to establish the *normative* meter, for no true poet writes always in regular measures" (1968:17). Alfred North Whitehead, speaking of rhythm in general, has it this way: "The essence of rhythm is the fusion of sameness and novelty. . . . A mere recurrence kills rhythm as surely as does a mere confusion of differences" (quoted in Wimsatt 1972:230). As we have already seen, triplets are the commonest variation on the couplets that dominate Quiché verse, but Ajxub has gone this variation one better by merging the two forms in such a way as to produce five parallel stichs that are inextricably woven together. Once we accept these stichs as they are rather than viewing them as flawed, we can see that they have an internal formality of their own: The dropping of *c'o in* halfway through what could have been a perfect *chac/ patan* couplet is echoed by the omission of the second half of what could have been a *bára/púnto* couplet. As for Ajxub's delivery, he ran off all five stichs as a single line with five cola, emphasizing their unity, and we may guess that the reader of the Popol Vuh might have done something similar with the five interwoven stichs quoted earlier.

The stichs of most Quiché quatrains, like the stichs of the Arabic rubai and a number of Celtic verse forms, have an AABA pattern, though here (as with Quiché couplets and triplets) the pattern is accomplished through parallelism rather than being marked by a rhyme scheme. The variation in the third line, where syntactical changes occur, suggests that the Quiché quatrain is a sort of resolution of the triplet, in which the fourth line restores the pattern of the opening pair of stichs and returns the count to an even number. In the following example from the Popol Vuh (1r), the variation in the third line consists of simple deletion:

ucaj tzuc'uxic,	fourfold siding,
ucaj xucutaxic,	fourfold cornering,
retaxic,	measuring,
ucaj che'xic,	fourfold staking,

A contemporary quatrain with a shortened third stich is illustrated by the following passage from a narrative by de León, given in its scanned form:

Xepicha ri chicop,	The animals carved them out,
xech'olic escaléta,	they were picked down to the skele-tons,

xecanaja, bay!	they were left, well!
Xec'ajtaj pura escaléta chique.	They were broken down into sheer skeletons.

All four of these stichs were run off as a single line embracing two complete periods (marked above by an exclamation point and a period). Like Ajxub, de León had an audience of several nearby persons; supposing, once again, that the reader of the hieroglyphic Popol Vuh had a similar audience, we may guess that his quatrain, like de León's, might have been contained within a single line, all the more so because de León got past his third stich without a pause even though he treated that stich as the end of a period.

In some quatrains the variation in the third line is more marked than in the examples so far given. This next passage from the Popol Vuh (1r), which gives both the proper name and a series of three epithets for the Popol Vuh itself, retains semantic parallelism in the third line but introduces a considerable syntactic change:

Xchikelesaj rumal majabi chic	We shall bring it out because there is no longer
ilbal re Popol Wuj,	a way to see the Council Book,
ilbal "Sak Petenak ch'aka Palo,"	a way to see "The Light from across the Sea,"
utzijoxic "Kamujibal,"	the account of "Our Darkness,"
ilbal "Sak C'aslem,"	a way to see "The Dawn of Life,"

The following contemporary passage, from the same de León narrative that was quoted above, is introduced by a word that stands alone, followed by a quatrain with a markedly changed third stich and then by a series of words I have chosen to scan as a triplet followed by a singular closing stich:

Cacho'maxic	A decision is being reached
chi jasa rumóda wa ri',	as to what the nature of that thing is,
jasa ri cabanok chech,	what must be happening to them,
de que consíste,	de que consiste,
jasa rumóda ri quesach	what is the nature of that loss
ralcalte,	of the mayor,
rejidor,	the manager,
ajch'amiy,	the staff bearer,
i tódos.	y todos.

Note that the third stich in the quatrain remains parallel with the other three stichs in taking an interrogative form; its variation from these stichs consists in a code switch to Spanish. The stich that follows the triplet could be reckoned as the the fourth stich of a quatrain, but the switch from Quiché to Spanish, the addition of a conjunction (*i*), the change to the plural, and the change from a noun to a pronoun make it sufficiently different from the preceding three stichs to suggest that it is better scanned as a singular stich. The way the passage is actually delivered (see below) lends support to such a reading, in that the last stich is spoken as a line to itself while the preceding three are run together within a single line. The word that introduces the passage, treated as a singular stich above, is also given a line to itself.

Cacho'maxic	A decision is being reached
chi jasa rumóda wa ri',	as to what the nature of that thing is,
jasa ri cabanok chech,	what must be happening to them,
de que consíste,	de que consiste,
jasa rumóda ri	what is the nature of that
quesach ralcalte, rejidor, ajch'amiy,	loss of the mayor, the manager, staff bearer,
i tódos.	y todos.

The four stichs of de León's previous quatrain were run off as a single line, whereas those of the present one are divided from one another by line breaks. A possible explanation lies at a broad semantic level: In the present passage de León expresses puzzlement and uncertainty, pausing as if waiting for an answer to each of the questions he raises. In his earlier quatrain, on the other hand, he expresses a single and quite definite action. Presumably the Popol Vuh quatrain giving the name and three epithets of the Popol Vuh itself is not meant to express uncertainty, so perhaps it would run off as a single line, given an intimate audience.

At the point of transition between the quatrain expressing uncertainty and the triplet that follows it, de León's delivery creates tension where there could have been a sharper boundary. Note that *quesach*, which we had earlier scanned as belonging to the last stich of the quatrain, is joined to the same line (the next-to-last) that contains the triplet, leaving *ri* hanging in the line preceding it. In terms of the timing of the delivery of the quatrain as a whole, this displacement of a line break into the midst of a stich (and a colon) might be termed *syncopation*.

Elsewhere in his narrative, de León recombines *ralcalte, rejidor, ajch'amiy*, and *sach* (all used in the triplet quoted above) to produce a new triplet, only this time he delivers each stich as a distinct line:

Sach ri alcalte,	The mayor is lost,
sach ri rejidor,	the manager is lost,
sach ajch'amiy.	the staff bearer is lost.

We cannot explain the delivery of this triplet by the fact that a verb has been introduced into each of its stichs, since the stichs of the first of the two quatrains quoted from de León were run on as a single line, despite the fact that each of them carried a verb. There is a solution, but it lies in taking account of the fact that the present passage is a quotation from the words of an *ajk' ojom*, a "player of the slit-drum" or "town crier," rather than in considering its internal features by themselves. Town criers deliver most of their lines phrase by phrase and colon by colon; they may run parallel nouns or noun phrases together in a closing line, but not even that line will carry more than one verb.

Although de León's use of three separate lines is indeed correct for a public announcement, he did not attempt a full imitation of the intonations of a town crier, which will be described below. Here we have a reminder that if our poetics is to take account not only of scannable features, which may be found in transcriptions of bare phonemes and words, but of features like pausing and intonation as well, the common linguistic notion as to what constitutes "direct" or "indirect" reporting of discourse must change. In the present case, de León may be said to be quoting a town crier directly when we consider his words and even his pause-divided lines, but he remains indirect in not adopting a crier's intonations. In this sense he is reporting *what* a crier would say rather than saying it.

The announcements made by the Quiché town crier resemble the prayers of the professional Quiché singer in having a singular opening phrase followed by parallel stichs, but they contrast in matters of contouring and timing. Except (on occasion) for the very end of an announcement, each stich corresponds to a single intonational colon, and each colon corresponds to a single line. In the case of the opening and closing cola, the final syllable or (in the case of words with nonfinal stress) syllables are lengthened so as to last two or three seconds; sometimes there is a lesser lengthening at the ends of other cola, most likely to occur in the second and penultimate cola. Except for the lengthened syllable or syllables of the closing colon, all pitches are stabilized (though not as much as in a singing voice) and reduced to two levels, three or four halftones apart. In a given colon, everything up to the final syllable lengthening is delivered on the lower of the two levels, while the lengthening itself occupies the higher level. The final line is the same as the others up to the point where the step to the higher level is taken at the end, but once that point is reached the lengthening itself is done with a rapidly descending glissando that reaches well beneath the lower of the two stable pitch levels.

The following announcement occurred when a stray cow knocked a child into a gulch and the mayor of Momostenango issued a proclamation. The crier quoted the mayor's words from various hilltops, calling out to the people down below. His lengthenings are shown by repetitions of the affected vowels, his stable pitches by split levels within the lines of type, and his glissando by descending steps of type:

"Caquita ri wi ^{naaaaaaaak}

caquiyokuba' ri quiwa ^{caaax}

caquiyokuba' ri qui ^{quej}

caquiyokuba' ri qui ^{tz'i' "}

cacha ral ^{cáa} a

       a

        al

         de

          e

          e.

"The people ^{heeeeeeeear}

they tie up their ^{cooow}

they tie up their ^{horse}

they tie up their ^{dog"}

says the ^{maa} a

       a

        ay

         y

         o

         or.

Note that each line (and colon) corresponds to an independent clause. The three lines between the opening and closing lines constitute the three stichs of a triplet, but the transitions into the first line of this triplet and away from its third line are not marked differently from its internal transitions. In effect, the only unifying thing about the sheer *sound* of this triplet remains at the level of the phonemic repetitions that result from parallel syntax and the repetition of the verb.

In a general way each line in an announcement, up to the last one, is something like the opening line of Ajxub's prayer, with its emphatic incompleteness, and the last line is like his closing lines, in which the long-delayed drop in pitch that marks the end of a period is more pronounced than it would be in narrative or conversation. In both cases, even though a strictly syntactical treatment could divide the discourse into a number of sentences, it is delivered as a single period made up of various cola. Sometimes a crier speeds up at the end of an announcement, just as Ajxub speeds up as he moves through a prayer, by increasing the length of the final line. In the following example of such a line, two cola are run together:

"roxej Wéves Cajib ^{Iiik' "} cach'a ral ^{cáa} a

               a

                al

                 de

                  e

                  e.

"three days frrom now Thursday Four ^{Wiiind"} says the ^{maa} a

                            a

                             ay

                               y

                                 o

                                 or.

In this example there is a further compression, even beyond the combination of two cola in a single line, in the sense that the first colon could be scanned as a triplet. It fixes the effective date of the mayor's proclamation in three different ways: "three days from now" (*roxej*), "Thursday" (*Wéves*), and "Four Wind" (*Cajib Ik'*), this last being a date from the 260-day cycle that forms the foundation of Maya calendrics. Although these three stichs are compressed into a single colon in actual delivery, while the colon in turn is compressed into a single line with the one that follows it, the resultant line remains consistent with other announcement lines on one point: It does not contain more than one verb.

In contemporary proclamations, the sender (the mayor) speaks about the addressee in the third person; for his part, the message bearer (the crier) quotes exactly what the sender said to him rather than switching into the second person. The same thing happens when messages are sent in Popol Vuh narratives, where they sometimes end up as double- and even triple-embedded quotations. But the Popol Vuh messages are all delivered to audiences of one or two people from close range and therefore do not call for the redundant wording, frequent pausing, and exaggerated intonations that characterize the performances of a crier. The crier's announcement quoted within de León's narrative and the actual announcement concerning stray animals both contain triplets in which a verb is repeated in each stich (and line) while a noun changes, but in the following sentence from a quoted message in the Popol Vuh (13r), a verb that has three parallel nouns as its object is given only once. It is the kind of sentence that might well be run off as a single line by de León:

> Chiquic'am c'u ulok ri quichokonisan, quibate, quipach'k'ab.

> And they must bring along their playthings, their yokes, their arm guards.

A form of oral delivery that stands in an intermediate position with respect to the prayers of professional singers like Ajxub and the announcements of a town crier may be found among the speeches made by actors in contemporary dramas. Since colonial times most such speeches have taken the form of flowery Spanish quatrains with a line-ending rhyme scheme (ABAB), recited in such a way as to give each rhyming word a semiterminal intonation followed by a pause, but a few speeches are in Quiché. The present example of a Quiché speech is from the Xajoj C'oy, or "Monkey Dance," as performed in Momostenango; it happens to be a prayer addressed by an actor to unseen gods rather than part of a conversation between two actors, but it is very much a part of the action of the drama. I take it as evidence for what dramatic speeches in general may have been like when they were all in Quiché. The intermediate style of its delivery befits the acoustical situation confronted by an actor in making himself heard by his audience.

At one end of the acoustic scale are the prayers of Ajxub and the narratives of Xiloj and de León, addressed to audiences of several nearby people; both kinds of performance are longer winded than those of a town crier. At the other end of the scale is the crier, with his short lines, sustained pitch levels, and lengthened vowels, calling to the people in the houses, patios, and streets below the hill where he stands. His long terminal glide, which is necessarily accompanied by diminishing amplitude (since he is running out of breath), signals people that they can stop straining to understand him; everyone knows all too well that his final words will be "says the mayor." The situation of the actors in the Monkey Dance falls in between. They attempt only to reach each other and those gathered immediately around them; outdoors and amid the general din of a crowded fiesta, it would be impossible for them to make themselves intelligible to everyone in the plaza, but they do make their voices carry farther than a singer reciting a prayer for clients standing right next to him.

The one Monkey Dance speech that is given in the Quiché language resembles public announcements in that all cola (except for those that end periods) are treated as independent lines, and in that nearly all lines that precede a period-ending line end with a rise. On the other hand, the speech resembles Ajxub's prayers in that the intonational pitches are not stabilized, and in that line-final rises are unaccompanied by lengthening. It is spoken by a character identified in the manuscript of the drama only as Viejo, or "Old Man," who has trapped a deer at this point in the action. The particular performance transcribed and translated here was given as a demonstration for tape-recording purposes by Paulino Ixchop, who is the *tijonel* 'teacher' for the Monkey Dance and possesses a copy of its manuscript. He knows all the parts by heart, but he prefers to have the text open in front of him while he recites.[8] He delivers the speech in two separate periods; as with the opening section of many a prayer in contemporary "real life," the first period deals with the celestial deities (which today largely coincide with the Christian pantheon):

Jesus María Joséfa,	Jesus Mary Joseph,
pa ri Dios Kajawixel –	for God the Father –
i Dios C'ojolaxel –	and God the Son –
i Dios Uxlabixel –	and God the Breath –
i Dios Espíritu Sántos amen, Jesus i María.	and God Holy Spirit amen, Jesus and Mary.

Note that the first line is a triplet with three stichs, recited as a single unbroken colon. The joining of three proper names in Quiché, divine or otherwise, predates the coming of the Christian trinity; again and again the Popol Vuh text joins the three names of the patron deities of the leading Quiché lineages together, and they may well have been recited as a single colon rather than three cola: "Tojil Awilix Jacawitz." The present triplet suggests that in speaking of singular or unparalleled introductory phrases in Quiché discourse, we should rather speak of singular or unparalleled *lines*. The present line has an *internal* parallelism, one that Ixchop deemphasizes by treating all three stichs as a single colon, but the parallel stichs that follow it are quite different in syntax, pausing, and intonation.

There is a tension between the last two lines: in one sense the words *i Dios Espíritu Sántos*, in the last line, constitute the second stich of a couplet, produced by means of a code switch from Quiché to Spanish, but in another way the words of the penultimate line, *i Dios Uxlabixel*, form a triplet with the two preceding lines. The words of the last four lines (up to *amen* in the final line) might be scanned as a quatrain, but the extra words added to the final line (from *amen* to the end) set the whole of that line apart on the Spanish side of the code switch. The increased length of the last line recalls Ajxub's tendency to accelerate, except that the acceleration has been held back until the very end of a period, just as it was in the case of the crier's announcement that ended with two cola in a single line.

The second of the two periods in Ixchop's speech, like the second part of many contemporary real-life prayers, deals with the earthly deities; a third period (if the present speech had one) would be devoted (like the earlier of the prayers quoted from Ajxub) to the ancestors. Note that the first line is without parallel, which fits the general pattern for introductory lines in Quiché discourse; in this case, unlike that of the introductory line of the previous period, it is also without internal parallelism. The fifth line completes a sentence but is given the same emphatic incompleteness as the lines before and after it; the sixth line serves as the unparalleled introduction for a further sentence.

Wacamic –	Today –
quimban ri nuchac –	I'm doing my work –
ri nupatan –	my service –
chupam Lok'olaj Juyub –	within the Sacred Mountain –
chupam Lok'olaj Tak'aj –	Within the Sacred Plain –
xewi pu lo –	and furthermore –
xinc'olibej junrakan balam –	I trapped one jaguar –
junrakan coj –	one puma –
junrakan masat –	one deer –
ri' mixinc'olibej –	that's what I've trapped –
chuwa Lok'olaj Juyub –	before the Sacred Mountain –
chuwa Lok'olaj Tak'aj –	before the Sacred Plain –
tan la ri Dios –	forgive it God –
Kajawixel –	the Father –
Dios C'ojolaxel –	God the Son –
Dios Espíritu Sántos, amen Jesus.	God Holy Spirit, amen Jesus.

Unless we count "amen Jesus" in the last line as the fourth stich in a quatrain, this passage never joins two successive stichs in the same line, whether they belong to the same couplet or triplet or to different ones; in this it is very different from Ajxub's prayers. But as in the first period of the present speech (except for its first line), the transition from one stich of a couplet or triplet to another is not marked differently from the transition between one couplet or triplet and the next.

Note that the first stich of the couplet occurring in the second and third lines above is seamlessly joined to the verb of which it is the object, as is the first stich of the triplet in the seventh to ninth lines. Except in the third and fourth lines from the end, where a noun phrase is split between two lines, the transition from one line to the next never occurs within a verb phrase, noun phrase, or prepositional phrase. In those two lines it is as if the opposite gravitational pulls of the verb phrase (*tan la*) and the parallelism that follows it had torn the stich consisting of *Dios Kajawixel* in half. Here is another example of syncopation, first noted above in the case of one of de León's two quatrains, only this time both a line break and a colon boundary have been displaced to the middle of a stich.

In general, the paradigmatic or vertical movement of verse in this speech from the Monkey Dance is limited to producing two or three parallel stichs before the syntagmatic or horizontal force of prose moves the next group of stichs forward within the particular independent clause or sentence of which it is a part, creating a diagonal trajectory. Ajxub's real-life prayers also have diagonal passages, but these are combined with lengthly vertical runs that are absent here. Passages in which the forces of verse and prose continue to be approximately balanced in the making of two or more independent clauses or sentences in succession are practically nonexistent in the dialogues within contemporary narratives, and they are quite rare in the narrative dialogues of the Popol Vuh as well. For a close structural analog to Ixchop's Monkey Dance speech we must turn instead to the text of the ancient drama called "Man from Rabinal."

The Rabinal speeches, like contemporary prayers and announcements, frequently open with the naming of the addressee; the naming is sometimes double, but more often it is triple, as it is in the Monkey Dance speech already quoted. In the following excerpt (Brasseur 1862:112), a Rabinal lord with the calendrical name Job Cawuk, or "Five Rains," speaks to the person he triply names ("Brave Man" and "Cawek" and "Quiché Person") in the first line, a captive warrior who will soon be sacrificed by priests costumed as eagles and jaguars. I have joined stichs together in the same line only in the opening line and at the closes of two of the periods.

Oyew Achi Cawek Qu'eche Winak,	Brave Man Cawek Quiché Person,
La cach'a na c'u ri atzij –	Are these the words you speak —
chuwach caj –	before the sky –

chuwach ulew –
"Chincajta na chi ech la –
ri cablajuj uk'anal cot –
uk'anal balam."
Cach'a ri tzij la –
canuya ba chi ech la –
ri cablajuj uk'anal cot –
uk'anal balam –
ri' caraij la –
ri' catz'onoj la –
chi nuchi', chi nuwach.
Ix bala nucot –
nubalam –
chibana c'o ta –
quel ri oyew achi –
quixretz'abej ulok –
chupam ral uch'ab –
chupam ral upocob –
chi cajpa, chi cajxucutal.

before the earth –
"Lend me what is yours sir –
the twelve yellow eagles –
yellow jaguars."
Since you speak these words sir –
I give you what is yours sir –
the twelve yellow eagles –
yellow jaguars –
just what you wanted, sir –
just what you requested, sir –
right in my teeth, in front of me.
Come on my eagles –
my jaguars –
let it be done –
the brave man comes out –
he plays a game with you here –
closed in by darts –
closed in by shields –
from all four directions, from all four
corners.

We could go on seeking analogies between contemporary Quiché discourse and that found in texts from the early colonial period, but it is already possible to venture some general statements. Despite what appears to be an extreme contrast in delivery between the discourse of the town crier and the dramatic actor, on the one hand, and that of the professional prayermaker, on the other, there is a common unifying force at work from one end of the spectrum of Quiché discourse to the other. At both extremes, most lines end with an incomplete intonational contour that serves to join one line to the next; even a line that could be reckoned as completing a sentence may be treated in this way. The very short lines that predominate in the discourse of the crier and actor, which could have a fragmenting effect, are bridged by emphatically incomplete intonational contours, while the longer lines that provide continuity in the discourse of the prayermaker require only mildly incomplete contours.

In the matter of scansion there is again a tendency to unification. Whether most parallel stichs get lines to themselves, as with the crier and actor, or are run together to form long lines, as with the prayermaker, the boundary between one couplet or triplet and the next is given the same treatment, more often than not, as the boundary between two successive stichs within a couplet or triplet. Where scansion is ambiguous the manner of delivery may leave the ambiguity intact, as it does when Ajxub unifies five stichs that have an uncertain triplet–couplet boundary by treating them as a single line with five identically intoned cola. Where stichs consist of uninflected nouns the unifying force may eliminate the marking of cola and lines between them, even in an actor's speech, the case in point being Ixchop's "Jesus Mary Joseph" triplet. And where two uninflected nouns total no more than four syllables, even the boundary between words may disappear, as in the case of *cajulew* 'sky-earth'.

In a context where stichs, cola, and lines are generally in close coincidence, the unifying force may take the form of syncopation. Near the end of Ixchop's dramatic speech, the line break and colon boundary that might have fallen after "forgive it," neatly marking off "God the Father" as the first stich in a triplet, are displaced to a position between "forgive it God" and "the Father," uniting "God" with the unparalleled verb of which it is the subject. In the solitary example of a relatively long parallel run in narrative, where de León follows a quatrain with a triplet, he neatly marks the first three stichs of the quatrain as both cola and lines, but then displaces his next line break to a position in the midst of the fourth stich. Then, not content with merely uniting the remaining part of the last stich of the quatrain with the first stich of the triplet, he runs off the entire triplet before reaching his next line break.

It is near the beginning of major segments of discourse delivered by the actor or prayermaker, where parallelism is just getting under way, or in the midst of a narrative, where a brief paradigmatic interlude may modify a predominantly syntagmatic movement, that a couplet, triplet, or quatrain is most likely to be rendered in a way that simultaneously calls attention to its internal unity and cleanly separates it from the surrounding discourse. In Ajxub's prayer to the ancestors, "all six generations, / all six jarsfull" contrasts with all the couplets that follow it in being given two full lines to itself, and the next couplet, "all mothers, all fathers," contrasts with all the other couplets of the prayer in taking the form of one line with two cola. In de León's narrative, the quatrain concerning the animals that reduced people to skeletons is set off as a single line with four cola, though its internal unity is somewhat disturbed by the fact that a period-ending intonation marks not only the last stich but the third one as well.

The periods of the Quiché prayer, announcement, and dramatic speech are always opened by lines that display some kind of singularity, and this is often the case with narrative periods as well. Singularity may take the form of a purely syntagmatic movement, producing a phrase that is unlike other phrases in having no parallel, or it may take the form of an intonational contour not heard in any other line in the period, or both. The incompleteness of contour in an opening line takes its strongest form in the case of the public announcement, where the pitch of the final syllable is not only raised but drawn out, more so than in the case of succeeding lines; a less emphatic incompleteness, with a rise but without lengthening, marks off the opening line of Ajxub's prayer to the ancestors and constrasts it with the mild falls that mark the following lines. In the narratives of Xiloj and de León, incompleteness in opening lines takes the form of a simple interruption of contour, without a rise or a fall.

In the case of the opening lines of the two periods in Ixchop's dramatic speech, there seems to be an economy that balances off singularity of phrasing against singularity of intonation. The line that opens the first period begins with a triplet rather than with a singular phrase, but it contrasts with succeeding lines in ending with a mild drop in pitch rather than a rise. The reverse is true of the line that opens the second period: It has the same rise that marks the lines that follow it, but it contrasts with those lines in its lack of participation in parallelism. In Quiché opening lines in general, whatever the details, an incompleteness of contour reaches forward to what follows; when Ixchop opens with a three-word triplet or Ajxub opens with a line that includes half a potential couplet, the parallelism that follows each of these openings reaches backward.

Let it be said that what those who read are apt to tear asunder, those who speak may join together. What looks like two words may sound like one, what looks like three one-word stichs may have the sound of a single colon, colon and line boundaries may sustain an ambiguity of scansion rather than resolving it, the eight stichs that make up four couplets may be treated as eight identical cola and run off in a single line, the end of a perfect sentence may be marked by an emphatically incomplete intonation, and so forth. It is also sometimes true that what those who read are apt to join together, those who speak may tear asunder, as when initial particles with meanings like "and this," or proper nouns that are introduced into a narrative for the first time, are given lines all to themselves. Such are the lessons to be learned when the ear of the ethnopaleographer is tuned to the contouring and pacing of actual performances.

The lessons with which we began this exploration, in which ambiguously written words were made phonetically clear with the help of a contemporary speaker of Quiché, are less of a departure from ordinary linguistic research than the lessons concerning the larger dimensions of oral performance. But there are two major considerations that unite the lexical and performance aspects of ethnopaleographic work. The first is that both aspects require collaborators whose competencies go beyond those of an ordinary native speaker of a language. The Popol Vuh and the Rabinal Achi are not mere collections of lexical items and sample sentences, but are works of art that are shaped by specialized performance skills and filled with specialized knowledge of the world of experience. The second consideration is that both aspects of ethnopaleographic work serve the end of understanding the meaning of ancient texts.

The contribution to meaning made by the solution of lexical problems is obvious, but it remains on a rather concrete level. The contribution made by the recovery of contouring and pacing, on the other hand, has potential implications of a more general nature. It might have turned out that oral performance intensified structural partitions of the kind that can be read in

Quiché texts; for example, the first stich of each couplet might have carried a rise and the second a fall, and there might have been a pause between the second stich of each couplet and the first stich of the next. Every line of a Quiché announcement (and not just the last) might have been treated as a complete period, as happens in some forms of Zuni oratory (D. Tedlock 1983:chap. 6). Instead, the Quiché performer tends to downplay structural partitions.

What I have called the unifying force in Quiché discourse is intelligible in terms of Quiché philosophy and religion. Quichés are dialectitians, but they understand proper dualities to be complementary rather than opposed, interpenetrating rather than mutually exclusive (B. Tedlock 1982:176–7). The "sky" and "earth" of *cajulew* are joined by a mutual attraction, though a structuralist might regard them as opposites. From a Quiché point of view the relationship between these two terms is different in degree, but not in kind, from the relationship between near-synonyms such as those in Ajxub's "this work, this service." Quiché triads come about not through the introduction of an ambiguous mediating term, but through the addition of a further shade of difference, as in de León's triplets combining "mayor," "manager," and "staff bearer," or through the addition of a third term that encompasses the other two, as in Ajxub's "world where the sun rises, world where the sun sets, all worlds."

I hope the present effort will be taken as an invitation by all who deal with New World native-language texts from the past. If sound recordings can help us hear a voice in the Popol Vuh, a Quiché Maya text that first took alphabetic form more than four hundred years ago, they can help us with the vast corpus of ancient texts from other Mesoamerican languages, to say nothing of North American texts taken down in dictation not so long ago. Ethnopaleographic enterprises are properly part of a larger reshaping of anthropological and linguistic field research along dialogical, collaborative lines, only in this case even the dead will be heard from.

Notes

The research that made this chapter possible was supported, in part, by a fellowship and translation grant from the National Endowment for the Humanities. I have benefited from discussions with Joel Sherzer, Barbara Tedlock, and Anthony Woodbury.
1 Parenthetical Popol Vuh references are to the manuscript, which is reproduced in Ximénez 1973 and accurately paleographed in Schultze Jena 1944; "r" and "v" refer to the recto and verso of a folio. In quotations from the texts of the Popol Vuh and the Rabinal Achi and in transcriptions from my own field tapes I have adopted the Quiché orthography currently in use in Guatemala, except in a later passage discussing the orthography of the Popol Vuh manuscript. The five vowels are approximately like those of Spanish; I have dispensed with a lax-tense distinction

that is missing in colonial texts and carries only a small semantic load. The velar stop is *c* (before *a*, *o*, *u*) or *qu* (before *i*, *e*), and the uvular stop is *k*. With the following exceptions, the remaining consonants are as in Spanish: *b* is a glottalized *p*, *l* is like *ll* in Welsh "Lloyd," *tz* is like English *ts*, *w* is like English *w*, *x* is like English *sh*, and ' is the glottal stop, which glottalizes other consonants when it follows them. Stress is on the final syllable of a word except where marked by ´.

2   The only available version of the complete text of the Rabinal Achi is the one published by Brasseur (1862); Acuña has published a partial paleography of a colonial manuscript of the drama that is in the possession of a citizen of Rabinal (1975:181–4). The drama was performed only rarely even in Brasseur's time and scarcely at all during the past forty years; I know of no sound recording.

3   Harrington's transcription of the Popol Vuh text (n.d.), together with Gates's explanation of the manner in which it was made, are in the collection of Harrington's papers at the Smithsonian Institution, in the National Anthropological Archives.

4   See D. Tedlock (1977:507–8) for my argument on this topic. The only present-day performances of epics with long metrical runs come from folk traditions within larger literate cultures; epics from non-Islamic Africa are not metrical. Claims for the antiquity and oral pristineness of the Homeric and Vedic texts rest on classical and brahmanical tradition.

5   The Spanish version of León-Portilla's *Pre-Columbian Literatures of Mexico* appeared in 1964.

6   This and subsequent English translations of the Popol Vuh text are taken, with minor changes, from my own complete translation of the work (D. Tedlock 1985).

7   In the Popol Vuh there are only a handful of Spanish words; Nahuatl is the major source of the foreign words occurring in the text, but there are no passages in which a simple code switch to Nahuatl is used to fill out a parallelistic scheme. This suggests that despite all that has been said about Nahuatl influence on the culture of the Quiché elite during the centuries immediately preceding the Spanish conquest, the members of the Quiché nobility who wrote the Popol Vuh were not bilingual in Nahuatl.

8   Bode, who dealt with various teachers of the Quiché drama whose subject is the Spanish conquest, also reports recitals that were given from memory but in the presence of open manuscripts (1961:77).

References

Acuña, René. 1975. *Introducción al estudio del Rabinal Achí*. Instituto de Investigaciones Filológicas, Centro de Estudios Mayas, cuaderno 12. Mexico City: Universidad Nacional Autónoma de México.

Bode, Barbara. 1961. The Dance of the Conquest in Guatemala. In *The native theatre in Middle America*. Middle American Research Institute Publication 27. New Orleans: Tulane University, pp. 204–296.

Brasseur de Bourbourg, Charles Etienne. 1862. *Rabinal-Achi ou le drame-ballet du tun*. Collection de Documents dans les Langues Indigènes 2, pt. 2. Paris: Arthus Bertrand.

Burgess, Dora M. de, and Xec, Patricio. 1955. *Popol Wuj*. Quezaltenango: El Noticiero Evangélico.

Chávez, Adrián I. 1979. *Pop Wuj*. Mexico City: Ediciones de la Casa Chata.

Edmonson, Munro S. 1971. *The Book of Counsel: the Popol Vuh of the Quiché Maya of Guatemala*. Middle American Research Institute Publication 35. New Orleans: Tulane University.

Garibay K., Angel María. 1953. *Historia de la literatura nahuatl*. Mexico City: Porrua.

Harrington, J. P. N.d. Popol wuh. Manuscript (1922) in the Harrington collection at the National Anthropological Archives, Smithsonian Institution, Washington, D.C.

Hymes, Dell. 1980. Particle, pause, and pattern in American Indian narrative verse. *American Indian Culture and Research Journal* 4(4):7–51.

1981. *"In vain I tried to tell you": essays in Native American ethnopoetics*. Philadelphia: University of Pennsylvania Press.

León-Portilla, Miguel. 1969. *Pre-Columbian literatures of Mexico*. Norman: University of Oklahoma Press.

Mace, Carroll Edward. 1970. *Two Spanish–Quiché dance-dramas of Rabinal*. Tulane Studies in Romance Languages and Literature 3. New Orleans: Tulane University.

Schultze Jena, Leonhard S. 1944. *Popol Vuh: Das heilige Buch de Quiché-Indianer von Guatemala*. Stuttgart: W. Kohlhammer.

Tedlock, Barbara. 1982. *Time and the highland Maya*. Albuquerque: University of New Mexico Press.

1983. El c'oxol: un símbolo de las resistencia quiché a la conquista espiritual. In Robert M. Carmack and Francisco Morales Santos, eds., *Nuevas perspectivas sobre el Popol Vuh*. Guatemala City: Piedra Santa, pp. 343–357.

Tedlock, Dennis. 1977. Toward an oral poetics. *New Literary History* 8:507–519.

1983. *The spoken word and the work of interpretation*. Philadelphia: University of Pennsylvania Press.

1985. *Popol Vuh: the Mayan book of the dawn of life and the glories of gods and kings*. New York: Simon and Schuster.

Turco, Lewis. 1968. *The book of forms: a handbook of poetics*. New York: Dutton.

Wimsatt, W. K. 1972. *Versification*. New York: New York University Press.

Ximénez, Francisco. 1973. *Popol Vuh*. Facsimile edition with paleography and notes by Agustín Estrada Monroy. Guatemala City: José de Pineda Ibarra.

6

RHETORICAL STRUCTURE IN A CENTRAL ALASKAN YUPIK ESKIMO TRADITIONAL NARRATIVE

Anthony C. Woodbury

1. Rhetorical structure

In the last decade or so a number of scholars have discovered systems of recurrent hierarchic organization in Native American oral narrative and used them in creating line-and-verse poetic transcriptions and translations. An astonishingly diverse range of linguistic phenomena underlie their similar-looking transcriptions. For instance Dennis Tedlock, in his work on narrative in Zuni and later Quiché, starts a new line each time the speaker pauses, ending up with transcripts organized in terms of *pause phrasing* (Tedlock 1972, 1983, this volume). Joel Sherzer (1982, this volume) too has used pause phrasing to shape transcripts of Kuna discourse. A second, more extensive, phonological criterion is *prosodic phrasing*, defined in all languages by formal features of intonation and rhythm (see Halliday 1967; Selkirk 1984) and consisting of a hierarchy of prosodic units from words, to groups of words spoken with a unitary intonation contour, to periods, to prosodic paragraphs. It is used by, among others, William Bright (1979, 1980) in his transcriptions of Karok myth, by Sally McLendon (1982) for Eastern Pomo, by Ron Scollon for narrative in several Northern Athabaskan languages (Scollon 1979), and by me for Central Alaskan Yupik Eskimo (Woodbury 1984).

Very different from these phonological criteria for line-and-verse analysis are criteria of content and syntactic form. Dell Hymes (1981), in work with Chinookan and other (mostly) northwestern American narrative recorded from dictation, makes use of *syntactic constituency*, according a line to each clause or other unitary predication and then building on this by locating larger units in global patterns of parallelism and recurrence in content, lexical choice, syntactic form, and (when present) use of adverbial particles with meanings like "and then," "so," and "now again." I will call this *global form–content parallelism*, and recognize *adverbial-particle phrasing* as an important subcase within it. In summary, there are at least five potentially independent types of recurrent, hierarchic organization on which poetic representation has been based: pause phrasing, prosodic phrasing, syntactic constitutency, global form–content parallelism, and adverbial-particle phrasing.

In many oral texts these organizations do not coincide. In such circumstances line-and-verse transcription then forces a choice, since a single transcription (or translation) cannot make opposing organizations overt simultaneously. Perhaps because of this limitation of the medium, there has been a tendency to take one type of organization as more central to verbal artistry and discourse structure than the others. For example, Tedlock has argued for the primacy of pause phrasing while Hymes has regarded syntactic constituency and global form–content parallelism as more basic (Tedlock 1977; Hymes 1977). The issue may be mitigated when organizations happen to coincide, as Bright (1979, 1980) has shown for prosodic versus adverbial particle phrasing in some Karok narratives, but the basic problem must still be addressed.

It seems to me one should not have to make such choices, for it is quite clear that each type of organization mentioned carries out major communicative functions. Thus Tedlock has demonstrated that pause phrasing – as well as prosodic phrasing and such auditory features as loudness, pitch, and voice quality – is part of the basic texture, artistry, and ambience of individual Zuni and Quiché narrative performances, inseparable from the lexical and syntactic face of any text one hopes fully to understand. On quite a different level, McLendon and I have argued that prosodic phrasing – along with syntactic constituency and adverbial-particle phrasing – organizes information in Eastern Pomo and Central Alaskan Yupik Eskimo discourse by introducing cohesion and disjunction (cf. Chafe 1980 and Halliday and Hasan 1976 for related discussion of English). Yet another significant linguistic function that has been implicated is the regulation of back and forth in interactive discourse: It has been argued that pause phrasing does this in Kuna (Sherzer 1982, 1983, this volume) and prosodic and adverbial particle phrasing do it in two Northern Athabaskan languages (Scollon 1979) and Central Alaskan Yupik Eskimo (Woodbury 1985). Finally Hymes has suggested that global form–content parallelism reveals a type of literary and conceptual organization that he has called "underlying rhetorical form," governed by a "logic of narrative action" (Hymes 1980b, this volume). All of these – the texture and ambience of performance, the organization of information, the regulation of interactive discourse, and the logic of narrative action – are critical elements in verbal art as well as in linguistic communication more widely. It follows then that an adequate approach to discourse form would accommodate each equally. As a corollary, no one line-and-verse representation can be wholly adequate, given the many competing dimensions of meaningful form present in a single narrative performance.

This point is made all the more compelling when one considers that not just the competing organizations themselves, but their interactions with one another, may be communicatively significant. Hence Hymes (1980b), while still insisting on his primacy argument, has suggested that pause and/or adverbial-particle phrasing may create a further expressive dimension when it operates in counterpoint to global parallelism. And Tedlock (this volume), while still taking speaking versus silence as the fundamental opposition, carefully points out the value of such interaction in Quiché, devoting considerable attention to all five of the types of organization cited above (see also Tedlock 1983:55–61 on enjambment). If interaction is meaningful, then it certainly cannot make sense to focus on one type of organization at the expense of the others, for interaction presupposes communicative unity among formally distinct and logically separate types of organization.

My central claim in this chapter is that such organizations are equal components in a larger whole I call *rhetorical structure* (see also Woodbury 1983, 1985).[1] Specifically, I take a rhetorical structure *component* to be any well-defined recurrent, hierarchic organization that is present in a stretch of discourse and distinct from other such organizations. By "recurrent, hierarchic organization" I mean something similar to what Jakobson (1960:358) meant in his well-known formal definition of the "poetic function" of language as that which "projects the principle of equivalence from the axis of selection into the axis of combination." (Cf. also Hymes 1981 and Silverstein 1981, 1985a, which explore different linguistic implications of Jakobson's formula for discourse study.) In spite of Jakobson's use of the term "function," it should be realized that his definition (as well as mine) actually describes a class of purely formal objects, independent of the linguistic functions they may ultimately serve.

Given this broad definition for them, rhetorical-structure components will be of many diverse types, encompassing many different kinds of phenomena. The recurrence (or "equivalence") in "recurrent, hierarchic organizations" could be framed in poetic lines or verses, or in phrases, clauses, sentences, or episodes. And the recurrent material itself could be as concrete as the repeated words in a case of lexical parallelism, or it could be as abstract as the finite set of basic English sentence structures repeated over and over in any piece of English discourse. We generally regard the more concrete instances as properties of speaking, and the more abstract instances as properties of grammar, although the difference is ultimately one of degree. Thus in a given stretch of discourse some rhetorical-structure components will be particular to the text, some attributable to genres or subcodes, and some general in the grammar of the language as a whole. (The notion of "hierarchy" intended here is developed in later sections.)

In practice, this definition would identify prosodic phrasing, pause phrasing, and syntactic constituency as the minimum rhetorical-structure components in nearly any discourse, since it is difficult to think of discourse without them (except that songs and chants using nonsense words have prosodic and pause phrasing but may lack syntactic constituency). Adverbial-particle phrasing and global form–content parallelism, the other organizations cited earlier, would be identified as separate components only in those discourses in which they occur.[2]

One prediction that the notion of rhetorical structure makes is that rhetorical-structure components in texts, genres, and languages will be isolable and formally distinct, that is, that rhetorical structure will be *modular*. But the notion also predicts (or at least implies) that rhetorical structure will be more than just an array of similarly organized but otherwise unrelated modules, that is, that rhetorical-structure components in texts and in languages will somehow *interact*. That interaction may be of two major kinds. One is *formal* interaction, in which units from distinct components align with each other in a predictable way. An example of this is the reinforcement Bright found between prosodic and adverbial-particle phrasing in Karok narrative. Another kind of interaction is interaction of several components toward a single *communicative* end. In this case, alignments of units from distinct components may not be predictable. Instead, each different allowable alignment would convey a different meaning. Tedlock's and Hymes's examples of enjambment, where alternative alignments of pause phrases and syntactic constituents have different dramatic and rhetorical force, illustrate this. Empirical investigations of rhetorical structure in many languages and genres must seek both of these kinds of interaction. If the search fails and if relations between components turn out to be essentially arbitrary, then it will be enough for us to recognize each rhetorical-structure component as entirely separate. But the more the various kinds of interaction are found, the stronger the argument becomes for a larger, interrelated system of systems.

As a model, rhetorical structure involves autonomous components that segment the stream of speech simultaneously into different kinds of units according to different kinds of criteria. The ways in which units in those components can align, or do align, constitute their interaction. In recent years, the idea of simultaneous autonomous components in linguistic structure has become increasingly fruitful in explaining patterns of linguistic form. It was pioneered by Goldsmith (1976) for the relationship between segmental phonology and tone (among other things) with an approach that has come to be known as "autosegmental phonology," and for the relationship among intonation, prosody, and syntax by Liberman (1978). It was then extended to the relationship of phonology to morphology by McCarthy (1981), Halle and Vergnaud (1980), and others, and most recently to the relationship of morphology to syntax by Sadock (1985). Rhetorical structure represents an attempt to extend this type of approach to discourse. However, because of the nature of discourse and our relative ignorance of it, there are some differences in the way rhetorical structure should be understood. The approaches above are all *theories* of linguistic structure in the sense that they include general principles predicting exactly how the autonomous components they deal with may and may not align in natural languages. But rhetorical structure as I am proposing it here is a theory only in the sense that it predicts *that* there will be autonomous components in discourse and *that* they will somehow interact in the ways outlined above. Beyond that, it is intended more as a *framework* for textual (including grammatical) description that may serve as a basis for inductive, phenomenon-oriented theory building. I conceive it in this way partly because we are concerned here with a relatively neglected area of language use and grammatical form, and partly too because the ratio of variability to universality across languages, cultures, and genres is likely to be much higher here than for core areas of grammar.

My goal in what follows is to support the basic claims of a notion of rhetorical structure and to elaborate the framework it provides by considering a Central Alaskan Yupik Eskimo (hereafter CAY) *quliraq* (traditional tale) as an extended example. I will isolate and justify its major rhetorical-structure components on strictly internal grounds (to avoid circularity), emphasizing modularity. Then, once each component is identified, I will demonstrate its interactions with the components previously isolated. This second step supports the claim that rhetorical structure is more than the sum of its parts. At the same time, it provides insights into the nature of interaction among components, and the textual and pragmatic meaning of that interaction, which I think are of considerable general interest.

The *quliraq* to be considered is Evon Mezak's *Tutgara'urluqelriik* (Grandchild and Grandmother), presented in the Appendix in its entirety. I chose it because it has, along with the basic prosodic phrasing, pause phrasing, and syntactic constituency discernible in any CAY discourse, a special type of global form–content parallelism manifested in recurrent groupings of three and five. Hymes (1981) has discovered this and other types of numerically constrained parallelism elsewhere in North America, but it has not previously been reported for any Eskimo narrative. It is especially important to scrutinize the relationship of numerically constrained form–content parallelism to other rhetorical-structure components, since it has occupied an important role in the recent work on North American oral literature represented in this book and elsewhere, and its status has been controversial.

CAY is one of five languages in the Yupik branch of Eskimo. It is spoken in southwestern Alaska from Norton Sound to Bristol Bay along the coast and for some distance up the major rivers of the region. At present there are around 18,000 Yupiit in the region, about 13,000 of whom speak the language. They live mainly in village groups of under 500 with mixed subsistence and cash economies. (Bethel, with a native population of ca. 3,000, is an exception.) Important reference works on the language include Jacobson 1984, Miyaoka 1983, and Reed et al. 1977. Mezak's *quliraq* is in a variety of the General Central Yupik (GCY) dialect of CAY, one of four now spoken. This work is directly based on fieldwork done in Bethel in 1983 and 1984 with other GCY speakers, and indirectly on fieldwork on the Hooper Bay–Chevak dialect done in Chevak in 1978, 1980, and 1983.

A note on interdisciplinary context is in order. Part of the wonder of rhetorical structure is that it is a relatively difficult-to-analyze aspect of language that nevertheless makes an enormous contribution to textual meaning and verbal art. As such, it holds interest for all serious interpreters of oral text, including literary scholars, cultural anthropologists, and folklorists. But in order to undestand it in texts from other cultures, we must first know what it is, how to find it, and what to expect of it. This is the goal toward which I am working here. To meet it in a scientifically useful way, it is necessary that I give analyses detailed enough to be replicated, and formulations explicit enough to be falsified (although in doing so, I will try not to presume more than a very basic linguistic background). Amidst this detail, I will still try to emphasize the importance of rhetorical structure to textual interpretation by using it as a route to a rudimentary literary interpretation of Mezak's *quliraq*. Although I will probably fail to convey a full native's appreciation of this work to nonnative readers, I do hope (limited by my own nonnative understanding) to convey enough so as to give a sense of curiosity about rhetorical structure and to make clear my hope that it will be attended to with the care and detail that it deserves, from a range of disciplinary perspectives.

2 Some basic components of CAY rhetorical structure in Evon Mezak's *Tutgara'urluqelriik*

In this section I will consider four basic components of CAY rhetorical structure in Evon Mezak's *Tutgara'urluqelriik*: prosodic phrasing, pause phrasing, syntactic constituency, and adverbial-particle phrasing. I begin by presenting a detailed analysis of CAY prosodic phrasing on its own terms, showing that a hierarchy of prosodic units is inherent in the text and can be defined without reference to such other rhetorical structure features as syntactic constituency (sect. 2.1). From there I will discuss the other three, first independently and then in terms of their interactions with components previously discussed (sects. 2.2–4).

2.1 Prosodic phrasing

CAY prosodic phrasing consists of a basic hierarchy of *lines, subgroups, groups,* and *sections*.[3] In the Appendix, lines are transcribed as lines of print, groups as print verses (with arabic numbering above), and sections as stanzas (separated from each other with three asterisks). Groups may be *simple* or *complex*. A complex group consists of two or more *subgroups*. In transcription, the first line of each subgroup begins at the left margin, with following lines successively further indented. For example, [6] is a complex group with two subgroups and [18] a complex group with three (the second and third having only one line each). Simple groups such as [1–5] contain a single subgroup.

All of these units – lines, subgroups, groups, and sections – are signaled through intonation, rhythm, and other aspects of prosody in ways that are intuitively clear to native listeners and yet are challenging to describe precisely.

(It is now suggested that the reader read through the English translation of Mezak's *quliraq* before proceeding.)

Lines are stretches of speech terminated by characteristic pitch sequences and followed usually, but not always, by pauses. They are not restricted to single words, nor do they pertain to any one level of syntactic constituency. As in most languages (Bolinger 1978), a relatively high pitch at the end of a line indicates that the speaker has more to say, while a lower (or steeply falling) pitch indicates that nothing more need follow. This allows us roughly to define subgoups – whether occurring in simple or in complex groups – as the units that continue after a higher terminal pitch and end after a lower terminal pitch.

Let us consider this in Mezak's group [1], a simple group – and hence also a single subgroup – whose three lines are repeated in Ex. (1) (pause length between lines is given in angled brackets):

(1) (= [1])

Nunát ˄ukut ⟨0.⟩	úitaúrá'rqélriit ⟨0.⟩	kúigém ˄cęñíini. ⟨2.8⟩
village this	which.lay	river's on.its.bank
There was once a village	which lay	on the bank of a river.

Each line has a discrete intonation contour (represented above the text with a leading vertical staff). Each contour rises and then falls. The second contour is aligned with a single word; the first and third, with two. (The intonational clisis this creates is indicated in transcription with a ligature (ˆ).) Notice that only the last line is followed by a pause, but all end with characteristic terminal pitches. At the end of the last line there is a steep fall beginning at the last stressed syllable. (Stress, which is assigned by automatic rules, is marked here with acute accent.) This falling terminal pitch characterizes *core* contours and (as noted) indicates that nothing need follow in the subgroup. At the ends of the other two lines pitch still falls after the last stress, but to a much lesser extent. Little or no final fall is characteristic of *lead* contours, which indicate that there is something more to follow in the subgroup. I symbolize lead and core contours with A and B respectively. For example the three-contour sequence aligned with the three lines in (1) is A – A – B. We will call that the *contour pattern* of (1). Contour patterns for all subgroups in the Appendix are shown to the right of the CAY text.

Since leads mean that more is to come and cores mean that nothing need follow, we should expect all A's to precede all B's in any subgroup's contour pattern. The exact sequencing is specified by the following, which refers to subtypes of the two basic contours. It serves as a precise description of well-formed subgroups:

(2) $(A_-) - A* - B(+) - B°*$
(Read $X*$ as "any number of lines (including zero) with final contour type X".

(2) says that such sequences as $A_- - A - B$, $A - A - B+ - B°$, and B would be well-formed subgroup contour patterns, but that $A_- - B - B$, A, and B – A would not. As the reader may verify, all but two of the subgroups in the text conform to it (cf. note 6). The unannotated lead (A) and core (B) contours shown in (2) are already familiar. (2) also indicates that the first line in a subgroup may optionally be a *low lead* (A_-), where the entire contour has low-level pitch. While we might expect such low pitch to be interpreted as a B-type contour, low leads are clearly A-type contours because they occur initially, introduce shifts in time or action, and often occur with initial adverbial and expressive particles like *tua=i* 'well, now, then' and *Aren!* 'Oh!' Examples are found at the beginnings of [4, 6, 13, 15, 16, 19, 20, 23, 27, 29, 33, 34, 42, 54, 57, 74]. The first – and usually only – core in a subgroup is either an ordinary core (B) or an *emphatic core* $(B+)$. An emphatic core has a terminal fall greater than that of an ordinary core and often is preceded by a greater than ordinary rise. It functions as an emphatic closure for a subgroup or larger unit (see discussion of sections below), or may introduce direct speech, as in [5] and [43]. Finally, subgroups may end with any number of *core supplements* (B°), which echo the contour of the entire preceding core line and often have attenuated pitch range or amplitude.[4] The B° contour marks phrases as additions, supplements, or afterthoughts, including (but not limited to) appositional modifiers and constituents postposed by syntactic transformations. It occurs only in [54] and [63] in this text, the former of which is repeated in (3). (In this and following examples, the English gloss consists of calques only. For free translations, see the Appendix. Exclamation point (!) marks added exclamatory intonation, described below.)

(3) (= [54, subgroup 2])

Nutaan ˆatam	!A	Voila! Hey!
angalkungciqialriakut,	!B	we.are.going.to.get.a.sha-man,
alailngurmek,	!B°	who.can.be.seen
tuunralegmeg alail-ngurmek!	!B°	spirit.owner who.can.-be.seen!

The two core supplement lines contain three nominal elements in apposition: an adjectival participle (*alailngurmek*), a noun (*tuunralegmeg*), and the adjectival participle again. All three modify *angalkuq* 'shaman', which is incorporated in the participial verb in the second line.

It will be noted that the class of units that (2) defines – subgroups – corresponds usually to one but occasionally to two or three morphosyntactic sentences (transcribed in the Appendix with initial capitalization and final period). More will be said about this in section 2.3.

Complex groups contain two or more subgroups obeying (2). They are bound together by intonational parallelism, rhythm, downdrift, emphatic core (B+) contours, or a combination of these. For example:

(4) ([34])

Aa^h!	!A_ ⟨0.4⟩	Oh!
Tutgara'urlullraam pikili-		Poor.little.grandson said.-
kek:	B ⟨0.5⟩	to.them:
"Aa^h ^kitaki ^tua=i anitek!	!B ⟨0.9⟩	"Oh! ^please ^then go.out!
An'ariatek!	!B ⟨0.6⟩	It.is.time.you.go.out!
Canritutek!"	!B ⟨1.9⟩	There's.nothing.more.for.-you!"

This complex group has four subgroups, each clearly ending in a core contour. Nevertheless the last three of them, each just one line long, are bound together by intonational parallelism: In addition to sharing B-type terminal pitch, the bodies of the contours they bear are very similar in shape. At the same time, an overall rhythmic regularity binds together all five lines in the complex group in (4): Pause length between lines is short and regular (0.5 to 0.9 seconds), while the pause at the end of the group is much longer (1.9 seconds). Another interesting example of a complex group is:

(5) (= [22])

Aren:: peka!	!A ⟨1.4⟩	My! what.a.journey!
Ununrakun tekicami,	A ⟨1.0⟩	during.night when.he.-came.home,
tua=i nerurall'rarraar-		then poor.little.he.first.-
luni,	A ⟨1.1⟩	eating,
qasgiūrlurtuq.	B ⟨0.7⟩	poor.he.went.to.qas-giq.
Aren ^qasgiūrlurtur=am ^im',	A ⟨1.1⟩	My! ^poor.he.went.to.qasgiq.-but ^that
ik'iki tua=i ^tang angal-		Lots! then ^look they.had.-
kulilriit ^ukut!	!B+ ⟨0.6⟩	many.shamans ^those

This complex group has two subgroups. The emphatic core (B+) contour ending the second "outweighs" the plain core ending the first, implying a broader nonfinal-to-final progression between the subgroups. The relatively short pause (0.7 seconds) between the two subgroups also enhances the impression of unity.

So far, we have examined the prosodic basis for lines, subgroups, and (simple and complex) groups, and have identified five intonation contours: (plain) leads (A), low leads (A_), (plain) cores (B), emphatic cores (B+), and core supplements (B°). Nevertheless CAY intonation – and Mezak's remarkable use of it in this text – is far more complicated than it will be possible to describe here. Formally, lines may contain more than one contour (in which case the value for the whole line is reckoned as that of its final contour (cf. Woodbury 1985 for discussion of this for the HBC dialect).[5] Intonation is also complex in allowing numerous modifications of canonical contour types to express affective values and illocutionary force. A frequent such modification in this text is one that imparts exclamatory force, marked here with preceding !, as in !A_ and !B. (Contours so modified retain a significant initial rise but from there narrow the pitch range and transpose it upward relative to what is standard in declarative sentences.) Finally, there are many variations in tempo and voice quality – especially in direct quotation – which convey sociocultural and expressive dimensions of characters and their actions while at the same time reinforcing groups and other units. For example, in the *quliraq* Mezak uses a falsetto voice quality that is nothing short of phenomenal. Marked in the text and translation with italics, it is occasionally used in direct quotation, as one might expect, but is used most notably in the narrator's own voice to frame certain units of form–content parallelism and bring to them a delightful movement and humor (further discussed in sect. 4.1.1). Clearly, a study doing full justice to a work of CAY oral literature would have to take all such intonational complexities into account.

The *section* is the largest unit of prosodic phrasing I am able to isolate. The transition from one section to the next may be marked in several ways: (i) closure of the first section with an emphatic core (B+) contour; (ii) opening of the next section with a low lead (A_) contour; (iii) a sudden slowing of tempo. (i) – (ii) are easy to recognize in the transcript. (iii) is indicated there by length marks (:) on segments held especially long in the course of a general tempo slowing, e.g. $tua::=i^h$ in [4] from $tua=i$ 'then now'. The section-marking pattern of Mezak's *quliraq* is shown in (6), where numerals indicate the first group of each section; trailing + indicates a final B+ contour; leading _ indicates initial A_ (or B_)[6] contour; leading "s" indicates initial slowing; and parentheses indicate features occurring in quoted speech:

(6) 1 3 _s4+ 7+ 10+ 14 _16+ _s19 s22+ _s23 (s)24 _s27 _s33+ 36
     s40 _42(+) _s45 _s54+ _s57 s60+ (s)63 s69 _s71 s73+ s76

(6) shows that all section boundaries but the one at [3] are demarcated. (It is marked instead by a lead contour in the first line of [3] which rises to a high and relatively steady terminal pitch, a section-opening device common in other genres and dialects but infrequent in this text.)

Tempo slowing and A_ and B+ contours do not occur only at the edges of sections; they can also occur inside them, at times establishing section-internal parallelism by echoing primary section transitions. For example, the A_ contours on *Tua=i=ll'* 'well' in [29] and on Aa^h in [34] echo the A_ contours on *Aren tua::=i ˆaa* 'Oh my then' in [27] and on Aa^h in [33] respectively.

On the other hand, B+ contours sometimes mark provisional transitions within sections. In [42] the B+ contour looks as if it closes a section. But since the B+ contours in [43] and [44] repeat its pattern, it is best to take those two groups as supplements to the old section rather than as the start of a new one. (In section 4.1 we will find that these examples of anomalous A_ and B+ contours directly reinforce independent features of form–content parallelism.)

Another factor that complicates section marking is direct quotation: A_ and B+ contours and slowing of tempo may occur within quotes ([5, 6, 12, 15, 20, 21, 24, 54, 55, 61, 63, 67, 74]) without affecting the sectioning of the embedding narrative; and B+ contours sometimes introduce quotes, though only infrequently ([5, 43]) in Mezak's text. Once we recognize the section-internal contexts and uses of tempo slowing and A_ and B+ contours, we can better see how native listeners distinguish them from markers of section boundaries (see Woodbury 1985:159 for evidence that sections and other CAY prosodic units have reality for native speakers).

2.2   Pause phrasing

All CAY discourse is divided into alternating periods of speech and silence. In most narrative and conversation the pauses are long by English standards, giving English speakers an impression of slowness even when the pause phrases in between are spoken rapidly. This is clear when the Appendix translation is read in English using original pause times.

At very least, pausing implies a simple division of discourse into a series of pause phrases. But from there it would be an oversimplification to categorize pauses as either short or long, and based on that to define a discrete hierarchy consisting at the lowest level of pause phrases separated by the short pauses, and at a higher level of groupings of pause phrases separated by long pauses. Though such a move may be useful in analyzing material of a certain kind,[7] it would not grapple with the most basic fact of pause length, its *gradience*. In fact, there can be no discrete groupings of pause phrases. Pause phrasing instead shows a different kind of recurrent, hierarchic organization, here to be called *nondiscrete hierarchy*. There we observe not clear grouping but rather loose clustering of pause phrases, as when several of them are separated by shorter pauses and surrounded by longer ones, or when a series of them establish their unity by coming at rhythmically regular intervals over a stretch of time. Such units, which I will call *pause-phrase clusters*, are nondiscrete in the sense that rather than being simply present or absent in a stretch of discourse, they will be well defined and present to a greater or lesser degree.

In the rest of this section, we will concentrate on the interaction of pause phrasing and prosodic phrasing in Mezak's *quliraq*. The following is a partial hypothesis of that interaction:

(7) In the default case, lines and pause phrases will correspond one-to-one; when more than one line occurs in a pause phrase an impression of

rapidity, leading to a variety of special interpretations in context, will be conveyed.

(8) In the default case, subgroups and well-defined pause-phrase clusters will correspond one-to-one; that is, the pauses between lines within a subgroup will be roughly equal to each other but shorter than the pauses at the subgroup's edges. In nondefault cases, unusually short pauses will create cohesion while unusually long pauses will convey disjunction or, in connection with core (A) contours, dramatic anticipation (especially section-initially).[8]

In positing *defaults*, I am predicting that certain pause–prosody alignments will be unmarked, expected, and expressively neutral in ordinary contexts, while all others will be marked, motivated, and communicatively significant.

Some texts and genres – especially basic expository narrative – fit the defaults quite closely. In Mezak's highly complex and expressive *quliraq*, however, well-behaved groups are hard to find (but some good examples are [16, 20, 34, and 59]), and nondefault groups are abundant. By diverging from default pause–prosody relations they convey extra meaning.

For example, the default in (7) is overturned in [1] (quoted in (1)), giving an impression of rapidity typical to *quliraq* openings, which are formulaic (see sect. 3.2). It is overturned with different effect in:

(9) (= [68 subgroup 2])

| "Nengugciu! | ⟨0.⟩ | "Stretch.him! |
| Nenguciu atra'rrluku! | ⟨0.4⟩ | Stretch.him get.him.down! |

The lack of pause adds urgency and fierceness to the shaman's threats. Finally, the (7) default is overturned when a pause occurs line-medially in the middle of an intonation contour (not attested in Mezak's *quliraq*). While sometimes merely a "performance error," such pausing also has many expressive uses.

(8) sets a default of one-to-one correspondence between subgroups and clusters of pause phrases. That default is overturned when pauses between subgroups are shorter than those within them, creating cohesion among the subgroups. We saw this in (4), where the short pause between the two subgroups tightens the overall complex group. The (8) default is also overturned when an unusually long pause occurs group-internally. Following a lead (A) contour, such a pause imparts a sense of anticipation:

(10) (= [4])

Tua::=iʰ,	A_ ⟨1.4⟩	Well,
asgurturaqerluni,	A ⟨3.1⟩	him.traveling.upriver.a.-little.ways,
*qangqii*regnek,	A ⟨1.7⟩	two.*ptarmigan*,
callulriignek ˆ*tekituq*.	B ⟨1.8⟩	two.*fighting* ˆ*he.ar-rived.(at)*

The longest pause establishes suspense as the audience waits to hear of the protagonist's first experience in his trip upriver. This use of longer pauses is common at the beginnings of sections (see those beginning at [3, 4, 7, 10, 14, 16, 19, 22, 23, 27, 40, 42, 45, 73]), where it seems to accentuate the stage setting done in the initial lines by giving them time to sink in. It is undoubtedly related to the section-initial tempo slowing discussed in section 2.1.

Notice that (7) and (8) do not exhaust all possible prosody–pause relations. They say nothing of the absolute timing of pauses, and hence nothing of the overall tempo that pause phrasing may be expected to follow. These are choices within the pause-phrasing component which are entirely left to the speaker, and which, as tempo changes from group to group, have enormous expressive potential. It remains for future research to determine whether in fact further defaults are implicit in this apparent freedom. It is necessary too to allow for entirely extraneous influences on pausing, such as hesitation due to memory lapse, interruptions, and such afflictions as coughing. Even so, there is a fine line between what is part of narrative competence and what is an artifact of performance, as in the case of Mezak's coughing at the end of his story (see [55–6; 64–61]). The coughing is a fixed part of the story, as shown by the fact that it occurs in exactly the same places in the "Materials" performance (see the introduction to the Appendix): it is the grandson's excuse for avoiding another shamanistic display. Nevertheless at one point at least ([64–6]) the coughing gets out of hand and afflicts Mezak himself. (See sect. 3.5 for more on coughing.)

In summary, the pause-phrasing component of CAY rhetorical structure interacts with the prosodic-phrasing component in part by fixed one-to-one alignments between units, as when the defaults in (7)–(8) are obeyed, and in part by meaningful departure from those defaults.

2.3   Syntactic constituency

CAY discourse is divided into a discrete hierarchy of syntactic constituents from lexical categories (nouns, demonstratives, verbs, etc.) to maximal phrasal projections (verb phrases, noun phrases, and particles) to clauses to sentences. The hierarchy itself is already well established in Eskimo linguistics on morphosyntactic grounds (Kleinschmidt 1851; Reed et al. 1977), and does not need to be recapitulated. Here I will demonstrate its interaction with other rhetorical-structure components.

Prosodic phrasing is partly predictable from syntactic constituency. One generalization is:

(11)   In the default case, sentences and prosodic subgroups will correspond one-to-one; in nondefault cases, special cohesion will be signaled when different sentences (or parts thereof) occur in the same subgroup, while

special disjunction will be signaled when the same sentence occurs over more than one subgroup.

Most subgroups in Mezak's *quliraq* follow the default in (11) (see [1, 3, 4, 5, 7, 8, 10], and others). But nondefault subgroup–sentence alignments also occur, and they appear to signal "cohesion" and "disjunction" (notions discussed in detail by Halliday and Hasan 1976 and McLendon 1982). An example where one subgroup is aligned with more than one sentence, creating cohesion, is:

(12) (= [15])

"Aa[h]!	!A_ ⟨1.3⟩	"Oh!
Aullu=wa=i! Aullu=wa=i!	!A ⟨1.6⟩	Watch.out! Watch.out!
Tuantevkenatek ciunem-		Don't.be.there in.front.-
ni!	!A ⟨1.9⟩	of.me!
Utertek!	!A ⟨2.2⟩	Go.home!
Pisqekumtek ˆta-		When.I.tell.you
ūgaam piniartutek!"	!B ⟨1.5⟩	ˆbut you.will.do!"

By occurring in one five-line subgroup rather than in several separate subgroups, the grandson's six separate commands to the young caribou constitute an especially cohesive battery, during which the grandson holds the floor by continuing to indicate (with !A contours) that more is to come. A further interesting aspect of this passage is its relatively long pauses. On the one hand, they create dramatic tension by offsetting the prosodic cohesion that is present (contrast (8)); on the other, they reinforce existing sentence boundaries (except within line 2). In all, (12) shows a remarkable three-way interaction of syntactic constituency, pausing, and prosody.

An example of the opposite case, where a single sentence is spread over more than one subgroup and creates disjunction, is:

(13) (= [21])

"Aa ˆtua:=i=w' tangenrril[ngua] ˆcamek!"	A ⟨1.2⟩
"Aling aren piyagaat=llu=ggem amllelartut;	B ⟨0.6⟩
lagiyagaat=llu,	A ⟨0.6⟩
mat'um nalliini."	B ⟨1.3⟩

"Oh ˆwell.but I.didn't.see ˆanything!"
   "Dear me! My! but.baby.ones.after.all they.are.abundant;
and.baby.geese,
   of.this at.its.time."

The sentence in question begins in the second line of the first subgroup and continues through the second subgroup. By putting them in their own subgroup, these two lines are marked as supplementary "afterthoughts" to the syntactically complete main clause in the previous subgroup which they modify. (In less marked contexts, such afterthoughts are expressed with core supplement (B°) contour lines in the same subgroup as what precedes it, as discussed above for (3)). As in (12), pause phrasing tends to reinforce syntax: sentence-final pauses are longer than sentence-medial pauses.

Especially in *qulirat*, speakers may create nondefault enjambment or *disalignment* by putting parts of different sentences in a single line:

(14) (= [2])
Tutgara'urluqelriigneg ilaluteng. Tutgara'urlurlua ˆim',   A ⟨1.5⟩
tan'ga'ūrlull'rauluni angutnguluni=w'.   B ⟨2.5⟩

and.two.in.grandchild.relationship they.included. Her.poor.grandchild ˆthat, he.was.a.poor.little.boy he.being.a.male.though.

Notice that the first line consists of the entire first sentence and the initial, old-information portion of the second while the second line expresses further new information. Narrative tension is created as information structure rather than syntactic constituency is carried by the prosodic component. Notice that this time pausing reinforces prosody and not syntax.

Within the sentence there are some fairly rigidly observed rules of prosodic phrasing. (For example, possessors and possessed nouns, and demonstratives and their head nouns are grouped together prosodically, usually in the same contour.) But there is also much freedom, as these four renditions of a formula in Mezak's *quliraq* suggest:

(15)
(a) (= [37, lines 1–2])
"Arenqiapaa=ll'!   "Oh.my.goodness!
  Nutaan ˆatam angalkungciqialriakut!   Voila! now we.are.going.to.get.a.-
                                                shaman!

(b) (= [44, lines 1–3])
"Arenqiapaa=ll'!   "Oh.my.goodness!
Nutaan ˆatam,   Voila! now,
  angalkungciqialriakut alailngurmek.   we.are.going.to.get.a.shaman

(c) (= [54, lines 1–7])
Tua::=i=am,   Then.indeed,
  anngan: when.he.went.out:
    "Arenqiapaa=ll'!   "Oh.my.goodness!
Nutaan ˆatam,   Voila! now,
  angalkungciqialriakut,   we.are.going.to.get.a.shaman,
    alailngurmek,   who.can.be.seen,
      tuunralegmeg alailngurmek!   a.spirit.owner who.can.be.seen!

(d) (= [63])
"Alingnaqvaa=ll'!   "Oh.dear.me!

Nutaan ˆatam angalkungciqialriakut,   Voila! now we.are.going.to.get.a.-

alailngurmek!   shaman,
                                                who.can.be.seen!

In (15a), the earliest of these, *arenqiapaa=ll'* 'oh my goodness' is part of the same subgroup as what follows; but as the boy's shamanistic prowess becomes more evident, the drama is increased by giving it more prominence, either by isolating it (or *alingnaqvaa=ll'* 'oh dear me') in its own subgroup, as in (15b) and (15d), or by enjambing it with a preceding subgroup, as in (15c). Within the second sentence of the formula, notice that (15c) achieves maximum disjunction by according separate lines to *nutaan ˆatam* 'voila! now' and *angalkungciqialriakut* 'we are going to get a shaman'. A lesser degree of disjunction occurs in (15b), where only *nutaan ˆatam* is accorded a line of its own.

A full treatment of defaults and permissible variants in sentence-internal prosody would take us well beyond the scope of this chapter. Even so, (11) alone is enough to show that syntactic constituency significantly interacts with prosodic phrasing and by extension (given (7) and (8)) also pause phrasing. We also saw cases where pause phrasing reinforces syntactic constituency while offsetting prosody ((12) – (13)), offering some evidence of a more direct pausing–syntactic constituency interaction.

2.4 Adverbial-particle phrasing

CAY as a whole makes significant use of adverbial-particle phrasing though its rich system of free and enclitic adverbial particles (Woodbury 1985). In this particular text, however, adverbial particles elaborate and reinforce other rhetorical-structure components more than they create a distinct hierarchical organization of discourse in and of themselves. Nevertheless, the relationship of the placement of adverbial particles to other rhetorical-structure components here is revealing.

Adverbial particles introduce both syntactic and prosodic discourse units, relating them to other discourse units or to the context of speaking. Some indicate the sequencing of narrative events in time: *tua=i* 'then; now', *tua=i=ll'* 'and then; well', *piqerluni/caqerluni* 'then at one/some time he/she . . .', and *=llu* 'and' ('=' = enclitic boundary); some also address audience expectations about the course of narrated events: *tuamte=ll'* 'then again', *taugaam* 'however', and *=am* 'again; but'; and some are interjections, portraying evaluations by the speaker, or short commands: *aa* 'oh!', *ik'iki(ka)!* 'how many!; how much!', *alingnaqvaa=ll'!* (lit.) 'how frightful!', *aling!* 'dear me!', *arenqiapaa=ll'!* (lit.) 'how unsettling!', *aren!* 'my! . . .', and *tua=i!* 'enough!'

There are sentence-internal syntactic constraints on adverbial particle order, formulated in (16) and illustrated with examples from Mezak's *quliraq*:

(16) Sentence-initial particle order:

    (Int.) + (PT$_1$(=E) (ˆPT)) + (PT$_2$(=E) (ˆPT)) + Word(=E) (ˆPT))

	Example	*Structure*
[6]	Aren imkug=am My! these.two again	Int. + Word=E
[9]	Pisqekumci ˆtau̅g̅aam when.I.tell.you but	Word ˆPT
[16]	Aren tuamte=ll' =am ayakarluni My! then.again again he.went.off	Int. + PT_1=E + Word
[40]	Tua::=i=ll' =am arenqialatni =am and.then again because.he.had.no.choice again	PT_1=E + Word=E
[57]	Tua::=i=ll' piqer:luni =am arenqialatni =am and.then once.he again [see above] again	PT_1 + PT_2=E + Word=E
[68]	Aa tua=i ˆtang qusrem =llu Oh! well see cough and	Int. + PT_1 ˆPT + Word=E

The interjection (Int.) occurs first (but may also stand as a separate sentence, as in (15)). Then follow two particle positions (PT_1 and PT_2), each of which may be followed by enclitics (=E) and certain particles (ˆPT, shown with sandhi ligature since they must appear in the same intonation contour with what precedes them). After that the first nonparticle occurs (labeled "Word"), optionally followed again by enclitics and particles. (Occasionally particles will also introduce noninitial main clauses, e.g. [22], last line.)

Adverbial particles also pattern with prosodic phrasing, being most frequent section-initially, and increasingly less so group-initially, subgroup-initially, and line-initially. In Mezak's *quliraq*, every section-initial sentence but the first begins with a particle; every group-initial sentence but those in [1] and [2] does; most subgroup-initial sentences do; but a good many group-medial sentences do not. (For some speakers and genres, particles or enclitics can even be the rule at the beginnings of sentence-medial lines; for others, they appear only section-initially.) No one particle consistently introduces sections in this text, but by far the most prevalent is *tua=i(=ll')* 'then, now, (and then, well)', often bearing an A_ contour and undergoing lengthening to *tua:=i* or *tua::=i* (see sect. 2.1). Also significant is the use of interjections, especially *aren!* 'my! . . . ', for introducing groups in this text. Thus nearly every group attributed to the narrator from [16] to [22] and from [27] to the end of the text begins with an interjection. Mezak uses these interjections partly to express the drama and surprise of these parts of his story, but at the same time they reinforce prosodic groups. In this way they are similar to the more obviously conjunctional particles. (In other texts the quotative enclitic *=gguq* 'it is said' carries out this same demarcative function; see Woodbury 1985.)

In short, adverbial particles are by nature syntactic, yet serve to introduce prosodic units in addition to syntactic ones. The fact that adverbial particles do the same thing for different rhetorical-structure components provides further evidence that prosodic phrasing and syntactic constituency are parts of a larger interdependent system.

2.5 Conclusions

We have considered four components of CAY rhetorical structure, and have established that three of them – prosodic phrasing, pause phrasing, and syntactic phrasing – present distinct and well-defined organizations of Mezak's *Tutgara' urluqelriik*. (The fourth, adverbial-particle phrasing, reinforces prosodic and syntactic units without offering a clear hierarchic structuring of the text of its own.) This along with the lack of completely predictable alignment among components demonstrates the modularity of CAY rhetorical structure.

At the same time, we have seen significant interactions among components of two major kinds: communicatively neutral default alignments, and communicatively significant departures from default alignments. All of the default patterns we have found happen to involve one-to-one correspondence, and hence reinforcement, between units of separate components: (7) aligns lines and pause phrases; (8), subgroups and pause-phrase clusters; and (11), subgroups and sentences. If these are correct, they show some formal unity for rhetorical structure. Further, they provide very specific hypotheses of the levels at which separate hierarchic structures intersect, to be tested in other CAY genres and eventually other languages.

The nondefault situations here involve one-to-many, many-to-one, or entirely disaligned correspondences between units of the different components. These departures from the one-to-one defaults were found to have meanings that included "cohesion," "disjunction," and "anticipation," leading to fairly specific textual interpretations *in situ*. This interaction of distinct formal components in carrying out communicative goals supports the communicative unity of rhetorical structure.

3 Numerically constrained form–content parallelism

Our final component is based on *numerically constrained form–content parallelism*, a type of global form–content parallelism (see sect. 1) where repetitions occur in fixed numbers. Before considering it in Mezak's *Tutgara' urluqelriik*, let me say more about it, its empirical status, and its meaning in discourse.

The notion originated (under other names) with Hymes (1976, 1977, 1980a and b, 1981), who first found it in Chinookan myth narrative. Analysis starts by looking for recurrence and hierarchical patterning among lines (reckoned as semantic predications), sentences, and larger groupings. Hymes (1980b: 8–9) describes the results as follows:

> [The nature of narrative verse in American Indian languages] depends upon a conception of narrative action as fulfilling a recurrent formal pattern. All American Indian narrative, I believe, will prove to be organized in terms of lines and verses, and sets of verses. Where syntactic particles are present, they will play a role, often a major role, as is the case in Wishram Chinook; but the fundamental con-

sideration will not be the presence of any particular linguistic device. The fundamental consideration will be the presence of a certain conception of narrative action. That conception, which can be called a rhetorical conception, will have it that sequences of action will satisfy one or another of two basic types of formal pattern. In Zuni, Karok, Takelma, and Tonkawa, the formal pattern is built up of pairs and fours. In the Chinookan languages, and in the neighboring Sahaptin languages, the formal pattern is built up of threes and fives.

The main methodological question raised is this: How can one be sure that the numerically constrained form–content parallelism discovered is immanent in the text, and not one's own construct? It seems to me that the more concrete its recurrent factor is, the surer one can be of its authenticity. One can therefore be surest in cases where there is a fixed number of verbatim repetitions of whole stanzas (as in songs and chants in most cultures), since the recurrent factor then is the entire textual unit. One can also be quite sure in narratives in which successive story divisions have as their common factor a fairly specific series of actions and events, expressed with only relatively minor changes in content or form from one division to the next. As we shall see, "episodes" in Mezak's *quliraq* are a case in point, as are the superordinate-level divisions in John Rush Buffalo's Tonkawa myth Coyote and Eagle's Daughter (Hymes this volume). However, when the recurrent factor is abstract, both discovery and verification of numerically constrained form–content parallelism can be difficult. This is the case for the tripartite conception of narrative action Onset–Ongoing–Outcome that Hymes (1977) posits to unify sets of threes in Chinookan myth narrative. It is also the case for the tripartite scheme proposed in Ex. (24) to account for lower-level form–content units in Mezak's *quliraq*. Adverbial-particle and prosodic phrasing can help one generate hypotheses, though caution is needed, since – as Hymes points out – these logically distinct rhetorical-structure components need not be aligned one-to-one with form–content units. Hence the more abstract types of form–content parallelism must ultimately be weighed carefully and critically on their own terms, for that is the only way noncircular generalizations about its interaction with other rhetorical-structure components can be reached (see e.g. Hymes's [1980a, this volume] descriptions of the evolution of his thinking on two particular texts). In the analysis of *Tutgara'urluqelriik* that follows, I hope to show by example the kinds of argumentation that I think are essential to such demonstrations.

A special feature of Hymes's hypothesis is its specification of *numerical constraints*. Numerically constrained form–content parallelism differs from ordinary global form–content parallelism – where stanzas, verses, etc. come in varying numbers – in that it involves *numerically constrained hierarchy*, a subcase of the formal type called *discrete hierarchy* in section 2.2. (We now have a three-way formal typology of *nondiscrete hierarchy* as in CAY pause phrasing, *discrete hierarchy* as in syntactic constituency, and *numerically constrained (discrete) hierarchy.*) Numerically constrained hierarchy can of course be imposed on organizations other than global form–content parallelism: For example, the dactylic hexameter of Homer imposes recurrent groupings of six at the level of the foot in the prosodic phrasing component.

A major question about numerical constraints concerns the meaning and communicative function they might have. Hymes has argued that these constraints will be based on *pattern numbers* known to be significant in the broader culture (e.g. five in the case of the Chinookans and four in the case of the Tonkawa and others), thus representing a remarkable convergence of linguistic structure and cultural patterning. But CAY culture has many numerical patterns, each with somewhat different symbolic and contextual associations. (It is likewise in European-based cultures where three, five, seven, ten, twelve, and thirteen each has special significance in a variety of well-known contexts.) The question then is not only whether numerical constraints on rhetorical structure and numerical patterns elsewhere in the culture converge – although they do to a significant degree – but how these patterns may convey sociocultural meaning by selectively mobilizing participants' knowledge of numerical patterns and numerical symbolism in their culture (where the culture is taken as a whole that includes language). That is, the patterns themselves would be linguistic, but in their use and interpretation they would draw in different ways on elements of the total system of numerical symbolism operative in both linguistic and nonlinguistic aspects of the culture.

Let me now summarize some of what is known about CAY numerical patterns and symbolism so that we have a background against which to interpret the numerical constraints we find in Mezak's text. Based mainly on Lantis's (1947:98) thumbnail summary of Alaskan Eskimo "ritual numbers," Mather's (1985) and Morrow's (1984) extensive discussions of CAY ceremonialism and traditional religion, evidence from CAY oral narrative, and my own inquiries, I would identify at least the following:

(i) *Four entities and a dissimilar fifth, symbolizing incompletion versus completion* (discussed by Morrow). Examples: the recurrent motif in CAY art of the thumbless versus complete hand (counting always begins with the little finger and ends with the thumb), corresponding to incomplete grasp (as of things of the spirit world) versus complete grasp (as of things in the real world) (see also Fitzhugh and Kaplan 1982:202); rituals repeated first in four corners (of house, grave, etc.) and then once in the middle; four brothers and their younger sister as characters of many myths. (In some myths, five-plus-one configurations are also found.)

(ii) *Four versus five.* Associated with: male versus female (Lantis; Morrow), e.g. setting down body of male four times and female five times on the way to the gravesite; overt aspects of ceremonial activity (four performers, four repetitions, etc.) versus life crises and religious belief (Lantis; but many counterexamples also exist). Four is far less important than five in the Nunivak

Island (Lantis) and Hooper Bay–Chevak areas, although musical verse structuring in all areas shows patterning in twos and fours (see transcriptions in Johnston and Pulu (1982) and Woodbury and de Reuse (in preparation)). Five comes up in many daily-life contexts and personal-experience narratives.

(iii) *Three*. Associated with: repetitions in narrative; repetitions in dance and songs; number of days in some ceremonies. (Yet since three shares all of these domains with five and the last two also with four, specific distribution and meaning have yet to be formulated.)

These patterns will give us some basis for interpreting the numerical constraints we find in Mezak's *quliraq*. At the same time, since there has been nearly no linguistic data on CAY number patterns, I hope that what is found in discourse here and elsewhere may in turn contribute to the overall elucidation of this interesting facet of CAY cultural symbolism.

3.1 Mezak's *Tutgara'urluqelriik*: broad architecture

We now turn to a detailed internal justification of numerically constrained form–content parallelism in the text. As we go along I will attempt to fill in some presuppositions that native listeners bring to this *quliraq*, relying on discussions with native speakers of it and other texts, and on generalizations that can be made about CAY and other Eskimo oral literature. In this way too I will use the analysis to develop some rudimentary literary interpretation of this excellent piece of CAY narrative performance.

Mezak's *quliraq* has three central parts, framed by a short opening and closing:

(17) 0   Introduction   Groups 1–2
          I   Grandson goes upriver   3–18
          II Grandson goes home   19–21
          III Grandson goes to the *qasgiq*   22–75
     IV   Ending   76

The main evidence for this analysis comes in parts I and III, which have nearly identical internal structure. In part I, the grandson encounters two ptarmigans, a flock of dunlins, two cranes, two young caribou, and two wolves in five highly similar episodes; in III, he summons each species into the *qasgiq* (men's communal house), again in highly similar episodes. The Introduction and Ending may then be defined at the edges of these sequences, while part II – which is also integral on its own terms – stands between them. (The reader is now urged to read the translation of Mezak's text through again, paying attention to these major units and to the sets of five episodes within parts I and III. It will also be useful for the reader to speculate on the import of the lower-level divisions labeled A, B, and C (and subdivided further in III into Aa, Ab, Ac, Ba, Bb, Bc, etc.).)

3.2 Introduction and Ending

Parts 0 and IV – the Introduction and Ending – are short and formulaic. The Introduction consists of three sentences ([1–2]). As noted in section 2.2, the first is a standard *quliraq* opening: "There was a village of people (/husband and wife, grandmother and grandson, etc.) who lived on the banks of a river (/on the sea shore, etc.)." The principal characters are introduced in the second and third sentences ([2]). Grandmother and grandchild – where the grandchild is assumed to be an orphan – is a very common character configuration in CAY and other Eskimo traditional narratives, part of a larger complex of orphan and poor-boy stories.[9] It is apparent that orphans had low social status in traditional Eskimo societies, having no one on whom they could reliably depend for food or protection from abuse. (The shamans' behavior toward the grandson in part III of Mezak's *quliraq* is a mild case in point.) In many stories, the orphan rises above his tormenters with the help of a protector or through magical powers gained by contact with the animal or spirit world. This sometimes involves bloody revenge, but in Mezak's story the grandson's gain is gentle and ironic. Mary Gregory (personal communication 1983) of Bethel comments that the grandson's unwillingness to brag or show off his considerable abilities represents the very model of correct personal conduct, allowing him to triumph simply in the contrast he offers to the crude taunting of the shamans (who in the end turn out to be less proficient than he in mobilizing the spirit world).

Part IV, Ending, is actually an announcement of the end to the audience; this is common in performance. This ending comes abruptly by CAY (as well as European) standards, following directly upon the departure of the fifth and final set of animals, the wolves. There is no summary statement of how the grandson or his fellow villagers lived after that event, as is frequently made in *qulirat*, nor any explication of the story's didactic message, as is also made occasionally (e.g. Thomas Moses's *quliraq* in Woodbury 1984:59–63). This seems to accentuate the story's form–content parallelism by replacing overt conclusions with the simple fact of pattern completion, implying in turn that the pattern and its content are enough to convey the essential message.[10]

3.3 Part I

Here the grandson travels upriver alone, encountering five animal species in five separate episodes:

(18) Part I: Grandson goes upriver
	[Introduction]	[3]
i	Encounters two ptarmigans	[4–6]
ii	Encounters flock of dunlins	[7–9]
iii	Encounters two cranes	[10–13]

iv Encounters two young caribou   [14–15]
v Encounters two wolves   [16–18]

The species are arranged in a significant *five-member sequence of narrative participants*, clearly manifesting an important pattern number. In it, the species are ordered from least to most formidable: Even though ptarmigans are larger than dunlins, they are regarded as stupid, easy prey. (The fact that dunlins are more gregarious than the other species may account for the flock, as against the solitary pairs elsewhere.) There is some internal evidence (to be noted) suggesting that the sequence here may resolve into the widespread four-plus-one number pattern noted above: The first four species are routinely hunted as game; the last is a carnivore dangerous to humans and hunted primarily for its fur.[11]

The five units are clear because the episodes are highly similar in content, including even verbatim repetitions in certain places. Based on that, it is possible to infer, through comparison, three episode-internal divisions (labeled in the transcript in the left margin without titles):

(19) Part I: Divisions within episodes
    A   Traveling upriver, grandson finds animals carrying on in his path
    B   Charms animals and orders them off
    C   Animals leave

(Although division A involves mating behavior between male and female in (iii) and perhaps mating-related conflict between males in (iv), what is important in all five episodes is that the animals make some spectacular display of behavior that will impress the people in the *qasgiq* in part III.) The divisions are not as easily justified as the five higher-level episodes. But if we take syntactic sentences as our basic unit, we find that A is a minimal part of episodes (i), (iv), and (v), where it occurs as a single sentence, and expands to two sentences in (ii) and (iii); B has integrity as a direct quotation (preceded in (i), (iii), and (v) by an introduction); and C – which is absent from (iv) but still implicit there – occurs everywhere else as a single sentence. We could conceivably merge B and C as a paired action and response, as indeed is implied prosodically in some episodes (see sect. 4.2); but we will see indirect evidence from a parallel situation in part III that they are separate.

Within divisions A, B, and C in each episode, there is no clear segmentation into a fixed number of subdivisions. As noted, A consists of one or two sentences. By Hymes's method of segmentation into predications, the first sentence always consists of two parts: an optional particle and a verb in *-qar-luni* (just-APPO[SITIONAL MOOD].he) 'when he just . . . -ed (i.e. a little ways further)' governing an adverbial clause, and an instrumental case (*-nek*) complement followed by *ciunrani* 'in front of him' and/or the verb *tekite-* 'come (upon)' in the third person singular indicative (*-(t)uq*). Hence this part of (i), (iii), and (v) might be divided into two lines as follows:

(20) (a) Episode (i) (= [4])
Tua::=i, asgurtura-qer-luni,
qang:qiireg-nek, callul:riig-nek ˆtekit-uq.

Then, travel.on.upriver-a.little.ways.further-APPO.he,
two.ptarmigans-INST,fighting-INST he.came.upon-IND.he

(b) Episode (iii) (= [10])
Ayagtura-qer-luni,
qucillgaag-nek tekit-uq.

Going.on-a.little.ways.further-APPO.he,
two.cranes-INST, he.came.upon-IND.he.

(c) Episode (v) (= [16])
Aren tuamte=ll'=am aya-kar-luni,
qeglunreg-nek, ciunrani.

My! and.then.again going-a.little.ways.further-he
two.wolves-INST, in.front.of.him

All five A divisions contain this putative couplet. But it is followed by nothing
in (i) and (iv); by one-line verses in (ii) and (v); and by what amounts to a
four-line verse in (iii), since the first two lines of [11] have four predications.
There is thus no clear basis for recurrent numerical configuration *within* A.

The situation is similar for B. Even if we simplify our task by considering
only the grandson's quoted speech, we get structure but no numerical pattern.
These English calques of the CAY illustrate:

(21) (a) Episode (i) (= [6])
"Hey! Enough!
When.I.tell.you.to.do ˆbut
you.will.do!
Hey enough
return – you.return!"

(b) Episode (ii) (= [9])
"Watch.out! Watch.out!
In.front.of.me don't.you.stay!
Hey enough,
when.I.tell.you.to.do ˆbut
you.will.do!"

(c) Episode (iii) (= [12])
"Hey enough enough
from.there you.be.gone!
But when.I.tell.you.to.do
you.will.do!"

(d) Episode (iv) (= [15])
"Hey! Watch.out! Watch.out!
Don't.you.be.there in.front.of.-
me!
You.return!
When.I.tell.you.to.do ˆbut
you.will.do!"

(e) Episode (v) (= [18])
"Oh.my.goodness ˆenough,
you.return!

You.return
in.front.of.me don't.you.-
stay!
When.I.tell.you.to.do ˆbut
you.will.do!' "

We can distinguish three potential subdivisions, represented by the indentation pattern in (21): (a) the order to get out of the way, (b) the order to return home, and (c) the order to obey future commands. But the subdivisions vary in length from one to three lines, depending in part on the presence of an initial interjection; some quotations employ two subdivisions and others three; and the subdivisions are deployed in different orders, namely c–b, a–c, a–c, a–b–c, and b–ba–c respectively. Perhaps it is significant that the inventory of potential subdivisions fits the pattern number three which is emerging in this text, but I do not think there is enough evidence to posit it as an underlying structure for the grandson's speech in B. It is also unlikely that the different orderings of the subdivisions are random effects of performance, for in the "Materials" version of the text, they are exactly the same, word for word and morpheme for morpheme.

3.4   Part II

Unlike part I, part II does not have episodes corresponding to each of the five animal species. But in an abstract way it seems to parallel the episode-internal structure in part I as follows:

(22) Part II: Grandson goes home

  A Grandson returns home to grandmother,
     who asks why he is so late   [19–20]
  B Grandson excuses himself   [21, line 1]
  C Grandmother is skeptical   [21, lines 2–4]

Division A is structurally analogous to the first sentence of A in the episodes of part I, as shown by a comparison of (23) with the items in (20).

(23) Tua:=i=ll' uterr-luni,   Then return-APPO.he,
     maūrlurlumi-nun teki-lluni.   his.grandmother-to arrive.APPO.he.

The grandmother then verbally challenges the grandson, building on the presupposition that small birds are the natural first hunting and stalking targets for a child. If we liken this to the animals' challenges to him in the A divisions in part I, then we may consider it and (23) as an A division in part II. To continue the analogy, the grandson's response corresponds to his reactions in B in part I and may thus be called the B division of II. This then highlights the contrast between the grandson's bold response to the animals in the B quotation in part I, as against the laudable meekness and modesty about his shamanistic prowess shown in his verbal response to his grandmother. Finally, the grandmother's disbelieving response may be seen as a kind of reverse C division for part II: Whereas the C divisions in part I show just the desired response to the grandson's utterances in the B division, the grandmother's response in II is (on the surface) an undesired one. The tripartite scheme of action implied by this set of analogies for both I and II is thus:

(24) Tripartite scheme of action, division-level
    A Grandson comes and is challenged
    B Grandson reacts masterfully (portrayed in quoted speech)
    C His reaction gets the desired (or undesired) response

Within the A, B, and C divisions of part II, I find no obvious numerically constrained form–content parallelism.

3.5 Part III

Like part I, part III has highly similar episodes organized around the five-member sequence of narrative participants:

(25) Part III: Grandson goes to the *qasgiq*
    [Introduction]   [22]
      i Calls in the two ptarmigans   [23–35]
     ii Calls in the flock of dunlins   [36–42]
   iii Calls in the two cranes   [43–53]
   iv Calls in the two young caribou [54–62]
    v Calls in the two wolves   [63–75]

Yet these episodes are longer and more complicated than those in part I. I propose the following hypothesis of their internal divisions:

(26) Part III: Divisions within episodes

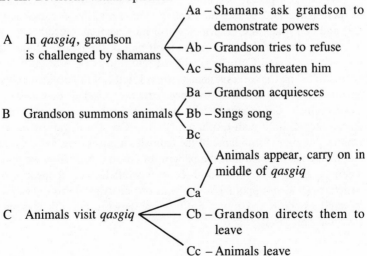

A In *qasgiq*, grandson is challenged by shamans
    Aa – Shamans ask grandson to demonstrate powers
    Ab – Grandson tries to refuse
    Ac – Shamans threaten him

B Grandson summons animals
    Ba – Grandson acquiesces
    Bb – Sings song
    Bc – Animals appear, carry on in middle of *qasgiq*

C Animals visit *qasgiq*
    Ca –
    Cb – Grandson directs them to leave
    Cc – Animals leave

(26) differs from anything we have considered up to now, since it crossclassifies a form–content unit: The appearance of the animals is both Bc and Ca simultaneously. Hymes (1977) has discovered such latching of triplets in Chinookan and taken it as the specific mechanism for the frequent groupings of five in Chinookan poetics. Given the patterns found elsewhere in Mezak's text, however, the most important feature of (26) is the similarity of the triplets, at two distinct levels, to the generalized tripartite scheme of action posited in (24). As we shall see, this is especially clear for divisions A, B, and C, where the song constitutes the grandson's masterful response to the challenge, and for subdivisions Ca, Cb, and Cc. Within A, Aa and Ab fit clearly, while Ac is a departure (it relates the opposite of the desired response); within B, Bb and Bc fit clearly, but Ba is a departure. Methodologically, the more evidence that can be found in favor of relating all A's and a's, all B's and b's, and all C's and c's, the better the case is for (26). I will proceed with the basic arguments and then account for the divergences from (26) in the text.

The analogy between divisions A, B, and C in part I and Bc/Ca, Cb, and Cc in III is quite striking. Where A in I begins with a one-sentence statement of arrival followed optionally by a description of the animals' carrying on (or its effect on the grandson), Bc/Ca begins with a syntactically similar one-sentence statement of "bursting in" followed (but in (iii) preceded) by a description or even rendition ((i), (iii), and (iv)) of their carrying on and a description of the effect on the crowd (in (iv) and (v)). Cb is clearly analogous to B in I, since in both cases the boy orders the animals off with a series of commands. And Cc, a single sentence, is very similar to the single sentence found in the C divisions of I. These parallels argue by analogy for the tripartite subdivision of C.

However, the pattern described for C is violated in three ways. Least serious of these is the lack of Cc, the explicit response to the grandson's words, in (iii) and (v): Since a C division is also missing from episode (iv) of part I, it is likely that its dispensability is itself part of the pattern. More serious is the lack of Cb and Cc in (ii), which I return to later. The third divergence occurs in (v) and involves a phenomenon I will call *pattern extension*. In that episode, division C has a five-part structure labeled Bc/Ca–Cb–Bc/Ca–Cb–Cc. In it, the grandson tries once without resolution (Bc/Ca–Cb) and then a second time with resolution (Bc/Ca–Cb–Cc) to rid the *qasgiq* of the wolves, the most formidable of the animals. It thus seems to be a meaningful and deliberate extension of the pattern set out in (26), which we may take as a default strictly within the form–content parallelism component of rhetorical structure. (It also supports the four-plus-one analysis of this *quliraq*'s episode structure, since it constitutes a difference between the fifth episode and the four that precede it.)

We next consider the internal structure of division A, which can be summarized as follows:

(27) Scheme for Part III, Division A
    Aa   Shamans challenge grandson to drum
    Ab   Grandson tries to excuse himself
    Ac   Shamans reject excuses with threats

In episode (i), Mezak introduces Aa – and indeed sets the stage for all of part III – by implying that the shamans have been frustrated in their attempts to contact the spirit world (they are "tired of drumming"). This is followed by two direct quotations: The first contains the initial challenge to the grandson, *Cauyarcetqerciu!* 'Let him drum!', and an explanation for why he is being asked; the second, by a different shaman, echoes it with *Cauya-qaa!* 'Drum!' (drum-POLITE.IMPERATIVE!). Episodes (ii) – (v) are very similar to each other, but different from episode (i) in that they lack the stage-setting introduction found there and contain only one direct quotation. That quotation corresponds most closely to the second shaman's challenge in episode (i) (*Cauyaqaa!* 'Drum!') because it is nearly identical to it in form: *Cali tua=i pi-qaa!* 'Again now do-POLITE.IMPERATIVE!', where *pi-* 'to do' is interpreted as *cauyar-* 'to drum' (word order varies slightly from episode to episode). The Aa subdivisions in episodes (ii)–(v) are different from the one in episode (i) in another respect, namely that they begin with a formulaic prediction that the grandson is on his way to becoming a great shaman. On a more abstract level, however, this corresponds quite closely to the surmise of the first shaman in (i) that the grandson might have some songs to use with the drums. In conclusion, the fact that two challenges in the Aa division of episode (i) are telescoped into single challenges in the Aa divisions of episodes (ii)–(v) makes it reasonable to regard the original challenges in (i) as part of a single subdivision (perhaps further subdivided so that [23] would be a minor pattern extension). In subdivision Ab the grandson responds with an excuse. This occurs at least once in each episode. Notice that it fits the broad pattern in (24) of masterful response to a challenge; in its evasiveness and modesty, it is especially similar to division B in II. Finally, subdivision Ac also occurs at least once in each episode. Like the C divisions in part II but unlike the C divisions anywhere else, it involves an undesired rather than a desired response to what the grandson says just before.

A feature of division A in episodes (iv) and (v) is the grandson's use of a cough to excuse himself from drumming. We know that the cough is part of the story itself because (with two exceptions) it occurs in exactly the same places in Mezak's "Materials" version. In both versions, the cough leads to extensions of basic pattern in (27) by adding further exchanges between the grandson and the shamans. After Ac in (iv) ([56]), the grandson coughs as a delay tactic and then repeats the essential content of Ab (I label this Ab'). In (v) (both versions), the cough leads to a repetition of a full exchange, the grandson's Ab and the shaman's Ac (labeled Ab' and Ac'). Both Ab' in (iv) and Ab'−Ac' in (v) may be viewed as pattern extensions that depart from the default pattern established in the first three episodes (summarized by (27)). All of these pattern extensions should be treated as motivated departures from the default. They are telling testimony to the expressive flexibility of form−content parallelism.

The present version of the story is different from the "Materials" version in having two coughs that are unanticipated. They occur in the Aa subdivision of episode (v) in group [64], during the shaman's quotation. Mezak comments in [65] that now he is catching the cough himself (eliciting laughter from his audience), and a partial repetition of Aa then occurs in [66] (labeled Aa'). In this way, pattern extension is also a device for responding to the exigencies of performance.

Division B is centered on the song, which in all five episodes is introduced with a sentence that is some variant of *Tua=i arenqialatni qiivciuq* 'Now because.he.had.no.choice he.started.a.low.rumble.on.the.drum'. Episode (i) is unusual in that while the formal introduction occurs in group [29], the theme of having no choice, giving in, and preparing to drum is taken up already in [27−8], suggesting that B in (i) begins there and not in [29]. This is at least some evidence for positing a Ba subdivision, rather than having just an unlabeled introduction to the song. But as noted, there is little that is parallel between the content of Ba and the content of other A divisions, as hypothesized in (24). Subdivision Bb, the song, is discussed at length in section 3.6. It is the mainstay of parallelism in the episodes of III, and, as (24) would predict for a b subdivision of a B division, it is the quintessential piece of masterful verbal action by the grandson in the entire text. Finally, there is good reason for the Bc/Ca subdivision to be classified as Bc/Ca rather than just Ca: Like C in part I and Cc in part III, it consists of the animals' response to the grandson's words. Notice too that the "bursting in" sentence in Bc/Ca is also quite similar to the single sentences of division C in I and subdivision Cc in III. There is therefore good reason for regarding Bc/Ca subdivisions as members of divisions B and C both.

I have saved for last the most serious departure from (26). In episode (ii), subdivisions Cb and Cc are missing; in episode (iii) just after that, there is the odd sequence Aa−Cc−Ac−Ab−Ac. On internal grounds, this seems to be an error, hinging on the similarity between the point in Ca where the narrator marvels at the animals' carrying on (cf. [33] in (i), [52] in (iii), and [61] in (iv)) and the point at beginning of Aa in the following episode where he marvels at the grandon's prowess (cf. [36] in (ii), [54] in (iv), and [63] in (v)). That is, I infer that in [43], Mezak has run two similar points in the story together, depriving (ii) of Cb and Cc. He "repairs" this in (iii) by reciting subdivision Cc of episode (ii) at [45] and then going back to finish division A in (iii) at [46] in the order Ac–Ab–Ac′. While one would expect only Ab–Ac at this point – grandson's evasion followed by shaman's threat – the first Ac seems to renew the shaman's challenge offered in Aa, group [44]. If these inferences are correct, the episode transition here provides further insight into the actual performance of narrative with highly complex global form–content parallelism while at the same time maintaining the correctness of the scheme in (26).[12]

3.6 The grandson's song

The song consists of a four-line *ayagneq* 'beginning', a verse of meaningless song words, and a three-line *apalluq*, a verse with words. The fullest renditions occur in episodes (iii)–(v); the renditions in (i) and (ii) lack all or part of the *ayagneq* verse. (I think it is unlikely that such shortening has special significance.)

The song shows numerically constrained form–content parallelism in several rhetorical structure components: prosodic phrasing, which in a song must include meter, rhythm, and musical pitch; pause phrasing; segmental phonology (in the form of assonance); and lexical choice, including both real and song words. But unlike anything else we have seen in Mezak's *quliraq*, the pattern is in pairs, and pairs of pairs.

In the prosodic component, the overall repetition pattern is:

(28) [aa ba′] [aa c]
      (Square brackets mark verses; a, a′, b, and c are melodic phrases; couplets are shown as pairs of melodic phrases [e.g. aa, ba′].)

Through parallelism, pair-of-pairs configurations are established both within and across verses. (However, c by itself creates an asymmetry within the *apalluq* verse.) In (28) the melodic phrase itself is clearly defined rhythmically, since each one (except c) consists of three two-beat measures plus, in b and a′, a sort of metrical tag lasting two measures in the former and one measure in the latter. The prosodic parallelism in the song is even more extensive than (28) suggests in that the main three-measure sequence in b is a fairly simple transformation of the corresponding sequence in a. On the other hand, c is strikingly different from a, a′, and b in several respects: It is melodically different (e.g. having an ascending fifth); its metrical length depends on the length of the name of the animal being called; and with its final pitch drop it seems more chanted than sung.

The song words too show a pattern of numerically constrained form–content parallelism very close to the prosodic one just described:

(29)

Ayagneq:	[₁ Nga yaa=i]	[₁ nga yaa=i]	[₁·ngay hyaa----------- a]!	a ⎤
	[₁ Nga yaa=i]	[₁ nga yaa=i]	[₁·ngay hyaa----------- a]!	a ⎦
	[₁ Nga yaa ------------------i]		[₂ ua------a]!	[ᴛᴀɢ Aa ngaa!]	b ⎤
	[₁ Nga yaa=i]	[₁ nga yaa=i]	[₁·ngay hyaa]!	[ᴛᴀɢ Aa=i!]	a' ⎦
Apalluq:	[₃ Nani--mi]	[₄ qama--ni]	[₁·ngay hyaa----------- a]?	d ⎤
	[₅ Kangi-mi]	[₄ qama--ni]	[₁·ngay hyaa----------- a]!	e ⎦
	[₆ Keglunra ------------------ag	iterlii-----k]!	c

ASSONANCE: a {a/i} i   a a i   a   a-----------a

(*Note:* Numbered bracketings mark lexical units; lines are metrically aligned.)

The main difference between the lexical repetition pattern in (29) – namely [aa ba'] [de c] – and the prosodic repetition pattern in (28) is that the first two lines of the second verse are different both from each other and from the first two lines of the first verse. Nevertheless, there is still considerable similarity in that the lexical units of these four lines are metrically aligned (shown in (29) by the vertical stacking of the brackets around them); they all end with lexical unit 1'; the first two lines of the second verse also share unit 4, *qamani* 'upriver'; and – most remarkably – *nanimi* (unit 3) is a kind of artificial word consisting of the ordinary word *na-ni* (where?-LOC) 'where?' plus a further locative suffix *-mi*, which would be ungrammatical in ordinary speech but which here serves a dual purpose: It fills out the line-internal metrical pattern, and it establishes parallelism to unit 5 in the next line, *kangi-mi* (source-LOC) 'at the source', which contains a legitimate instance of locative *-mi*. A further way in which the lexical pattern follows the the prosodic pattern is that the very last line, which calls the animals, is as new lexically as it is prosodically: It repeats no lexical units from the first lines, it contains no meaningless song words, and it varies from episode to episode. Finally, lexical parallelism is enhanced by the almost perfect vocalic assonance achieved through the choice of song words and real words. This is shown in (29) with shading.

In terms of rhetorical structure, we have seen that the prosodic and lexical/syntactic components are quite closely aligned in the song at the line, couplet, and verse levels; in both, numerical constraints in twos and fours are evident. (The reader may notice further evidence of this in (28) and (29) which I have not discussed here.) Within the line, however, the situation is quite different: There, rhythmic units (part of prosody) and lexical units are disaligned rather than aligned, and come in threes rather than twos. The following analysis of the first line illustrates this:

(30)

```
|x            |x          |x
|x     x      |x      x   |x   x        RHYTHMIC UNITS
```

[₁ Nga yaa=i] [₁ nga yaa=i] [₁,ngay hyaa-----a]!　　LEXICAL UNITS

(Bars mark measures, double x marks downbeat, single x marks upbeat.)

Here, it is seen that the prosodic and lexical units both involve triplets, but they are not in one-to-one alignment. Nevertheless, the disalignment that occurs is a regular one that is repeated in the following five lines. Hence, we must recognize that it is possible for *disalignment* to establish itself as a default within the context of particular texts or genres.

Interestingly, the melody reinforces lexical rather than rhythmic units here in that the first and second lexical units are carried, respectively, on ascending and descending melodic figures. This suggests, of course, that in a more complete analysis melody would not simply be lumped with prosodic phrasing.

In summary, then, several rhetorical-structure components converge in the song to arrange its lines into pairs and pairs of pairs. Below that, prosody and lexicon each divide lines into a basic pattern of three or three plus a tag, but instead of converging, these line-internal threes are regularly disaligned. It should also be seen from this discussion that the rhetorical-structure framework gives us useful ways to integrate our analysis of songs and other special genres with our analysis of discourse in ordinary spoken genres (see also Sherzer's and Tedlock's treatments of chanting in Chapters 4 and 5 of this volume).

3.7. Conclusions: the meaning of numerically constrained form–content parallelism

From this consideration of Mezak's *Tutgara'urluqelriik*, the first conclusion we can draw is that numerically constrained form–content parallelism does indeed exist in CAY *quliraq* narratives, and that it can be demonstrated in them rigorously and on its own terms. In the narrative portions of Mezak's *quliraq*, the phenomenon extends down only to a level somewhat above that of the sentence, whereas in the song, it (and numerically constrained prosody and lexical choice) extends down much further. It will thus be important to examine other *qulirat* and other songs carefully in order to discover its true range and extent in CAY oral literature.

Form–content parallelism is a major communicative resource. In the *quliraq*, the *five-member sequence of narrative participants* not only organizes parts I and III into episodes, but represents an increasing series of challenges to the grandson's abilities. The other generalization, the *tripartite scheme of narrative action* (24), organizes the episodes (and all of part II) into divisions and subdivisions, and at the same time puts forward again and again the concrete moral lesson contained in its abstract sequence of challenge–masterful reaction–desired response.

In addition to these face-value contributions to narrative meaning, the predictability of form–content parallelism makes it a basis for inference and interpretation on the part of listeners. It creates expectations in audiences (see Burke 1931) that increase as basic patterns are recognized more and more clearly. Thus by the time the grandson is in the *qasgiq* and is summoning the animals, we so fully expect the wolves to come last that once they are gone Mezak can leave us with no conclusion but "My, well now that's it, it's over," as if to say that we, as audience, know enough to recognize that completion of the pattern means the completion of the narrative and the drawing of its lesson.

Form–content parallelism is not always rigid. Its patterns can be extended to make a point, as when the grandson tries a second time to rid the *qasgiq* of the wolves in III:v:C. It can also be adapted in narrative "repair," as we saw in (ii) – (iii) in III. It can even be expanded to absorb unexpected problems of performance, such as Mezak's own coughing in III:v:A. In all these cases, divergence from rigid pattern is communicatively significant. It follows then that retaining errors and other features of "mere" performance in literary editions of texts may be part of preserving a narrator's original creativity, humor, and art.

Finally, I hypothesized that the numerical constraints themselves make important contributions to narrative meaning by mobilizing participants' knowledge of culturally significant number symbolism. The clearest case of this was the five-member sequence of narrative participants, since it almost certainly draws on the overt complex of fives found generally in CAY culture, and may even be segmented into the widespread pattern of four plus a dissimilar fifth to complete it. On that interpretation it was noted that the fifth trial, with two wolves, was put before us as a startlingly different encounter that completes the four earlier trials involving lesser species.

It is much more difficult to ascertain a connection to broader cultural patterns and symbolism for the tripartite scheme of narrative action in (24), mainly because it is quite abstract. That is, it is difficult to verify whether such an abstract use of three really calls to listeners' minds the symbolic values of overt patterns of three found in the culture generally (e.g. ceremonies said to last three days). It is even difficult to verify whether this use of triplets within narrative episodes is connected to the text's division into parts I, II, and III.

Still more difficult to interpret are the numerical patterns in the song. It seems unlikely that the pairs, and pairs of pairs, found there actually relate to the complex of fours in CAY culture: For one thing, the cultural pattern does not show subgrouping into twos; moreover, twos and fours are so widespread in musical traditions of the world that they may be somehow intrinsic to human music and lack any cultural symbolism whatever. It seems unlikely too that the line-internal patterning in threes in Mezak's song calls on the other threes that have been discussed (just as waltz time in European dance can hardly be said to call to mind the tripartite structure and symbolism frequent in European folktales).

It seems unsatisfactory to be drawing so few positive conclusions and so many negative ones. Nevertheless, the positive conclusions do show a definite relationship between number symbolism in the culture generally and numerically constrained patterns in CAY rhetorical structure. At the same time, my reservations serve to indicate the considerable richness and complexity of that relationship, as well as to underscore the importance for both linguistics and anthropology of studying such phenomena in greater detail.

4 Interaction of form–content parallelism with other components

In section 3 we looked at numerically constrained form–content parallelism strictly on its own terms as a component in rhetorical structure. Here we will consider its interaction with another component, prosodic phrasing. While that will be enough for our purposes, a more complete study would of course also treat its interaction with such components as pause phrasing and adverbial particle phrasing. (There would be little to say about interaction with syntactic constituency, since form–content parallelism in this text generally operates above the sentence level.)

4.1 Form–context parallelism and the prosodic section

Even a quick inspection of Mezak's *Tutgara'urluqelriik* shows that nearly all prosodic sections (see sect. 2.1) coincide with units of form–content parallelism: episodes in part I, divisions in part III, and the parts themselves in 0, II, and IV. The following therefore suggests itself as a working hypothesis:

(31) Prosodic sections will correspond one-to-one with units of form–content parallelism. Those units will reside at a hierarchic level that is consistent over a stretch of discourse.

Notice that (31) is stronger than any of our earlier alignment hypotheses (given in (7), (8), and (11)): (31) is a categorical rule, whereas the earlier hypotheses state default alignments that can be violated. Because of this I should like to maintain (31), if at all possible, by explaining the few apparent counterexamples to it not as violations of a default but as reflections of quite separate phenomena.

For the most part (31) is rigorously obeyed. Parts 0 (Introduction), II, and IV (Ending) each occur as single sections, and in part I units at the next level down – the five sections and the introduction in [3] – consistently occupy a section each. Part III, however, is more complicated. Divisions (A, B, C) there most often are sections, but there are some qualifications to that: Bc/ Ac is sometimes grouped with the rest of C and sometimes split between B and C; A in episode (i) and C in (v) are cut in half; and episode (iii) shows just a single section break, in the middle of A. Thus in order to maintain (31) categorically, it is necessary to argue that none of these facts constitute violations of it.

Bc/Ca subdivisions belong by definition to divisions B and C simultaneously, at once resolving the one and opening the other. Assuming that, (31) actually gives us more leeway than might appear: It predicts that Bc/Ca subdivisions, or parts of them, can be sectioned either with the rest of B or with the rest of C. In fact, three of the four logical possibilities this opens up actually do occur. The first possibility is for Bc/Ca to be cut in half, sectioned partly with B and partly with C. This is what happens in (i) and (iv). In (i), Bc/Ca consists of groups [31–3]. Of that, the ptarmigans' entry and call ([31–2]) are sectioned with division B and hence can be treated as the result of the song, while the description of their fluttering about ([33]) is sectioned with division C and can hence be treated as the opening challenge to which the grandson must respond. Form–content parallelism and prosodic phrasing thus interact to give the following composite analysis of this portion of episode (i):

(32)

BASIC ANALYSIS   COMPOSITE ANALYSIS [not in Appendix]

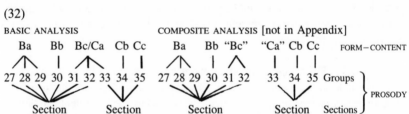

The situation is similar in (iv), where Bc/Ca ([59–61]) is resolved by a section break into [59] (composite Bc) and [60–1] (composite Ca). In effect, prosody resolves an ambiguity in form–content parallelism.

The second logical possibility occurs in episodes (ii) and (v), where the whole of Bc/Ca is sectioned with C, implying a composite analysis of it as Ca. The third occurs in (iii), where Bc/Ca is not in contact with any section break, leaving Bc/Ca ambiguous. And the fourth, where Bc/Ca would be grouped entirely with B, is not realized. (Given that C (sub)divisions are often dispensable in this text while A (sub)divisions never are, this is unsurprising.) In summary, the treatment of Bc/Ca subdivisions shows a type of interaction between form–content parallelism and prosodic phrasing where each contributes complementary information to a hierarchic organization of content at a higher level of abstraction. Mediated by that level, divisions and sections actually do show one-to-one correspondence.

The next challenges to (31) from part III are single divisions that are broken into two sections: division C in episode (v) and A in (i). But interestingly enough, these division-internal sections correspond to division-internal pattern extensions discussed already in section 3.5. In division C in episode (v) there are two sections, [71–2] and [73–5]. They correspond exactly to the two attempts by the grandson to get the wolves out of the *qasgiq*, labeled as Bc/Ca–Cb and Bc/Ca'–Cb'–Cc respectively. Since the second of these amounts to a complete version of division C as found elsewhere (and the first is simply the remainder), sectioning actually does correspond one-to-one to units of form–content parallelism, as predicted by (31). That is, sectioning highlights the division there between pattern and pattern extension. Division A in (i) offers a similar but somewhat less clear case: It is sectioned into group [23], an extension of Aa that is unique to episode (i), and [24–6], which by itself contains the complete division-A pattern (Aa–Ab–Ac) in very much the form it appears in later on.[13] But in spite of these two examples, it would be wrong to conclude that sectioning cordons off pattern extensions obligatorily. For example, the A divisions in (iv) and (v) also contain pattern extension (connected with coughing; see sect. 3.5) but they still correspond to just one prosodic section each. Sectioning is therefore a device both for highlighting and for merging pattern and pattern extension. We may account for this not by revising (31), but by recognizing that pattern extension makes form–content parallelism ambiguous to (31).

A final set of problems for (31) occurs in divisions C in (ii) and A in (iii), related no doubt to the skipping of Cb and Cc in (ii) and the "repair" of Cc after Aa in (iii) discussed in section 3.5. Prosodically, Bc/Ca in (ii) and Aa in (iii) are a section,[14] and a new section begins at the point of repair ([45]) with the sequence Cc–Ac–Ab'–Ac'. If, as I argued in section 3.5, this sequence functions as a "retake" of all of division A (where Cc–Ac substitutes for Aa), then the sectioning strategy is familiar: Bc/Ca–Aa is sectioned alone as a pattern extension – or, better, a false start – while the sequence beginning with [45] is the pattern itself. That leaves us with just one prosodic puzzle, the sectioning of divisions B and C together with the retake of A, giving an episode-long section. Since sections elsewhere in III correspond to divisions rather than episodes, this is a one-to-one correspondence between a section and a form–content unit at the wrong hierarchical level. Hence it is an actual counterexample to (31), which predicts that correspondences will reside at a consistent hierarchical level. I will provisionally call such cases "nondefault," thus weakening (31). In fact, though, I do not have enough information about them even to know whether "nondefault" is justified (i.e. whether speakers do in fact infer special meaning or effects from such occurrences).

Based on this discussion, the following revision of (31) is necessary to account for the genuine counterexample discovered:

(33) Prosodic sections will correspond one-to-one with units of form–content parallelism. In the default case, those units will reside at a hierarchical level that is consistent over a stretch of discourse.

In addition, the following statement of the consequences of (33) clarifies its application to the apparent counterexamples that were discussed:

(34) As a consequence of (33), alternative sectionings are possible when form–content parallelism is ambiguous due (a) to cross-classification or (b) to independently identifiable pattern extension. In the case of (a), a composite organization of discourse is created; in the case of (b), pattern and pattern extension can be sectioned separately to highlight them, or together to merge them.

Alhough (33) is slightly weaker than (31), it is still unique in that it specifies categorical one-to-one correspondence between units of two separate components. Because of this extensive reinforcement, the section (and the form–content units it coincides with) must be regarded as very central discourse units. As stated in (34), ambiguities in form–content parallelism and in pattern extension provide a constrained amount of leeway in the alignment of sections with form–content units. Because of this, sections themselves cannot be expected to obey numerical constraints, as indeed they do not in Mezak's *quliraq*.

4.1.1   *Other reinforcement of larger form–content units*
An unexpected further reinforcer of some larger form–content units in the text is a paralinguistic feature, falsetto voice quality, marked in the transcript and translation with italics. Mezak occasionally employs his falsetto to depict excitement in his characters' voices, but for the most part, those voices are relatively deadpan. In contrast, he often produces wild fluctuations in pitch in his own, narrator's voice. Several native listeners to the tape commented on this with great approval: It seems to bring surprise, excitement, movement, and humor to the discourse units it introduces or concludes. Of interest to us is the way in which the falsetto reinforces larger form–content units. In part I, Mezak's falsetto reinforces both episodes and sections, which are in one-to-one alignment there: He uses it in [3] to introduce the grandson's activity, at the beginning of each episode to introduce the animals and describe their doings, and occasionally at episode endings. He uses falsetto next in part III, but on a slightly different pattern: He uses it, optionally, to introduce or to follow up direct quotations that open a division (A, B, C) or in one case a subdivision (Cb); moreover, he does so whether or not the divisions or subdivisions are section-initial. Thus falsetto occurs at the beginning of Bc/Ca in all episodes but episode (ii), regardless of where section boundaries fall. It occurs twice (episodes (i) and (iii)) in introducing the grandson in Cb, which is never section-initial. It is used at the beginning of A in episodes

(i)–(iii) even though a full section boundary does not occur there in (iii) (but see note 12). And even though the song in (i) is introduced with falsetto in the middle of Ba (at [29]), just where a minor prosodic boundary begins, this location is also the boundary of a minor pattern extension (see note 14). It is clear then that while falsetto is a feature of sound, it reinforces form–content parallelism more directly than it does prosodic phrasing.

Another expressive feature picking out the episode – but also the section – as a unit is the use of interjections (a type of adverbial particle; see sect. 2.4). This is clearest in the wolf encounter in part I, where for the first time the grandson is actually frightened. There, interjections based on *arenqiaᵗᵉe-* 'to be uneasy' abound from beginning to end: *arenqiatuq* (lit. 'it makes one uneasy'); *arenqiapaa* (lit. 'how uneasy it makes one'); *aren!* (abbreviation of the preceding). By contrast, an interjection from this class occurs in earlier episodes only once (see C in (i)). We may regard this as a case in which adverbial particle phrasing reinforces both form–content parallelism and prosody. It also provides further support for the hypothesis that the wolf episode in part I is a dissimilar fifth, part of the four-plus-one pattern-number configuration discussed in section 3.

4.2 Form–content parallelism and prosody below the section

Units of form–content parallelism do not correspond to prosodic groups nearly as tidily as they do to sections. In part I, divisions A and B and C in each episode sometimes correspond one-to-one to complete groups, sometimes one-to-several. I find no evidence that either case is out of the ordinary and nondefault. Sometimes, however, two divisions (or parts of divisions) occur in the same group and a special meaning does seem to be involved. Part I has six such cases, four of which involve division C. Thus while C corresponds to a separate group in (iii), it attaches in the other four episodes to the group containing the end B, the grandson's quoted speech. Apparently this reinforces the interpretation of the grandson's orders and the animals' obedience as a linked action-and-response pair, in counterpoint to the A–B–C pattern that sets C on an equal basis with both A and B. The other two cases occur in (iii) and (v), where the introduction to the quotation in B is annexed by the group containing the end of A. Here too a special action-and-response interpretation is enforced, involving the animals' startling behavior or demeanor in A, and the grandson's verbal confrontation of it in B. Action-and-response is a type of marked cohesion that we may isolate as follows:

(35) In the default case, units of global form–content parallelism (at the levels discussed here – not at lower levels) must contain a whole number of complete prosodic groups. In nondefault cases, prosody conveys marked cohesion among (portions of) separate units joined within the same group, highlighting them as "action-and-response."

In parts II and III the default is largely followed, but we are provided with six revealing nondefault cases that further refine the action-and-response interpretation. In part III, episode (iv), Cb and Cc are grouped together much as B and C are in part I, episodes (i), (ii), and (v). The other five examples involve conversational adjacency pairs (see Levinson 1983:303–6) consisting of request-and-refusal or statement-and-rejoinder: in part II, the grandson's excuse in B is grouped in [21] with the grandmother's skeptical rejoinder in C; in part III, episode (ii), the shaman's request in Aa is grouped in [37] with the beginning of the grandson's first refusal in Ab; and the grandson's excuses in Ab are grouped with the shaman's denial of them in Ac in group [55] of episode (iii) and in groups [67] and [68] of episode (v). It thus seems that the joining of units of form–content parallelism within prosodic groups is a significant tool for representing conversation inside narrative.

4.3   Conclusions

In these interactions there is remarkable convergence at the top: Sections and units of form–content parallelism always correspond one-to-one; sections/episodes are reinforced in one case by the use of interjectional particles; and falsetto voice reinforces section-sized form–content units (but not sections directly). At a lower level, however, prosodic grouping operates within a rather broadly defined default relative to units of form–content parallelism, conveying special meaning with nondefault alignments.

5   Overall conclusions and outlook

In this investigation we have seen a number of ways in which rhetorical structure is modular in Mezak's *Tutgara'urluqelriik*, involving discrete, very different, components. Formally, three distinct types of recurrent, hierarchic organizations characterized the components: nondiscrete hierarchy (in pause phrasing), discrete hierarchy (in prosodic phrasing and syntactic constituency), and numerically constrained hierarchy (in form–content parallelism in the narrative, and in a variety of components in the song). The components were distinct too in that they were based on different types of formal features, from paralinguistic to phonological to syntactic to lexical. Most important, the components were distinct in that it was impossible accurately to predict the form or distribution of units of any one component given the distribution of units of the others. Indeed the most we could usually do was to specify certain alignments as default cases.

Along with this modularity, we have also seen evidence for the other essential feature of rhetorical structure, significant interaction among its components. Predictable alignments constituted a formal interaction, while meaningful departures from default alignments constituted interaction among different components toward special communicative ends. I will now draw conclusions about the nature of each of them.

Predictable alignments among units of different components were proposed in (7) and (8) for pause and prosodic phrasing, in (11) for prosodic phrasing and syntactic constituency, and in (33) and (35) for prosodic phrasing and form–content parallelism. All define a default alignment in which there is one-to-one correspondence – and hence mutual reinforcement – between units of different components, but they differ in how narrowly and strictly that alignment is actually followed:

(36)

Rule	Units	Alignment type			
		$1:1$	$1:n$	$n:1$	Disalignment
(7)	Line : pause phrase	D	+	+	+
(8)	Subgroup : pause-phrase cluster	D	+	+	+
(11)	Subgroup : sentence	D	+	+	+
(33)	Section : form–content unit$_i{}^a$	O	–	–	–
(35)	Group : form–content unit$_j$	D	+	D	+

Note: n is an integer greater than 1; D = occurs as default alignment; O = occurs as an obligatory alignment; + = occurs as nondefault; – = does not occur at all. Form–content units$_{i,j}$ are the regular correspondents of sections and groups, respectively, in a given stretch of discourse. (These differ in parts I, II, and III.)
[a] In nondefault case, 1:1 correspondence is with the next form–content unit up.

In effect, the strongest convergence is between sections and units of form–content parallelism, where we always found one-to-one correspondence. And the weakest convergence shown here is between groups and units of form–content parallelism at a lower level, where all possible alignments exist and the default is defined broadly.

This strong convergence with form–content parallelism at the top of the prosodic hierarchy makes the section (and its correspondents) a good candidate as a basic unit of rhetorical structure as a whole, abstracted from particular subcomponents (even though there would remain some problems). By contrast, such lower-level units as groups, subgroups, pause phrases, and sentences cannot be abstracted in this way, since they show much less absolute convergence. This has major implications, for while there has been important work done on the relation of prosody to sentence syntax in sentence-based grammatical frameworks (see esp. Selkirk 1984), it suggests that the sentence is a much less autonomous domain in which to study interaction of prosody and syntactic form than the section is. If so, it is further indication of a highly complex linguistic competence residing above the level of the sentence. One would predict that theories of sentence-internal syntax–prosody interaction would be simplified if contextualized in a section-level theory.

We turn now to the other type of interaction among components, in which meaning is conveyed by violating expected default alignments. In Mezak's *Tutgara'urluqelriik* such divergences were assigned invariant meanings or expressive values, but these values were remarkably abstract: "an impression of rapidity" in (7); "dramatic anticipation" in (8); "cohesion" and "disjunction" in (8), (11), and (35); "a composite organization of content in discourse" and "highlighting or merging" of pattern and pattern extension in (33) (as clarified in (34)); and "action-and-response" in (35). The same was so for much of the meaning within the form–content parallelism component, summarized in section 3.7. In spite of this abstractness, these forms are interpreted in context quite concretely by what must be complex processes of inference. From the "dramatic anticipation" we would associate (by rule (8)) with the long pause in line 2 of [4] (discussed as (10)), we infer that something interesting or unusual happened to the grandson as he went upriver; from the "action-and-response" we would associate (by (35)) with the two-unit conversational adjacency pair squeezed into a single group in [67], we infer the shaman's impatience and unwillingness to be tricked. Nondefault interactions among rhetorical-structure units must therefore be included among the growing list of formal linguistic devices found to play major roles in nonreferential aspects of discourse understanding, including intonation, paralinguistic features, non-verbal signs, and mid-utterance register switching and code switching. In most of these cases, very little invariant meaning or expressive force can be imputed to the form itself; instead, speakers construct and test possible inter-pretations of them almost entirely in context based on background knowledge, text content, situation, and community-specific "contextualization conventions" (see Gumperz 1982 for discussion of these kinds of form in discourse, and this approach to their interpretation; Levinson 1983 provides a context for it in linguistic and philosophical pragmatics). Clearly, a fully scientific account of rhetorical structure would need to go beyond positing the abstract char-acterization of nondefault alignments, and specify the actual mechanisms and details by which inferences and situated interpretations actually arise from them.

I have made my case for rhetorical structure from a single text. Yet as a framework, it should be useful far beyond that. For one thing, the pursuit of rhetorical structure raises hopes for a better understanding of genre differences both in CAY and in other languages. For example, rhetorical-structure analysis made it possible to characterize far-reaching similarities and differences between the narrative and song portions of the text within a single framework. Such characterization is important, since it leads one to ask a variety of interesting questions about the range of variation to be expected once many genres and styles within a given language are surveyed: Will sections (or their equivalent) be a major point of convergence in all more-or-less extemporaneous spoken language? (Investigation so far suggests this is the case in CAY.) Will units of different components always set their default alignments at one-to-one, and if so, will the units involved reside at some consistent level? To what degree will regular *dis*alignment along units of different components serve as the default in some genres (as it seems to do within lines in Mezak's song)?

More broadly, it is important to develop typologies of rhetorical structures across languages. (See Woodbury 1985:180–2 for a few suggestions about what this might look like.) These should specify what components are obligatory, what components are optional, and what components are possible at all; what kinds of hierarchical structure components may have; what kinds of alignments can exist between components; and what kinds of meaning individual components, as well as components interacting with each other, might convey. A full theory of rhetorical structure would have to make predictions on all of these questions and carefully rule out what does not actually occur. In this it must take its cue from the other simultaneous-autonomous-component theories now being discussed for alignments and interactions in phonology, morphology, and syntax. The present framework should be seen as a beginning to this, in serious need of further data and analysis in its terms.

Appendix: Evon Mezak's *Tutgara'urluqelriik* (Grandchild and Grandmother)[15]

The following is a transcript and translation of a *quliraq* (traditional tale) told by Evon Mezak (19??–74), known also as Aatacuar ("little father"), of Nunapitchuk, Alaska, in the variety of the General Central Yupik dialect of Central Alaskan Yupik that is native to that area. The recording was probably made in the early 1970s, probably in the presence of members of Mezak's extended family (including two women whose laughter is audible on the tape). It was brought to my attention by Irene Reed as part of a collection of Mezak materials taken by one of Mezak's grandchildren to the Yup'ik Language Workshop in Bethel, Alaska, while Reed was there in 1974–6. Mary Gregory, a GCY-speaker from Kipnuk and Bethel, dictated the text to me from the tape in March 1983, giving me word-by-word – and some sentence – translations. Later I made a few revisions in the transcript from the tape and prepared a translation based on Ms. Gregory's translations, the original text, and information from other speakers and scholarly sources. Chase Hensel, Phyllis Morrow, Irene Reed, and especially Elsie Mather provided valuable comments and suggestions on an earlier version of the transcript and translation.

Although Mezak does not give a title for his *quliraq*, I follow the standard CAY practice of using the designation of the first characters introduced, here *Tutgara'urluqelriik* (Grandchild and Grandmother). Furthermore, all subtitles and annotations were introduced by me, as guides to analysis, rather than by Mezak. The transcript's basic graphic organization follows prosodic phrasing (see sect. 2.1): prosodic "lines" are accorded lines of text, followed by indications of the intonation contours they bear (A, !A, B, B+, etc., discussed in sect. 2.1); "groups" of prosodic lines are numbered with arabic numerals in square brackets, from [1] to [76]; within groups, lines are successively indented except that the first line of a new "subgroup" within a group begins flush left (see [9]); and prosodic "sections" are separated with three asterisks (* * *).

Italics indicate falsetto voice quality. To the right of each line, the duration of the pause that follows it is given to the nearest tenth of a second (in angled brackets). Finally, numerically constrained form–content parallelism (see sect. 3) is indicated as follows: major parts (0, I, II . . .) and episodes (i, ii, iii . . .) are headed with mnemonic titles in square brackets; divisions (A, B, C) or subdivisions (Aa, Ab, Ac, Ba . . .) within them are indicated in the left margin. The transcription itself uses the standard CAY orthography (Reed et al. 1977), except that /v/ and /w/ (both *v* in the orthography) are distinguished as *v* and *v̄*, expressive vowel length (:) and aspiration (ʰ) are noted, and intonational sandhi is marked with a ligature (ˆ). In the translation I endeavored to follow the wording and structure of the original as closely as was possible while remaining consistent with the referential and expressive content of the original, as elucidated by Mary Gregory and Elsie Mather. In my view it would have been more of a disservice to withhold their insights in the interest of a better-calqued translation than it is to expect serious readers to keep an eye on the left-hand side of the page!

After this paper was substantially written, a transcript and translation of another performance by Mezak of this same story came to my attention. It is part of another set of Mezak tapes furnished to the Yup'ik Language Workshop around the same time as the set that includes the present tape. It consists of twenty stories transcribed and translated by several native speakers and Irene Reed, listed by title (along with transcript page lengths) on an undated sheet of paper headed "Materials from Evon Mezak: Traditional and historical tales." These materials are now in the archives of the Alaska Native Language Center. The "Materials" version of the story is entitled "*Nukalpiaq tuunrilek*" 'Youth with spirit powers' by its native transcriber. It is very significant that that version is nearly identical to the present one, even down to the minutest details of morphology, word order, and particle and enclitic usage, for it clearly indicates that Mezak had memorized the *quliraq* word for word. At the same time, however, the "Materials" version contains a sixth episode in parts I and III that alters the import of the story radically (see note 10).

[0. Ayagneq]			[0. Introduction]
[1]			[1]
Nunat ˆukut	A	⟨0.⟩	There was a village (of people)
uitaura'rqelriit	A	⟨0.⟩	who lived
kuigem ˆceñiini.	B	⟨2.8⟩	on the bank of a river.
[2]			[2]
Tutgara'urluqelriigneg ila-			They had *there* a grandchild

lu*teng*. Tutgara'urlurlu*a* ˆim',	A ⟨1.5⟩		and grandmother. And the grandchild
tan'ga'ūrlull'rauluni			was a poor little boy, a
angutnguluni=w'.	B ⟨2.5⟩		male.[16]

* * *   * * *

[I. Asgurtuq]		**[I. Grandson goes upriver]**
[3]		[3]
Tua=i=ll'=am caqerluni,	A ⟨2.3⟩	Well once upon a time,
kuigkun ˆ*e:–*	A ⟨0.⟩	*the river eh–*
kuimegteggun=am as-		*he took a trip up their*
gurtuq.	B ⟨1.5⟩	*river.*

* * *   * * *

[i. Qangqiiregnek tekituq]		*[i. Encounters ptarmigans]*
[4]		[4]
A Tua::=iʰ,	A_ ⟨1.4⟩	Well,
asgurturaqerluni,	A ⟨3.1⟩	traveling upriver a little ways,
*qang:qii*regnek,	A ⟨1.7⟩	*he came upon two (wil-low) ptar*migans,
callul:riignek ˆ*tekituq.*	B ⟨1.8⟩	*that were fighting.*

[5]		[5]
B Tua=i=ll' ketairamikek ce-		Well when he went by them
ñami ˆpiagnek:	B+ ⟨1.8⟩	on the bank he said to them:
[6]		[6]
"Aaʰ!	!A_ ⟨1.7⟩	"Hey!
Tua:=i!	!A ⟨2.4⟩	Enough now!
Pisqekumtek ˆtaūgaam		But when I tell you you
piniartutek!	!B ⟨1.8⟩	will carry on some more!
Aa tua=i uter– utertek!"	!A ⟨1.6⟩	Hey enough now, go– go home!"
C Aren imkug=am *qang*qiirek		My and sure enough *the*
niilluteg ˆayagtuk.	B+ ⟨1.7⟩	*ptarmi*gans obeyed and went away.

* * *   * * *

[ii. Ceremraagnek tekituq]

[7]
A Tuamte=llu,   A   ⟨1.0⟩
  ayagtura*q*erluni *cerem-*
  raagnek tekituq.   B   ⟨0.8⟩

[8]
  Ik':ikika amllerrarluteng!   B   ⟨1.3⟩

[9]
B "Aullu=wa=i! Aullu=wa=i!   !A ⟨1.2⟩
  Ciunemni uitanrici!   !B ⟨1.2⟩
  Aa tua=i,   !A ⟨0.3⟩
    pisqekum–   ⟨0.⟩
      *pis*qekumci ˆtaū̄gaam
      *pin*iartuci!"   !B ⟨1.8⟩
C Tua=i tayima.   B+ ⟨2.3⟩

* * *

[iii. Qucillgaagnek tekituq]

[10]
A Ayagturaqerluni,   A   ⟨1.8⟩
    qucillgaagnek tekituq.   B   ⟨1.3⟩

[11]
  *Ciun*rani=am *pil*riik pilriik   A   ⟨0.⟩

  *aren::qial*nguuk yu*ral*riik.   A   ⟨1.6⟩
B   Tua=i=ll'=am pikilikek: B   ⟨1.6⟩

[12]
  "Aa tua:=i tua=i tuaken aū̄g'-
  a'rlutek!   !A ⟨0.9⟩
    Taū̄gaam pisqekumtek,   !A ⟨1.1⟩
    piniartutek!"   !B ⟨0.9⟩

[13]
C Tuamte=ll'=am ˆtua=i–   A_ ⟨0.⟩
  aa tua=i ˆtang na– ˆnii-
  ga'rr*luteng* ˆ*ayagar*culriit.   B+ ⟨1.4⟩

* * *

[ii. Encounters dunlins]

[7]
Then again,
  going *a little ways further*
  he came upon two dunlins.

[8]
Boy there were lots everywhere![17]

[9]
"Watch out! Watch out!
  Don't you be in my way!
Hey, enough now,
  but when I–
    when I tell you you will
    carry on some more!"
And so they were gone.

* * *

[iii. Encounters cranes]

[10]
Going a little ways further,
  *he came upon two (sand-
  hill) cranes.*

[11]
In front of him they were
going, going,
  carrying on and *danc*ing.
  Well he said to them:

[12]
"Hey enough enough be gone
from here!
  But when I tell you,
    you will carry on some
    more!"

[13]
And so then once again–
  oh then they ob– *obeyed*
  him right away and left.

* * *

[iv. Tunturyuaryuugnek tekituq]

[14]

A Piqerluni=am,	A	⟨1.4⟩
*tuntur*yuaryuugnek,	A	⟨1.3⟩
*cirunermiar*autell*riig*-nek *ciun*ran' *tekiar*tuq.	B	⟨1.3⟩

[15]

B "Aa^h!	!A_	⟨1.3⟩
Aullu=wa=i! Aullu=wa=i!	!A	⟨1.6⟩
Tuantevkenatek ciunem-ni!	!A	⟨1.9⟩
Utertek!	!A	⟨2.2⟩
Pisqekumtek ˆta-ūgaam piniartu-tek!"	!B	⟨1.5⟩

* * *

[v. Keglunregnek tekituq]

[16]

A Aren tuamte=ll'=am,	A_	⟨0.9⟩
ayakarluni,	A	⟨1.3⟩
keglunregnek,	A	⟨1.0⟩
ciunrani.	B	⟨2.0⟩

[17]

Arenqiapaa^h!	!A	⟨0.2⟩
B Arenqiatuq alingerrlugtuq:	B	⟨0.2⟩

[18]

"Arenqiapaa ˆtua=i,	A	⟨1.0⟩
utertek!	!A	⟨1.9⟩
Utertek ciunemni uitav-kenatek!	!B	⟨1.1⟩
Pisqekumtek ˆtaūgaam pi-niartutek!"	!B	⟨1.5⟩
C Aren tua=i=am niilluteg ˆayagtuk.	B+	⟨0.8⟩

* * *

[iv. Encounters young caribou]

[14]

Then after a while,
    he suddenly *came upon two young caribou,*
        sparring with their *antlers in front* of him.[18]

[15]

"Hey!
    Watch out! Watch out!
    Don't be there in my way!
        Go home!
        But when I tell you you will carry on some more!"

* * *

[v. Encounters wolves]

[16]

My and then again,
    as he went a little ways further,
        (there were) *two wolves, in front of him.*

[17]

Oh my goodness!
    Goodness he was kind of scared:

[18]

"Oh my goodness enough now,
    Go home!
        Go home and don't be in my way!
But when I tell you you will carry on some more!"
My and sure enough again they obeyed and went away.

* * *

[II. Utertuq]

[19]

A Tua:=i=ll' uterr:luni,   A_ ⟨1.9⟩
   maūrlurluminun tekilluni.   A ⟨1.6⟩

    Tekican   maūrlurluan
    arenqialkii: B ⟨1.9⟩

[20]
"Aa[h]!   !A_ ⟨0.7⟩
   Cali'urlurluten ˆtanem
   ˆtua=i,   A ⟨0.8⟩
    muluv̄akarcit?   A ⟨0.6⟩
     Waqaa ˆtua=i canek
     =llu,   A ⟨0.6⟩
      piyagarnek=llu ta-
      ngerqanrituten?"   B ⟨0.9⟩

[21]
B "Aa ˆtua:=i=w' tangenrril-
  [ngua] ˆcamek!"   A ⟨1.2⟩
C "Aling   aren   piyagaat
  =llu=ggem amllelartut;   B ⟨0.6⟩

  lagiyagaat=llu,   A ⟨0.6⟩
   mat'um nalliini."   B ⟨1.3⟩

      * * *

[III. Qasgiuq]

[22]
Aren:: peka!   !A ⟨1.4⟩
   Ununrakun tekicami,   A ⟨1.0⟩

    tua=i   nerurall'rarraar-
    luni,   A ⟨1.1⟩
     qasgi'ūrlurtuq.   B ⟨0.7⟩

Aren ˆqasgi'ūrlurtur=am
ˆim',   A ⟨1.1⟩

[II. Grandson goes home]

[19]
Well then he headed home
   and reached his poor
   grandmother.
    When he got there his
    poor grandmother was
    worried about him:

[20]
"Oh!
    What were you doing
    now, poor one,
    that kept you so late?
    What is it now,

     didn't you even see
     any little birds?"[19]

[21]
"Oh well, I didn't see much
of anything!"
    "Dear me but I thought
    those little birds were
    abundant;
and baby geese too,
   at this time (of year)."[20]

      * * *

**[III. Grandson goes to the
    qasgiq]**

[22]
My what a journey!
    When he came home at
    night,
     and had taken his time
     eating,
      he shambled off to the
      qasgiq, poor guy.
My when he had shambled
off to the qasgiq,

ik'iki tua=i ˆtang angal-
kulilriit ˆukut!   !B+ ⟨0.6⟩

* * *

boy look how many sha-
mans they had!

* * *

[i. Qangqiirek it'resqak]

[23]
Aa Tua:::=i=ll',   A_ ⟨1.8⟩
   cauyalnguameng *angal-*
   kuit,   A ⟨0.7⟩
      iliit=am qanertuq: B ⟨0.4⟩
   "Aling,   A ⟨1.2⟩
      tutgara'urluq tang ˆuna,   !A ⟨1.0⟩
      cauyarcetqerciu!   !B ⟨1.2⟩
   Tayima yuarulluitenrituq.   !B ⟨1.4⟩

   Atumcinarqelartuq,   !A ⟨0.8⟩
   cailkami."   !B ⟨4.0⟩

* * *

[i. Calls in the ptarmigans]

[23]
Well,
   because their *shamans*
   were tired of drumming,
   one of them said:
"Hey,
   this grandchild here,
   let him drum!
He mustn't be entirely without songs.
One usually has to sing a bit,
out in the wilderness."21

* * *

[24]
Aren::qia ˆpia: (?)   A ⟨0.⟩

   "Ilumun! Ilumun ˆtang cauyaqaa!"   !B+ ⟨1.3⟩

[24]
Oh goodness (one of them)
said (?) to him:
   "Surely! Surely you will
   drum (for us)!"

[25]
Ab "Aren wii:nga=wa,   A ⟨1.0⟩
   eng–   ⟨0.5⟩
      cameg   ˆneq'ak'ngail-
   ngua!"   !B ⟨2.1⟩

[25]
"My but me,
   uh–
      I cannot remember a
   thing!"

[26]
Ac "Aa ˆqang'a! Qang'a!   !A ⟨1.1⟩
   Qessakan,   !A ⟨0.6⟩
      amigmun ciryaaruski-
   ciu!"   !B ⟨1.1⟩

[26]
"Oh no! No!
   If he is unwilling,
      throw him at the door
   head first!"

* * *

[27]
Ba Aren tua::=i ˆaa,   A_ ⟨1.6⟩
      tua::=i t(ang) ˆarenqialnguq: B ⟨0.8⟩
   "Cauyaqaa!"   !B ⟨1.3⟩

* * *

[27]
Oh my then,
   then he had no choice:
"Drum!"

[28]		
Aren tua=i iliit,	!A	⟨0.9⟩
iliita cauyamek cikiraa!	!B	⟨1.4⟩
[29]		
Tua=i=ll',	A_	⟨0.5⟩
arenqialami,	A	⟨0.1⟩
amigmun ciryaarucii-		
qelliniatni *qiiv*ciuq:	B	⟨0.8⟩

[30]

Bb Nani——mi qamani ngay
     hyaa–a?
  Kangi–mi qamani ngay
     hyaa–a!
  Qangqii——ra——ag
     iterlii——k!

[31]		
Bc/ Aren piqanratgun qangqiirek		
Ca ^un*kuk* al*pa*kartuk:	B	⟨1.0⟩
[32]		
"Qangqihihihi!	!B	⟨0.3⟩
Ca͞viituten!	!B	⟨1.2⟩
Ca͞viituten!"	!B	⟨1.0⟩

* * *

[33]		
Aa[h]!	!A_	⟨1.1⟩
Tua::=i una::=i arenqia-		
natek.	B	⟨1.1⟩
[34]		
Cb Aa[h]!	!A_	⟨0.4⟩
Tutgara' urlull' raam piki-		
likek:	B	⟨0.5⟩
"Aa[h] ^kitaki ^tua=i anitek!	!B	⟨0.9⟩
An'ariatek!	!B	⟨0.6⟩

[28]
My then one of them,
  one of them gave him a
  drum!

[29]
Well,
  because he had no choice,
  because they would
  throw him at the door
  head first he *started* a
  low rumbling on the
  drum:

[30]
At what place upriver ngay
  hyaa?
At the source upriver ngay
  hyaa!
May the two ptar-rmigan-
  n-ns en-nter![22]

[31]
My, at once the two ptar-
migans *burst* in *down* there
from nowhere:

[32]
"Qangqihihihi!
Ca͞viituten!
Ca͞viituten!"[23]

* * *

[33]
Oh!
  Then they were all aflutter
  down there.

[34]
Oh!
  The poor little grandson
  said to them:
"Hey come on enough now,
go out!
It is time you go out!

| Canritutek!" | !B ⟨1.9⟩ | There is nothing more for you!" |

[35]
Aren ˆpisqe◌̄ngatek   A ⟨0.⟩   My and when he said so
   an'uk.   B+ ⟨0.6⟩   they went out.

        * * *   * * *

[ii. Ceremraat it'resqak]   *[ii. Calls in the dunlins]*

[36]   [36]
[*:t]!   ⟨0.5⟩   [*:t]![24]
  Arenqiapaa=ll'!   !B ⟨0.⟩   Oh my goodness!
Iliit=am ˆ*taukut qanertuq*: B ⟨0.5⟩   *Again one of them spoke:*

[37]   [37]
"Arenqiapaa=ll'!   !A ⟨0.7⟩   "Oh my goodness!
  Nutaan ˆatam angalkung-   Now for sure we are going
  ciqialriakut!   !B ⟨0.6⟩   to get a shaman!
Cali ˆtua=i piqaa!"   !B ⟨0.7⟩   Do it once again now!"
"Aren ˆtua:=i,   !A ⟨0.6⟩   "My that's enough now,
  nangutuaʰ!   !B ⟨2.1⟩   I have no more.

[38]   [38]
Tua=i ˆwaten pilii!"   B ⟨2.5⟩   Enough of that for me!"

[39]   [39]
"Ahʰ ˆqessakan amig–   "Hey if he is unwilling, throw
amigmun ciryaaruskiciu!" !B ⟨1.1⟩   him at the d–door head first!"

        * * *   * * *

[40]   [40]
Aling::naqvaa=ll'!   !B ⟨1.2⟩   Oh dear me!
Tua::=i=ll'=am   arenqialat-   And so again because they
ni=am qiivciuq: B ⟨0.7⟩   gave him no choice he started
                            a low rumbling on the drum:

[41]   [41]
Nga yaa=i nga yaa=i ngay   (Song words)
    hyaa—a!
Nga yaa————=i ua———a!
    Aa ngaa!
Nga yaa=i nga yaa=i ngay
    hyaa! Aa=i!

Nani—mi qama—ni ngay
  hyaa—a?
Kangi–mi qama—ni ngay
  hyaa—a!
Ceremra————at iter-
  lii————t!

* * *

At what place upriver ngay
  hyaa?
At the source upriver ngay
  hyaa!
May the flock of du-u-u-un-
  lins en-nter!

* * *

[42]

Bc/   Aren ˆit'resqeng̅ateng aren-
Ca   qiapaa=ll',   A_ ⟨1.2⟩
        ceremraurtur ˆun'a,   A ⟨0.2⟩

        nacitet qaingat.   B+ ⟨1.7⟩

[42]
My, when he said to enter
oh my goodness,
    dunlins appeared down
    there,
        all over the firepit
        planks.

[iii. Qucilgaak it'resqak]

[43]

Aa   Ik'ikika *a*ren*q*iatut ta*ma*kut,   A ⟨1.1⟩

        *irr*iut: B+ ⟨1.6⟩

[iii. Calls in the cranes]

[43]
Boy there were lots and *those*
people,
    they were amazed:

[44]
"Arenqiapaa=ll'!   !B ⟨1.2⟩
Nutaan ˆatam,   !A ⟨1.0⟩
  angalkungciqialriakut
  alailngurmek!   !B ⟨1.2⟩
Tua=i cali ˆpiqaa!"   !B+ ⟨1.6⟩

* * *

[44]
"Oh my goodness!
Now for sure,
    we are going to get a sha-
    man we can see!
Now do it once again!"

* * *

[45]

Cc   Aren tua:=i=am imkut anes-
      qeng̅ateng an'ut.   B_ ⟨1.2⟩

[45]
My and sure enough when
he said for the dunlins to go
out they went out.

[46]

Ac   Aren tua=i ˆtaun':   A ⟨0.3⟩

        "Nengugeskiciu qessa-
        kan!"   !B ⟨1.1⟩

[46]
My then one (of the men
said):
    "Stretch him if he is un-
    willing!"

[47]

Ab   "Aren:qia:paa=ll'!   !B ⟨1.0⟩
      Tua=i neq'aq'ngairutua!"[25]   !B ⟨0.9⟩

[47]
"Oh my goodness!
I can't remember any more!"

[48]

c' "Qang'a! !B ⟨0.8⟩

Neq'aq'ngengqertutenˆcali! !A ⟨0.5⟩

Neq'aq'ngai– neq'aq'-
ngailkuvet, !A ⟨0.6⟩
    iteryanritut aūgkut! !A ⟨0.6⟩

Nengugciu! Nengu-
gciu!" !B ⟨0.8⟩

[49]

a Aren tua:=i=am arenqialatni, A ⟨0.3⟩

qiivciuq: B ⟨3.3⟩

[50]

b Nga yaa=i nga yaa=i ngay
    hyaa—a!
Nga yaa=i nga yaa=i ngay
    hyaa—a!
Nga yaa———=i ua———a!
    Aa ngaa!
Nga yaa=i nga yaa=i ngay
    hyaa! Aa=i!

Nani—mi qama—ni ngay
    hyaa—a?
Kangi– mi qama—ni ngay
    hyaa—a!
Qucillga———ag iter-
    lii——k!

[51]

c/ "Quter::!" ⟨0.⟩
a Ilait *tatamluteng tuaten*, A ⟨0.8⟩

    alpakartuk. B ⟨0.8⟩

[52]

Ik':iki*ka*, !A ⟨0.8⟩
    qecguag ˆu*na*ni! B ⟨0.8⟩

[48]

"No!

You still have some left in
your memory!
    If you didn't– if you didn't
    remember,
        those out there wouldn't
        have come in!
            Stretch him! Stretch
            him!"

[49]

My then again because they
gave him no choice,
    he started a low rumbling
    on the drum:

[50]

(Song words)

At what place upriver ngay
    hyaa?
At the source upriver ngay
    hyaa!
May the two cra-a-a-anes en-
    nter!

[51]

"Quter::!"
Startling some of them with
that,
    *they burst in from no-
    where.*

[52]

Boy they were something,
    jumping around *down*
    there!

[53]

Cb Arenqiapaa!   !A ⟨0.8⟩
    "Tua=i tua=i!"   !A ⟨0.9⟩
      Uum wani,   A ⟨0.8⟩
        *pi*kilikek.   B ⟨0.⟩
    "Tua=i tua=i,   !A ⟨0.6⟩
      pissiyaagpek'natek!   !A ⟨0.5⟩
      Amci aniteg maanel-
      kaunrirtuq!"   !B ⟨1.2⟩

               * * *

[53]

Oh my goodness!
  "Enough, enough!"
    The (grandson) *here*,
      was saying to them.
  "Enough, enough,
    don't carry on so much!
    Come on, go out, you
    can't be here any more!"

               * * *

[iv. Tunturyuaryuuk
it'resqak]

[54]

Aa Tua::=i=am:,   A_ ⟨0.4⟩
      anngan: A ⟨0.1⟩

      "Arenqiapaa=ll'!   B ⟨1.0⟩
    Nutaan ˆatam,   !A ⟨0.9⟩
      angalkungciqialriakut,   !B ⟨0.6⟩

      alailngurmek,   !B° ⟨0.8⟩
      tuunralegmeg alail-
      ngurmek!   !B° ⟨0.9⟩
    Aa^h ˆtua=i cali ˆpiqaa!"   !B+ ⟨0.4⟩

[55]

Ab "Aren ˆtua=i nangutua!"   !B ⟨0.7⟩

Ac "Qang'a ˆnangutenrituq!   !B ⟨1.7⟩
    Amigmun ciryaaruskiciu,   !A ⟨0.8⟩

      nenguggluku=llu aipaag-
      ni!"   !B+ ⟨0.6⟩
      ⟨qusngallagtuq⟩   ⟨6.0⟩

[56]

Ab' Arenqiatuq!   !A ⟨1.1⟩
      Qusngarcami ˆpiuq.   B+ ⟨1.1⟩

    Qusrem tuc'ani,   A ⟨1.5⟩
      qanerciigatur ˆav̄a=i.   B+ ⟨0.9⟩

               * * *

[iv. Calls in the young
caribou]

[54]

Well,
    when they went out (one
    man said):
    "Oh my goodness!
Now for sure,
    we are going to get a sha-
    man,
    one we can see,
      a spirit owner we can
      see!
Oh, now do it once again!"

[55]

"That's all, it has run out on
me!"

"No it hasn't run out!
Throw him at the door head
first,
    or else stretch him out!"

      ⟨coughs⟩

[56]

Goodness!
    Because a cough was com-
    ing on he coughed.
When the cough got him,
    he could not speak then.

               * * *

[57]

Tua::=i=ll'   piqer:luni=am
arenqialatni=am,   A_ ⟨0.8⟩
    nengugcuatni,   A ⟨1.3⟩

    qiivciuq: B ⟨1.4⟩

[58]

Nga yaa=i nga yaa=i ngay
    hyaa—a!
Nga yaa=i nga yaa=i ngay
    hyaa—a!
Nga yaa————=i ua————a!
    Aa ngaa!
Nga yaa=i nga yaa=i ngay
    hyaa! Aa=i!

Nani—mi qama—ni ngay
    hyaa—a?
Kangi– mi qama—ni ngay
    hyaa—a!
Tun–tur–yuar–yu————ug
    iterlii————k!

[59]

Aa ^piqanratgun=am *tun*tur-
yuaryuuk: B ⟨0.3⟩
"[h̄:]!   ⟨0.3⟩
    [h̄:]!   ⟨0.3⟩
        [h̄:]!"   ⟨0.3⟩
*Aren*qiatut ^imkut,   A ⟨0.3⟩

    ci*ru*nekek=ll' *arenqia*-
    lagnek.   B ⟨1.1⟩

            * * *

[60]

Tua::=i=ll' kanani ciruner-
miaraulluteg nacitet qai-
ngatni.   B ⟨0.5⟩

[61]

Arenqiapa'! Arenqiapaa!   !A ⟨1.2⟩

[57]

Well, soon after because they
gave him no choice,
    because they would stretch
    him,
        he started a low rum-
        bling on the drum:

[58]

(Song words)

At what place upriver ngay
    hyaa?
At the source upriver ngay
    hyaa!
May the two young ca-ari-
    bou-u-u en-nter!

[59]

Oh at once the two young
*ca*ribou (burst in, going):
"[h̄:]!
    [h̄:]!
        [h̄:]!"[26]
They were impressed those
people,
    because those *ant*lers *were*
    impressive.

            * * *

[60]

Well, they sparred with their
antlers down there on the
firepit planks.

[61]

Oh my goodness! Oh my
goodness!

Aren ˆukut *tua=i* qasgimiut
qaneqsaunateng,   A ⟨0.8⟩
  ilait   qanevyuaraqa'aq-
  l(uteng):   B ⟨0.8⟩
"*Ayayay ˆcaca ˆcak ˆtanem
kankuk!*   B ⟨0.4⟩

Ca– ˆcaugek ˆtanem *kankuk?*"   B+ ⟨0.7⟩

[62]
Cb "Aullu=wa=i! Aullu=wa=i!   !A ⟨0.8⟩
  Tuaten pivkenateg ˆamci
  anitek!"   B ⟨0.8⟩
Cc [*:t]!   !A ⟨0.3⟩
  Aren ˆtua:=i=am anesqe-
  n̄gateg ˆan'uk.   B+ ⟨2.4⟩

* * *

[v. Keglunrek it'resqak]

[63]
Aa "Aling:*naq*vaa=ll'!   B ⟨0.7⟩
  Nutaan ˆatam angalkungci-
  qialriakut,   !B+ ⟨1.0⟩
    alailngurmek!   !B° ⟨1.0⟩

[64]
  "Arenqiatuq!   B ⟨0.7⟩
  Cauyarualallerni ˆat' ˆkitak
  tangerciu!   !B ⟨0.16⟩
    ⟨qusngallagtuq⟩   ⟨4.6⟩
  Aʰ ˆcali– cali ˆtua=i piqaa!   !B ⟨1.3⟩
    ⟨qusngallagtuq⟩   ⟨3.8⟩

[65]
  (Arenqiatua ˆtang qusrem
  tullua qusriyungua!)   !B ⟨0.⟩

    ⟨ngel'allagtut⟩   ⟨3.8⟩

[66]
Aa' "Arenqiapaa cali piqaa!"   !B ⟨0.⟩

    ⟨ngel'allagtut⟩   ⟨2.5⟩

The qasgiq people *oh* they
did not speak
  until some mumbled:

"*Ayayay! Wh– wh– what in
the world, those two down
there?*
"*Wh–* what in the world are
those *down there?*"

[62]
"Watch out! Watch out!
  Stop carrying on like that,
  come on, go out!"
[*:t]!
  My and sure enough again,
  when he said to go out they
  went out.

* * *

[v. Calls in the wolves]

[63]
"*Oh* dear me!
  Now for sure we are going
  to get a shaman,
    one we can see!

[64]
"Goodness!
  You who merely play with
  the drums, take a look at him!
    ⟨coughs⟩
  Oh again– do it once again!"
    ⟨coughs⟩

[65]
(Oh goodness me, the cough
  is getting to me and now *I'm*
  doing it!)
    ⟨laughter⟩

[66]
"Oh my goodness do it
  again!"
    ⟨laughter⟩

[67]

o "Aren tua=i=w' nangutell-

riánga!"   !B   ⟨1.1⟩

c "Qang'a nangutenrituq!"   !B+ ⟨1.6⟩

⟨qusngallagtuq⟩   ⟨2.8⟩

[67]

"That's enough, it has really
run out on me!"

"No it hasn't run out!"

⟨coughs⟩

[68]

b' "Aa ˆtua=i ˆtang qusrem=llu

pivaqaanga,   !A   ⟨0.4⟩

nangutua!"   !B   ⟨0.9⟩

c' "Nengugciu!   !A   ⟨0.⟩

Nengugciu atra'rrluku!   !B   ⟨0.4⟩

Qeñarqelria ugna!"   !B   ⟨2.9⟩

[68]

"Oh now look this coughing
is getting to me,

I have run out!"

"Stretch him!

Stretch him, get him down
(on the floor)!

He is infuriating, this one!"

* * *

* * *

[69]

a Aren::qia ˆaren:qialatni=am

ˆtua=i,   A   ⟨1.6⟩

qiivciuq: B   ⟨2.7⟩

[69]

Goodness, because again
they gave him no choice then,

he started a low rumbling
on the drum:

[70]

b Nga yaa=i nga yaa=i nga

hyaa————————a!

Nga yaa=i nga yaa=i nga

hyaa————————a!

Nga yaa————=i ua————a!

Aa ngaa!

Nga yaa=i nga yaa=i ngay

hyaa! Aa=i!

Nani—mi qama—ni ngay

hyaa—a?

Kangi– mi qama—ni ngay

hyaa—a!

Keglunra————ag

iterlii———k!

[70]

(Song words)

At what place upriver ngay
hyaa?

At the source upriver ngay
hyaa!

May the two wo-o-olves en-
nter!

* * *

* * *

[71]

3c/ Aren ˆtua:=i=am piqerlutek

2a   ˆkankuk ˆkeglunreg alpa-

kartuk.   B_ ⟨0.8⟩

[71]

My, well soon two wolves
burst in down there from nowhere.

Ik'ikika am'amam ˆmakut
ˆatam cautaarlukek.   B   ⟨0.8⟩

Boy oh boy, ayayay! They
faced *the people*, going back
and forth.

[72]
Cb "Aullu=wa=i! Aullu=wa=i!   !A   ⟨0.7⟩
     Tamakut cautaarpek'nakek
     tamaani pitek!"   !B   ⟨0.9⟩

[72]
"Watch out! Watch out!
   Don't face them, just go
   about your business!"

* * *

[73]
Bc/ Aren::qiatut.   B   ⟨1.3⟩
Ca'

[73]
They were in awe.

[74]
Cb' Tua=i: A_ ⟨0.⟩
     "Arenqiatuq maancunai-
      rutaateg ˆamci anitek!"   !B+ ⟨1.0⟩

[74]
And so (he said):
   "Now you no longer have
   reason to be here, come
   on, go out!"

[75]
Cc   Aren tua=i=am pisqeṅgatek
     ˆtayim anqertuk.   B+ ⟨0.4⟩

[75]
My and sure enough again
when he said so they hurried
out and were gone.

* * *

[IV. Nangneq]

[76]
Aren tua::=i=ll' nang::qerr:-
lun'.   B+

[IV. Ending]

[76]
My, well now that's it, it's
over.

65 beats (♪) per minute
Up one semitone

Nga yaa =i nga yaa =i ngay hyaa!

Nga yaa =i nga yaa =i ngay hyaa!

Nga yaa -a -a =i u -a -a! Aa nga -a!

Nga yaa =i nga yaa =i ngay hyaa! Aa=i!

Na -ni -mi qa -ma -ni ngay hyaa?

Ka -ngi -mi qa -ma -ni ngay hyaa!

i. Qang -qi -ra -ag i -te -rl -iik!

ii. Ce -rem -ra -at ...

iii. Qu -cill -ga -ag ...

iv. Tun -tur -yuar -yu -ug ...

v. Keglun -ra -ag ...

Note: The song transcription is based in part on instrumental acoustic analysis (waveform display, pitch tracking, and sound spectrograph analysis) and was carried out with extensive guidance and collaboration from Steven Feld (who must not be held responsible for infelicities in the final product!). The tonal center is written as C; as Feld has noted, there is an ascending neutral third (between the major and minor thirds) written as E, an ascending perfect fifth written as G, and a strongly variable descending neutral second written as A. The meter, manifested most clearly by amplitude pulses, is quite asymmetric; thus although measures consist always of a strong and a weak beat (except in the last line), some beats add up to more than a quarter note and others to less than one. It would be wrong, however, to consider this an imperfection of performance. For one thing, the meter is always asymmetric in exactly the same places and in the same ways from one episode to the next. For another, the prosodic structure (see Reed et al. 1977) of the song words lends a considerable degree of predictability to the meter: For example, vowel clusters and closed syllables generally occur with irregularly dotted eighth notes rather than undotted eighth notes, suggesting that these dotted eighth notes are underlying undotted. Both these considerations suggest that beat irregularity is a fixed, patterned phenomenon and is intrinsic to the song.

234 ANTHONY C. WOODBURY

Notes

wish to thank Mary Gregory, Elsie Mather, Ida Alexie, and the many other native
CAY-speakers in Bethel who made substantial contributions to my linguistic investigations
there. Financial support for this research was provided by the National Science Foundation
(BNS-8217785), for which I am very grateful. I have benefited from discussion of
issues taken up here and (in most cases) of earlier drafts of this chapter with Chase
Hensel, Dell Hymes, Elsie Mather, Phyllis Morrow, Irene Reed, Jerrold Sadock, Joel
Sherzer, and Dennis Tedlock, and from extensive discussion and analysis of Mezak's
song with Steven Feld. I am especially grateful to William Hanks for his extensive
written comments on an earlier draft. Errors and infelicities that remain are, needless
to say, my responsibility alone.

1   "Rhetorical structure" here embraces less than "rhetoric" does in its traditional
    sense. I use it instead of "poetic function" or "poetics" in order to avoid the
    connotation of "poetry" as a set of genres: As Jakobson (1960) pointed out, poetic
    function may be present in such nonpoetry as campaign slogans. Moreover, the
    formal features that rhetorical structure embraces have functions beyond verbal
    art, such as organization of information and regulation of dialogic interaction,
    as already noted.

2   Many other components may occur. On the phonological side one might find a
    conflict (in certain verse passages) between imposed versus natural metrical or-
    ganization, where the oral reader must choose to render one overtly and leave
    the other implicit (Jakobson 1960:367). In such cases it is necessary to establish
    these as separate prosodic components. And one might distinguish a component
    for sandhi phrasing if it fails to coincide with intonationally defined prosodic
    phrasing. On the side of syntax and content – even restricting consideration to
    discourse above the level of the sentence – one would include divisions defined
    by speaking turns in conversation (cf. Sacks, Schegeloff, and Jefferson 1974;
    Silverstein 1985a); divisions defined by successions of framed quotations in
    narrative (Silverstein 1985b); and topic chaining, that is, the formal unification
    of sequences of sentences sharing the same topic noun phrase, especially clear
    in languages that mark it simply and overtly (e.g. Dyirbal topic chaining [Dixon
    1972], Algonkian "obviation" [Goddard 1985; Wolfart 1973], and the various
    "switch-reference" systems [Haiman and Munro 1983]). There is of couse no
    logical necessity for these different types of discourse segmentation to coincide;
    hence their treatment as separate rhetorical structure components is strongly
    indicated.

3   This discussion represents a first attempt at accounting for the prosodic system
    (above word level) of any variety of the GCY dialect of CAY. Prosody varies
    considerably from dialect to dialect: Compare this with my description of HBC
    dialect prosody (Woodbury 1985).

4   B° is much more salient in HBC dialect intonation; cf. Woodbury 1985. I have
    actually identified it in the GCY dialect only on partly functional grounds, in
    anticipation of an improved formal description.

5   The example in (1) happens to have just one contour per line. To determine the
    number of contours in any line of Mezak's *quliraq*, simply count the number of
    words not linked to a preceding word by a ligature (ˆ). (E.g. the contour count

for the six lines in (5) is $2-2-2-1-1-3$.) Interestingly, (2) governs the sequence of contours within a line just as it governs the sequence of lines within a (sub)group.

6   Multicontoured lines beginning with A_ and ending with B are marked as *low-core* (B_) lines (cf. [45, 71]). The low pitch of the first contour usually spreads rightward across the entire line.

7   Brown and Yule 1983:160–4 argue that in English very short pauses (under one second) tend to be hesitations, while medium and long pauses mark successively larger units. They can do this only because pause phrasing happens to *reinforce* units of prosodic phrasing at the two higher levels in the type of data they examined (certain varieties of informal spoken British English). But in much oral discourse, including Mezak's *quliraq*, pause phrasing *offsets* prosodic phrasing. In such cases it will be difficult if not impossible to calibrate short, medium, and long pauses.

8   In a formal grammar, a completely unconstrained rule of pause insertion might apply to prosodically phrased syntactic structures. Pause-prosody alignments falling within the defaults in (7) and (8) would then receive no semantic/pragmatic interpretation, since they would be taken as communicatively neutral. But nondefault alignments *would* receive interpretations, based first on their inherent meanings or forces, and second on the individual linguistic and situational contexts in which they occur. For example, "creates cohesion" is taken in (8) to be the inherent force when nondefault one-(sub)group-to-many-pause-phrase correspondences occur. However, the full interpretation of "cohesion" is calculated in context, as is done in the discussion of (10). Needless to say, a fully worked out account would have a great deal more to say about the principles guiding such interpretation than the present one does.

9   Orphan and poor-boy stories are well represented in Nelson 1899:450–518 for CAY and Inupiaq Eskimo just to the north, in Lantis 1946:264–313 for Nunivak CAY, in Mather et al.'s (1980–2) large collection for contemporary CAY, and, farther afield, in Boas 1888, Holtved 1951, and Rink 1875 for Inuit Eskimo of Baffin Island, North Greenland and West Greenland, respectively (including tales of such well-known pan-Inuit characters as Kâgssagssuk and Kivioq).

10 The "Materials" version of the story (see the introduction to the Appendix), in most respects identical to the present one, ends parts I and III with a final sixth episode. This episode involves a single huge supernatural being referred to as both Qanerpak (Big Mouth) and Sugg'evialuk (Ugly Lips). The grandson manages to charm him in part I, but in part III he is extremely reluctant to summon him. When the shamans actually have him down on the floor and are ready to stretch him he finally relents, but then tries to leave off the song's *apalluq* (verse with words). When the shamans take hold of him again, he finishes the song. Big Mouth then appears in the *qasgiq* and gobbles up everyone, including the grandson.

This short pair of additions to the text changes its interpretation greatly: The grandson now seems overreaching and self-congratulatory for having taken Big Mouth into his power in part I, daring to remark, "*Aling niisngalarmiatnga tang makut!*" (My, even these [=Big Mouth, metaphorical plural] seem to obey me!). Further, his reluctance to summon Big Mouth in part III stems from fear rather than exemplary modesty. On the other hand, the moral point about the shamans' conduct is unchanged, carried by violent retribution instead of delicate irony.

When two such different versions of the same myth are encountered, one is tempted to choose one as the "real" one. But I think it would be a mistake to regard the present version as incomplete, and a mistake too to regard the "Materials" version as a melodramatic revision of a myth that may have seemed too subtle for some tastes. The real point is that by adding and subtracting just a single pair of episodes, Mezak could elegantly transform and redirect the meaning of an entire myth, giving us unique insight into the relationship between text and performance.

11   Even more clearly, the "Materials" version displays a five-plus-one pattern. That pattern is frequent in *quliraq* character configurations, e.g. five brothers and a younger sister. Like the present one, the majority of tales in the "Materials" collection also involve sequences of narrative partipicants, ranging in number from sets of four (most common), to five, to five-plus-one, to seven.

12   To my great surprise, the "Materials" version also contained this exact same putative performance error, word for word and morpheme for morpheme. Nevertheless, there is especially interesting evidence that it still was an error, for in that version Mezak inserts an aside after Aa and before Cc (i.e. between groups [44] and [45]: *Anesqevvailemki=am pillinianka. Tua=i pilit.* 'Gee, I said that (sc., that the people were amazed) before having (the grandson) tell (the dunlins) to go out. Oh well, so be it'. Thus he too regards the sequence as being out of canonical order. It may still be significant, of couse, that the same "errors" should occur from one telling to the next, since Mezak conceivably learned and remembered the story with the error. But like the coughing sequences, this phenomenon reveals how fine the line may be between narrative competence and narrative performance.

13   This may actually explain the initial A_ contour in [29]. A_, which is ordinarily a marker of section openings, may here underscore the break between [29], which is common to all Ba subdivisions, and [27–8], which is unique in episode (i) and hence a low-level pattern extension. (Intonational considerations noted in section 2.1 argue against positing a full section boundary here.)

14   It might be argued that the episode-final B+ contour in [42] really does mark a section ending, but is later canceled by the more emphatic B+ in [44] once the skipping of Cb and Cc has been detected (see sect. 2.1). If this is so, then (27) is further supported.

15   Literally "Two who share the grandchild relationship," but implying a grandmother and grandchild in the context of *qulirat*.

16   Literally "Was a poor little boy, was a male." *Angute-* 'man; male' also implies that he is old enough to go out on his own (Mary Gregory personal communication).

17   From here on, he refers to the dunlins with plural rather than dual forms.

18   *Tunturyuaryuk*, which Mary Gregory (personal communication) translates as "yearling caribou," is a rare word occurring in this and a few other *qulirat* (Irene Reed personal communication) but unattested in the published CAY corpus. I use "young caribou" here, since Mezak's referents have well-developed antlers.

19   The grandmother is given a brittle voice with even, isochronic prosodic feet frequently characteristic of CAY women's speech. In the second line of group [21], the reappearance of this voice quality is the only overt signal that the grandmother is again the speaker.

20   Probably June, given that baby geese have hatched but cranes are still doing mating dances.

21 That is, sing minor power songs for luck in hunting.
22 Musical transcription is given at the end of the text.
23 A stylized imitation of a ptarmigan call, performed with low, creaky "burping" voice quality. The first part is based on the lexical form *qangiiq* 'ptarmigan'. *Caviituten*, the form in the second part, would mean "You have nowhere."
24 [*:t] is a longish, kisslike labiodental click terminated with apicodental occlusion. It functions as an interjection and is often said to mark a narrator's satisfaction with his/her story.
25 The *k* of *neq'ake-* 'to remember' is irregularly changed to *q* here and below.
26 [h̃:] is a voiceless epiglottal trill representing the grunting of the caribou.

References

Boas, F. 1888. The Central Eskimo. In *Sixth Annual Report of the Bureau of American Ethnology, 1884–85*. Washington, D.C.: Government Printing Office, pp. 399–669.

Bolinger, D. 1978. Intonation across languages. In J. Greenberg et al., eds., *Universals of human languages*, vol. 2 *(Phonology)*. Palo Alto: Stanford University Press.

Bright, W. 1979. A Karok myth in "measured verse": the translation of a performance. *Journal of California and Great Basin Anthropology* 1:117–123.

1980. Coyote's journey. *American Indian Culture and Research Journal* 4(1–2):21–48.

Brown, G. and Yule, G. 1983. *Discourse analysis*. Cambridge: Cambridge University Press.

Burke, K. 1931. The psychology of form. In Burke, *Counterstatement*. New York: Harcourt Brace, pp. 38–56. (Reprinted, Chicago: University of Chicago Press [Phoenix Books P14], 1957.)

Chafe, W. 1980. The deployment of consciousness in the production of a narrative. In Chafe, ed., *The pear stories: cognitive, cultural and linguistic aspects of narrative production*. Norwood, N.J.: Ablex.

Dixon, R. M. W. 1972. *The Dyirbal language of North Queensland*. Cambridge: Cambridge University Press.

Fitzhugh, W. and Kaplan, S. 1982. *Inua: spirit world of the Bering Sea Eskimo*. Washington, D.C.: Smithsonian Institution Press.

Goddard, I. 1985. The obviative in Fox narrative discourse. In W. Cowan, ed., *Papers of the Fifteenth Algonquian Conference*. Ottawa: Carleton University, pp. 273–286.

Goldsmith, J. 1976. An overview of autosegmental phonology. *Linguistic Analysis* 2:23–68.

Gumperz, J. J. 1982. *Discourse strategies*. Cambridge: Cambridge University Press.

Haiman, J. and Munro, P., eds. 1983. *Switch reference and universal grammar*. Amsterdam: Benjamins.

Halle, M. and Vergnaud, J.-R. 1980. Three dimensional phonology. *Journal of Linguistic Research* 1:83–105.

Halliday, M. A. K. 1967. *Intonation and grammar in British English*. The Hague: Mouton.

Halliday, M. A. K. and Hasan, R. 1976. *Cohesion in English*. London: Longman Group.

Holtved, E. 1951. *The Polar Eskimos, language and folklore*. Pt. I: *Texts*. Pt. II: *Myths and tales*. Meddelelser om Grønland 152(1–2). Copenhagen.

Hymes, D. 1976. Louis Simpson's "The deserted boy." *Poetics* 5(2):119–155. Reprinted in Hymes 1981.

　　1977. Discovering oral performance and measured verse in American Indian narrative. *New Literary History* 8:431–457. Revised in Hymes 1981.

　　1980a. Verse analysis of a Wasco text: Hiram Smith's "At'unaqa." *International Journal of American Linguistics* 46:65–77. Reprinted in Hymes 1981.

　　1980b. Particle, pause, and pattern in American Indian narrative verse. *American Indian Culture and Research Journal* 4(4):7–51.

　　1981. *"In vain I tried to tell you": essays in Native American ethnopoetics*. Philadelphia: University of Pennsylvania Press.

Jacobson, S. 1984. *Central Yup'ik Eskimo dictionary*. Fairbanks: Alaska Native Language Center, University of Alaska.

Jakobson, R. 1960. Concluding statement: linguistics and poetics. In T. A. Sebeok, ed., *Style in language*. Cambridge: MIT Press, pp. 350–377.

Johnston, T. F. and Pulu, T. L. 1982. *Yup'ik Eskimo songs*. Anchorage: University of Alaska, Rural Education.

Kleinschmidt, S. P. 1851. *Grammatik der groenlaendischen Sprache*. Hildesheim: Georg Olm.

Lantis, M. 1946. *The social culture of the Nunivak Eskimo*. Transactions of the American Philosophical Society, n.s. 35:3. Philadelphia.

　　1947. *Alaskan Eskimo ceremonialism*. Seattle: University of Washington Press.

Levinson, S. C. 1983. *Pragmatics*. Cambridge: Cambridge University Press.

Liberman, M. Y. 1978. *The intonational system of English*. Bloomington: Indiana University Linguistics Club.

McCarthy, J. J. 1981. A prosodic theory of nonconcatenative morphology. *Linguistic Inquiry* 12:373–418.

McLendon, S. 1982. Meaning, rhetorical structure, and discourse organization in myth. In D. Tanne, ed., *Analyzing discourse: text and talk*. Georgetown University Round Table on Language and Linguistics 1981. Washington, D.C.: Georgetown University Press, pp. 284–305.

Mather, E. 1985. *Cauyarnariuq*. Bethel, Alaska: Lower Kuskokwim School District.

Mather, E., Morrow, P., et al. 1980–2. [Transcripts and translations of taped Central Alaskan Yupik narratives.] Ms. Bethel, Alaska: Yup'ik Language Center.

Miyaoka, O. 1983. Sketch of Yupik, an Eskimo language. Ms. To appear in I. Goddard, ed., *Language* (Handbook of American Indians 17). Washington, D.C.: Smithsonian Institution Press.

Morrow, P. 1984. It is time for drumming: a summary of recent research on Yupik ceremonialism. *Etudes/Inuit/Studies* 8(suppl.):113–140.

Nelson, E. W. 1899. The Eskimo about Bering Strait. In *Eighteenth Annual Report of the Bureau of American Ethnology, 1896–97*, pt. I. Washington, D.C., pp. 3–518.

Reed, I., Miyaoka, O., Jacobson, S., Afcan, P., and Krauss, M. 1977. *Yup'ik Eskimo grammar*. Fairbanks: Alaska Native Language Center, University of Alaska.

Rink, H. 1875. *Tales and traditions of the Eskimo*. Edinburgh and London: Blackwood.

Sacks, H., Schegloff, E. A., and Jefferson, G. 1974. A simplest systematics for the organization of turn-taking in conversation. *Language* 50(4):696–735.

Sadock, J. M. 1985. Autolexical syntax: a theory of noun incorporation and similar phenomena. *Natural Language and Linguistic Theory* 3:379–439.

Scollon, R. 1979. The role of audience in the structure of Athabaskan oral performances. Paper presented at the 43rd International Congress of Americanists, Vancouver.

Selkirk, E. O. 1984. *Phonology and syntax*. Cambridge: MIT Press.

Sherzer, J. 1982. Poetic structuring of Kuna discourse: the line. *Language in Society* 11:371–390.

1983. *Kuna ways of speaking: an ethnographic perspective*. Austin: University of Texas Press.

Silverstein, M. 1981. Metaforces of power in traditional oratory. Ms. University of Chicago, Department of Anthropology.

1985a. On the pragmatic "poetry" of prose: parallelism, repetition and cohesive structure in the time course of dyadic conversation. In D. Schiffrin, ed., Georgetown University Round Table on Language and Linguistics 1984. Washington, D.C.: Georgetown University Press, pp. 181–199.

1985b. The culture of language in Chinookan narrative texts; or, On saying that . . . in Chinook. In J. Nichols and A. C. Woodbury, eds., *Grammar inside and outside the clause*. Cambridge: Cambridge University Press, pp. 132–171.

Tedlock, D. 1972. *Finding the center: narrative poetry of the Zuni Indians*. New York: Dial.

1977. Toward an oral poetics. *New Literary History* 8:507–519.

1983. *The spoken word and the work of interpretation*. Philadelphia: University of Pennsylvania Press.

Wolfart, H. C. 1973. *Plains Cree: a grammatical study*. Transactions of the American Philosophical Society, n.s., 63:5. Philadelphia.

Woodbury, A. C. 1983. Switch reference, syntactic organization, and rhetorical structure in Central Yup'ik Eskimo. In Haiman and Munro 1983, pp. 291–315.

1984. *Cev'armiut qanemciit qulirait=llu: narratives and tales from Chevak, Alaska*. Fairbanks: Alaska Native Language Center, University of Alaska.

1985. Functions of rhetorical structure: a study of Central Alaskan Yupik Eskimo discourse. *Language in Society* 14:150–193.

Woodbury, A. C. and de Reuse, W. In preparation. *Narrative and conversation in a Central Alaskan Yupik Eskimo qaygiq (men's house)*.

SUBJECT INDEX

INDEX OF NAMES

243

INDEX OF LANGUAGES

245